SOURCEBOOK OF MODERN FURNITURE

SOURCEBOOK OF MODERN FURNITURE

Jerryll Habegger
Joseph H. Osman

 VAN NOSTRAND REINHOLD
New York

To Nancy C. Los, Director of Education, Harrington Institute of Interior Design. She has provided an environment that nurtures the talents of others.

Copyright © 1989 by Van Nostrand Reinhold

Library of Congress Catalog Card Number 88-10895

ISBN 0-442-23276-4

Printed in the United States of America

Designed by Monika Grejniec

Van Nostrand Reinhold
115 Fifth Avenue
New York, New York 10003

Van Nostrand Reinhold (International) Limited
11 New Fetter Lane
London EC4P 4EE, England

Van Nostrand Reinhold
480 La Trobe Street
Melbourne, Victoria 3000, Australia

Macmillan of Canada
Division of Canada Publishing Corporation
164 Commander Boulevard
Agincourt, Ontario M1S 3C7, Canada

16 15 14 13 12 11 10 9 8 7 6 5 4 3 2 1

Library of Congress Cataloging in Publication Data

Habegger, Jerryll, 1944–
    Sourcebook of modern furniture / Jerryll Habegger, Joseph H.
    Osman.
        p.   cm.
    Bibliography: p.
    Includes index.
    ISBN 0-442-23276-4
    1. Furniture—History—20th century—Catalogs. 2. Architect-
    designed furniture—History—20th century—Catalogs. 3. Furniture
    designers—Catalogs. I. Osman, Joseph H., 1955–   II. Title.
NK2395.H34   1988
749.2'049—dc19
                                                    88-10895
                                                       CIP

CONTENTS

ACKNOWLEDGMENTS

We wish to express our gratitude to the following persons, whose assistance and support have been invaluable in the preparation of this book: Alfred N. Beadle; Howard Brown; Don Curtis; Jim Fagerburg; Linda Folland; Arthur and LaVaun Habegger; Judy Jacobs; Donald and Nancy Los; Robert J. Nedved; Sara K. Osman; Eli Prouty; Dorothy Spencer; Ida Stein; Larry Whiteley; the Staff of the Harrington Institute of Interior Design.

We also wish to thank the manufacturers, designers, and museums for providing photographs and product information.

PREFACE

The purpose of this book is to provide a concise reference of the works of industrial designers and architects whose ideas are widely considered to be the most influential in the development of modern furniture and lighting. It is intended to benefit the interior design and architecture professions as a sourcebook for high-quality products applicable to all design areas.

The products presented in this book are truly representative of creative design experimentation within the context of available technology. They reflect the design philosophy that the results of creative purpose and experimentation are superior to those of poor imitation (or kitsch) and misinformed historicism. To that end, this book is a celebration of both the works of dedicated designers and the vision of innovative manufacturers who have translated their works into reality.

The specific pieces in this book were selected on the basis of the integrity of their design philosophy, materials expression, and form content. While these criteria are interrelated, the individual definitions in use are as follows:

Design Philosophy: The products illustrated embody a philosophy that conveys values—an attitude attained through critical analysis, creative goals, and experimentation. The results of this design philosophy offer new experiences, thereby heightening visual responses and provoking thought.

Materials Expression: The materials technology and manufacturing methods employed in these products involve both innovative techniques incorporating traditional materials and novel production processes that utilize new materials. The materials detailer anticipates function and interprets it into new form.

Form Content: Each product presented has been analyzed for its visual expression (pure form, proportion, and scale) in space, for its direct relationship of shape configuration to human requirements, and for its physical utility and efficient function.

The following data are provided for each entry:

- Model name or number
- Year of design (entries are arranged chronologically)
- Designer(s)
- Manufacturer
- Materials
- Dimensions

The List of Suppliers provides manufacturers' names and addresses. There are three indexes, each listing a different aspect of the product: designer, model name or number, and manufacturer.

INTRODUCTION

Furniture design and production have undergone more dramatic progress in the twentieth century than at any other time in history. In the last 120 years, a truly modern idea of furniture has evolved. The acceptance of the machine as a positive and creative aesthetic force marked the beginning of the modern era. Resulting new techniques enabled creative designers to go beyond the imitation of historical forms.

In the mid- to late nineteenth century, the technology existed for mass production of objects. Mechanization yielded more economic and effective manufacturing methods. During the first part of the twentieth century, innovative design experimentation had its roots in the concepts of mass production and adaptive reuse of existing materials. It is thus fundamentally ironic that so many significant designs from this period were hand crafted.

Following World War II, new production techniques and industrial materials, such as aluminum alloys, curved plywood, and plastics, were adapted to domestic uses and became the standards. The principal attractions of these materials were mobility and lightness. The Americans and Italians led in the research and development of these new materials and technologies. Significant materials and components developed were: steel and aluminum frames, tension springs, rubber diaphragms, plastic foam cushioning, semirigid plastic shells, and synthetic resin adhesives. New fabrication techniques included: Fiberglas lay-up, thermal forming, extrusion, injection, and compression molding. In the 1980s the achievements of modern technology have made it possible to shape materials in such a way that an almost complete freedom prevails in the design field. The chronological evolution of materials detailing is evidenced in the descriptions of the selected works included as part of this introduction, and in the captions accompanying the photographs.

The following designs, presented in chronological order, represent the best examples of the modern idiom. The products illustrated range from those that are instructive of function and structure to others that are purely sculptural. Each design is referenced by designer in the book's index and by manufacturer in the list of suppliers.

1870

"CORBUSIER" DINING CHAIR

This Gebrüder Thonet-designed chair is the oldest modern chair in production. Because there was little appropriate modern furniture prior to 1925, Le Corbusier used this piece quite extensively in his earlier interiors. Hence, it has become known as the "Corbusier." The tight structural organic curves are achieved through the steam bentwood process, in which a thin, flexible strip of steel is clamped along the outside of the steamed wood. The bentwood process of 1840, developed by Michael Thonet, revolutionized the mass production of furniture. The advantages of steam bending over lamination were that the process required less work and the chairs were more durable. Lamination was not desirable because of the limitation of the glues available at the time. In addition, the elements could be disassembled and shipped knocked down.

This chair consists of only five elements of Carpathian beechwood, overlapped and joined with screws, eliminating complex joints. It expresses an unpretentious simplicity of construction and line in a sculptural, lightweight form (15 pounds/6.8 kilos).

1900

OPAL PENDANT HANGING LAMP

One of the first designs for a lamp employing electric light bulbs was the Opal Pendant. It consists of a chrome-plated tube with an opaque globe.

1903

HILL HOUSE I DINING CHAIR

Charles Rennie Mackintosh's tall, thin ladderback chair of ebonized ashwood is an ornamental and sculptural abstraction weighing 6 pounds (3 kilos).

1904

LARKIN SWIVEL-BASE DESK CHAIR

Frank Lloyd Wright's central-pedestal-base metal desk chair became the prototype for the task chair in the office furniture industry.

1910

D 51/2 SOFA

Walter Gropius's simple, geometrically constructed, 55½-inch-wide sofa with an ashwood frame achieves an open and lightweight feeling.

1918

RED AND BLUE LOUNGE CHAIR

Developed as an abstract sculptural form, Gerrit T. Rietveld's Red and Blue chair liberates the seat planes from the support structure—an aesthetic exercise that functions as an example of unimpeded horizontal, vertical, and diagonal elements.

1924

B 80 DINING CHAIR

Jean Prouvé's folding chair, designed for his sister's wedding, was the first modern experiment in flat sheet steel. The steel was folded and welded into a streamlined support for seating.

WAGENFELD TABLE LAMP

Wilhelm Wagenfeld's design represents a straightforward use of thick glass. The clear glass on the base and in the stem of the lamp reveals the interior workings.

1925

WASSILY LOUNGE CHAIR

Marcel Breuer designed this first modern lounge chair, constructed of tubular steel with a sled base. The skeletal framework is formed from a continuous line of tubing, providing solidity and visual lightness with intersecting support planes of canvas or leather.

CASIERS STANDARD STORAGE SYSTEM

Le Corbusier went beyond the idea of furniture as a collection of single items and developed a system of cellular containers with coordinated modular sizes, called the Casiers Standard storage system. The basic system consisted of four containers based on a 37.5-cm (14¾-inch) module. The Casiers Standard became the first example of a unit storage system, serving as a cabinet and a partition at the same time.

1926

LACCIO SIDE TABLE
Marcel Breuer's Laccio table/stool, turned on its side, was the inspiration for the cantilever (projection) principle in modern furniture design. It was originally designed as a stool for the cafeteria at the Bauhaus. Mart Stam's S 33 dining chair of the same year is representative of the tubular cantilever principle.

PH 4½-4 HANGING LAMP
Poul Henningsen's PH lamp applies a multishade principle. The size, shape, and position of the shades determine the distribution of the light and the control of direct glare from the lamp source. The color of the light is neutralized by adding color to some of the inner reflectors.

1927

MR DINING CHAIR
Ludwig Mies van der Rohe's design represents the first *resilient* cantilevered steel-tube chair. The design spreads the tension through a curve rather than a sharp angle, taking advantage of the spring-like quality of tubular steel. Thus, it allows the suspended seat to move freely, up and down. Knoll introduced stainless steel versions of Ludwig Mies van der Rohe's furniture in 1947.

TUBE LIGHT FLOOR LAMP
Eileen Gray's design is the first floor lamp to use a totally exposed incandescent tube as the light source, providing soft, nonglare general illumination.

1928

LC/2 GRAND CONFORT LOUNGE CHAIR
Le Corbusier's LC/2 chair is fundamentally different from previous upholstered designs in that the cushions are contained within the tubular framework rather than serving to conceal the structure. The exposed structure consists of a thick bar, which wraps around the frame and eventually forms the legs, and a thinner bar, which contains the cushions.

LC/4 CHAISE LONGUE
Le Corbusier differentiated strongly here between the cradle and the base support through the use of different materials and detailing to express distinct functions. The seat frame (cradle), which is totally adjustable, is raised on two gliding arcs of tubular steel. The sitter's body is supported by reinforced elastic straps. The cradle may also be used separately as a rocker. The cradle is supported on rubber-covered stretchers that are welded to the painted steel base.

LC/6 DINING TABLE
Once again, Le Corbusier differentiated between supported and supporting elements by giving the table top a floating quality. The supports and stretchers consist of oval metal sections with mitered and welded joints.

S 35 LOUNGE CHAIR
In this chair, made of one continuous piece of steel, Marcel Breuer achieved a double cantilever; that is, both the arms and the seat cantilever from the same bent tubular frame. Thus, the seat moves separately from the arms.

1929

BARCELONA LOUNGE CHAIR
Ludwig Mies van der Rohe's Barcelona chair, with a base of welded flat spring steel, flows from the floor plane, establishing structural clarity. The chair is one square meter in plan, is generous in scale, and weighs 84 pounds (38 kilos). Although the chair appears to be machine-made, it is manufactured almost entirely by hand.

"BARCELONA" COFFEE TABLE
Ludwig Mies van der Rohe's low table eliminates a sense of heaviness and achieves a simplicity of aesthetic and technological organization. Although the table was originally designed for the Tugendhat House, it has been erroneously labeled the "Barcelona" table because it is so frequently used with the Barcelona chair.

LIRA LOUNGE CHAIR
Piero Bottoni's curiosity is a double-cantilevered structure. It

consists of a cantilevered seat suspended by nylon threads from a larger cantilevered support structure.

1930

D 61 DINING CHAIR

El Lissitzky's design was originally executed in wood. In 1971 the Plexiglas version was introduced by Tecta Möbel.

BRNO (255) DINING CHAIR

By incorporating a noncontinuous flat steel frame, Ludwig Mies van der Rohe reduced the chair structure to two runners and a crossbar. The relationship of the seat thickness and the bar-stock width creates a harmonious proportion.

1931

CHAISE LONGUE (241)

Ludwig Mies van der Rohe's extended version of the MR lounge chair incorporates channeled foam cushions. The full lounge support moves freely up and down.

1932

PAIMIO (41) LOUNGE CHAIR

The arms and base of Alvar Aalto's chair are of laminated birchwood bent into a closed curve. Within the seat, strength is achieved through the varying thickness of the wood lamination. Added resilience is achieved in the scroll-shaped 3-mm plywood seat. This chair was designed for the Paimio Sanatorium in Finland.

1933

MULTI-SECTIONAL (4-905) DINING TABLE

Alvar Aalto's use of two semicircular and two rectangular table sections allows for versatility in arrangement. The sections incorporate the *bent-knee leg.* This leg is constructed by taking a solid piece of birch and sawing grooves in the end in the direction of the fibers. Thin pieces of wood are glued into these grooves, reinforcing the bend at its greatest point of stress. The wood is then bent to the desired angle.

The foot of the leg is left solid so that it does not splinter with age.

AALTO WING (401) LOUNGE CHAIR

This adaptation of the laminated cantilever principle in wood was developed by Alvar Aalto in 1931–32. The compressive spring of seven birch laminations provides precisely the right balance of flexibility and resilience.

BREUER SEATING COLLECTION LOUNGE CHAIR

In this early experiment in aluminum, Marcel Breuer incorporated grooved-out flat bands of aluminum to form the double U supports, one for the leg and seat, the other for the arm.

1934

EVA LOUNGE CHAIR

This design is the result of Bruno Mathsson's experimentation with basic anthropometric requirements in lounge seating. The laminated beech is shaped to the human body in a light and totally organic and harmonious form. The separation of the contoured lounge from the legs allows for compact stacking and hence, economical shipping and storage.

ZIG-ZAG DINING CHAIR

This stackable chair by Gerrit T. Rietveld had a revolutionary new structure. The diagonal cantilever incorporated a simple dovetailed and glued triangular joint.

1936

LARIANA DINING CHAIR AND SANT'ELIA LOUNGE CHAIR

Giuseppe Terragni used the reverse (double) cantilever in a truly graceful and lyrical manner.

TEA TROLLEY (98) SERVING CART

Alvar Aalto's service cart has a sled base of molded, laminated birch and very large, graphic wheels. The wheels are of painted wood and are banded with rubber to deaden the noise from movement.

1937

2633 COFFEE TABLE
This table represents Pietro Chiesa's contribution to the development of bent plate glass.

JOHNSON WAX DESK AND ADJUSTABLE DESK CHAIR
Both structures, designed by Frank Lloyd Wright, are constructed of cast aluminum and magnesite soldered rod. The chair has a self-adjusting and rotating back support and a three-point leg support. The casters and bronze feet are interchangeable. The desk has multitiered levels to keep the main cantilevered surface free for writing. The drawers are hinged and swing on pivots.

L1 TABLE LAMP
This Jac. Jacobsen design consists of a bell-shaped shade and a spring-balanced, 45-inch arm, which is totally adjustable. This was an altered design of an English lamp called the Anglepoise, for which Jacobsen secured patent rights.

CT SERIES COFFEE TABLE
William Armbruster's table consists of a thin (1-inch) angled steel (L-profile) frame with radius reinforcements at the corners.

1938

"WORK CHAIR" DINING CHAIR
This chair of spring steel is completely movable and was designed by Herman A. Sperlich for use with an ironing machine.

SPARTANA DINING CHAIR
Hans Coray's design was developed when "steel-hard" aluminum alloys were first becoming available. The Spartana seat shell is formed from a single piece of aluminum sheet that is stamped by a large drop press, then punched with holes. The frame is tempered by heat. Its discoloration is then removed, exposing a soft crystalline surface finish that is impervious to weather and cool in the sun. The use of stamped, welded, and spray-painted sheet metal components is the result of borrowing from the automobile industry. The chair weighs 6 pounds (2.7 kilos).

BUTTERFLY LOUNGE CHAIR
The Butterfly chair was designed by the Argentinian architects Jorge Hardoy, Antonio Bonet, and Juan Kurchan. The shape of this chair is based on an idea borrowed from a folding wooden chair used by British officers during the nineteenth century. The design is a continuous metal frame on which a fabric or leather seat is slung. Following World War II, the steel rod became the basis of many important design elements, placed within dynamic and organically conceived spaces.

1940

80 D DESK
Franco Albini achieved a lightness and simplicity for the desk function in his metal truss structure, which supports the glass top and the drawer unit.

1944

CHINESE DINING CHAIR (4283)
Until 1943, Hans Wegner was employed by Arne Jacobsen's design office in Århus, where he designed the furniture for the Århus City Hall. Simultaneously, he designed an interpretation of a Chinese chair, incorporating a steam-bent top rail in wood. This was Wegner's first chair for mass production, and it established the high standards of hand woodworking typical of modern Scandinavian design.

1946

LCM LOUNGE CHAIR
Charles Eames achieved both a thin structural frame in metal rod and a continuous body support of 5/16-inch, five-ply, laminated wood, subtly molded into two directional compound curves. The parts are attached to a rubber shock mount system, electronically welded to the wood. The design represents a major advance in the compound molding and bonding of materials.

1947

VAN KEPPEL-GREEN CHAISE LONGUE
Hendrik van Keppel and Taylor Green pioneered in the area of modern outdoor furniture with this early experiment in cord-wrapped tubular structures.

NOGUCHI COFFEE TABLE
The sculptor Isamu Noguchi used a triangular plate-glass top to reveal a biomorphic pivoting base. The soft angular configuration of the top makes it very versatile for space planning.

Y 805 COFFEE TABLE
Alvar Aalto originally made the *Y leg* by sawing the bent-knee leg into two parts. The two 90-degree laminated bends were then mitered at their juncture.

406 LOUNGE CHAIR
In this chair, Alvar Aalto incorporated the principles of the laminated birch curve and the flexible, resilient cantilevered structure, developed in 1931.

"THE CLASSIC CHAIR"
(JH 501) DINING CHAIR
Hans Wegner's "Classic Chair" achieves a spare, unified form in which all parts flow into each other. The visually light chair has simple sawtoothed joinery executed in solid wood

1948

WOMB LOUNGE CHAIR
Eero Saarinen's chair is very deep and wide, with ample room for changing seating positions. The thin-profile seat shell is molded from a Fiberglas, plastic, and wood particle mix and covered with foam padding. The seat shell is supported by bent steel rod.

1950

ROCKER LOUNGE CHAIR
The introduction of economical molded plastic chairs began with Charles and Ray Eames's one-piece, glass-reinforced polyester shell. It represents the first successful application of this material for furniture. The shell can be used with numerous other bases. The split-pedestal base was added in 1961 with the introduction of the "La Fonda" version.

NOGUCHI SIDE TABLE
Innovative technology and materials inspired many designers to a new level of enthusiasm resulting in creative yet straightforward pieces. An example of this is Isamu Noguchi's floating-top table. It is made up of a cast-iron base supporting a steel-wire column structure for the plastic laminate top.

TUBINO TABLE LAMP
With this design, Achille and Pier Giacomo Castiglioni introduced organic shapes to table lamps.

1951

ETR COFFEE TABLE
This long, low coffee table, with a surfboard-shaped top supported on wire bases, was first used in Charles and Ray Eames's 1950 LTR design.

CANAAN DESK
Marcel Breuer's wood desk, composed of a central square opening and cantilevered storage drawers, expresses a pleasing 1:2 proportional relationship.

PK 25 LOUNGE CHAIR
This chair was originally designed by Poul Kjaerholm as a master's thesis assignment given by Hans J. Wegner, while Kjaerholm was a student at the furniture department of the School of Arts and Crafts in Denmark. The chair frame was developed from one piece of spring steel, which was cut and bent to form the continuous linear structure.

1952

BUBBLE (CC 727) HANGING LAMP
George Nelson's hanging lamp represented a revolutionary application of a translucent self-webbing vinyl over metal ribs.

HIGH-BACK (423) LOUNGE CHAIR

Sculptor Harry Bertoia used steel rod here, hand shaped in a wooden mold and welded into a cellular structure. The high-back design is an open mesh in the shape of a bird.

1952–53

NEW YORK SEATING (161.000.0) DINING CHAIR; NEW YORK SOFA; NEW YORK CONFERENCE DINING TABLE

These three pieces, designed by Ross Littrell, William Katavolos, and Douglas Kelley, and originally manufactured by Laverne, express a strong clarity of structure and dimensions that fall within "The Modulor" proportions (dimension multiplied by .618) of Le Corbusier. Both the New York Sofa and the New York Conference dining table employ the cantilever. All the elements of the New York Seating dining chair are in a T formation. The scroll-shaped connection between the leather sling and the frame is achieved by wrapping and screwing the leather around the halved rods of the frame.

1954

FAN-LEGGED (X800) DINING TABLE

Alvar Aalto's fan-shaped leg is made by sawing a bent-knee leg into five parts and doweling them into the table top.

SOFA COMPACT

Charles and Ray Eames's application of human engineering is evident in the profile of this thin, two-part, sectioned, high-back sofa. It weighs only 140 pounds (64 kilos) and folds flat for shipping. With this design, the Eameses established the standard for the "modern" sofa.

A 805 FLOOR LAMP

The strong organic contour of this floor lamp by Alvar Aalto filters the light while maintaining a unity of form.

1955

SERIE 7 DINING CHAIR

Arne Jacobsen's laminated-wood-veneer stacking chair pro-vides good upper back support and flexibility through the freeform shape of the contoured shell.

COCONUT LOUNGE CHAIR

In George Nelson's sculptured design, the three points within the conical seat shell and the three support points come together to create a visual unity.

P 40 LOUNGE CHAIR

Osvaldo Borsani's versatile design, which incorporates totally adjustable elements, can take up to 486 distinct positions. The chair also features retractable and flexible rubber arms.

1956

PEDESTAL (151) DINING CHAIR

Eero Saarinen's chair fused four legs into one organically unified form.

1957

SUPERLEGERRA DINING CHAIR

Gio Ponti's chair is derived from the vernacular "Chiavari" chair. It weighs in at 4 pounds (1.85 kilos), probably the lightest of all modern chairs.

PK 22 LOUNGE CHAIR

Poul Kjaerholm's chair has neither a front rail nor a top bar. Stability is ensured by means of the clamp below the seat and the cross sewing of the upholstery. The attachment with raised Allen-head screws was innovative.

1958

ALUMINUM GROUP DESK CHAIR

Charles and Ray Eames originally conceived this as an outdoor chair. The chair's thin profile consists of one continuous seat and back plane suspended between structural ribs of polished die-cast aluminum. The "sandwich" sling consists of front and back layers of textile or vinyl and a reinforcement of vinyl-coated nylon with a 1/4-inch-thick layer of foam. The materials of the sling are welded together at 1 7/8-inch intervals through pressure and high-frequency current.

1959

SWAN LOUNGE CHAIR
Arne Jacobsen's soft and mature sculptural form expresses both comfort and stability.

CSS STORAGE
Based on the adjustable pole systems developed by Angelo Mangiarotti and Franco Albini in 1952, George Nelson's CSS (Comprehensive Storage System) consists of wooden components suspended on brackets between aluminum poles. The components can be adjusted to any height. As director of design at Herman Miller, George Nelson established the systems approach for corporate application.

1960

PANTON STACKING DINING CHAIR
Verner Panton's chair is made of rigid polyurethane foam, injection molded in one piece. It is the first one-piece chair made of plastic and manufactured entirely by machine. New developments in the plastics industry made many of the rounded and molded forms possible. It was not put into production until 1967, as no suitable materials were available in 1960.

AJ VISOR FLOOR AND TABLE LAMP
These lamps are two of the objects designed by Arne Jacobsen for the SAS Royal Hotel in Copenhagen. Each lamp has a strong profile, an angled base, and a support stalk. Each base contains a void and reflects the shape of the shade.

1961

OVAL (2481) DESK
This desk, designed by Florence Knoll, consists of a canted base structure and a beveled-edge oval top, which provides a significant savings of circulation space around the perimeter.

HALLER FURNITURE SYSTEM STORAGE
A variation on the Abstracta display system designed by Poul Cadovius in 1960, the Fritz Haller System employs a 19-mm steel tube (Abstracta uses 13- and 19-mm steel tubes). The corner connector is a 25-mm ball with six threaded openings.

1962

TOIO FLOOR LAMP
Achille Castiglioni's fixture, with its upward-directed light (actually an automobile headlight), introduced the ad hoc or ready-made methodology to design. The novelty of this design is not so much in the way it looks but in the way it is put together.

COLOMBO TABLE LAMP
The popularity of shiny surfaces during the 1960s was influenced by advances in the synthetic plastics industry. Joe Colombo, attracted by the technological aspects of futuristic design, chose a thick acrylic (Perspex) to transfer light throughout the form from its fluorescent source in the base of the lamp.

TACCIA TABLE LAMP
Achille Castiglioni's design consists of an extruded aluminum base, which houses the bulb and acts as a heatsink, allowing heat dispersion. An enameled spun aluminum concave reflector rests on a clear handblown glass bowl, both of which tilt to various angles, creating diffused indirect light.

TANDEM MODULAR SEATING
Charles and Ray Eames's Tandem Seating was designed for C.F. Murphy's O'Hare Airport in Chicago. The repeated component combines a soft, padded arm and interchangeable seat/back pads. The easily removable pads are sandwiches of heat-sealed vinyl materials with welts diagonally placed to increase strength. The seats are secured to a single, continuous steel T-beam and are strong enough to permit long spans (twelve components back to back) with minimum floor contact.

1963

CATENARY LOUNGE CHAIR
The frame of George Nelson's Catenary chair is made of steel-rod and flat-bar stock bonded with epoxy. The seat and back, made up of eight individual cushions, contain

two rubber-coated steel cables, which hang from the frame in a catenary (suspended) curve.

1964

DJINN CHAISE LONGUE
This Olivier Mourgue piece was the first to use flowing forms incorporating melted urethane foam over a tubular steel frame. The furniture is upholstered in brightly colored stretch jersey. The lounge chair (Low Fireside Chair Djinn), designed in 1965, was used in the interior of the Space Hilton in the 1968 movie *2001: A Space Odyssey*.

ACTION OFFICE DESK
As a component of the Action Office I system, created by George Nelson and Robert Propst, the Action Office desk incorporates integral top-loaded filing for easy access and provides a roll-top to cover up clutter. The 42-inch-high work surface offers a stand-up work option.

PERCH DESK CHAIR
The Perch chair was designed by Robert Propst to be used with the 42-inch-high Action Office desk. It was a new concept in seating, offering a stand-up position of 30 to 33 inches.

TULIP DESK CHAIR
The Tulip desk chair, designed by Jørgen Kastholm and Preben Fabricius, consists of a flexible Fiberglas frame clad in a seamless hide of leather, over which a padded leather jacket is placed. The extremely thin seat is supported on a steel tripod base.

40/4 DINING CHAIR
David Rowland solved the problem of efficient stacking by providing a design that nested closely. The frame is a thin ($7/16$-inch diameter), high-strength steel rod. The seat and back are made of hard, vinyl-coated, rolled-edge sheet metal. Forty chairs may be stacked within 4 feet. Flanges in the back of the structural frame incorporate male and female connectors. Four interlocked chairs may be gang-stacked for fast clearance.

KARUSELLI LOUNGE CHAIR
This Yrjö Kukkapuro design employs a glass-reinforced, molded polyester swivel base and seat shell, which is thinly padded with leather. The shape of the shell was determined through the use of flexible steel mesh formed to the human anatomy.

SLING SOFA
The frame of George Nelson's Sling sofa is chrome-plated, nonwelded (epoxy-glued) tubular steel. It is sprung on the back with fabric-reinforced rubber webbing and across the seat area with neoprene platforms. Multiple elements can be fastened together with epoxy glue to achieve sofas of various lengths.

LANDMARK SERIES (1074) DINING CHAIR (c. 1964)
The Landmark Series chair by Ward Bennett has a contained sculptural quality, expressed through the exposed wood frame. The top rail flows into the arms and legs in one sweeping, uninterrupted line. The chair is joined entirely with concealed dowel joints.

1965

PK 24 CHAISE LONGUE
Poul Kjaerholm's design utilizes the flexibility of stainless steel to its utmost, expressing the limitations of the material. The seat/back element may be adjusted to the angle of individual preference.

5/4867 DINING CHAIR
This stacking chair, designed by Joe Colombo, has flush sides for butting during installation. Originally, legs of different heights could be interchanged for use by adults or children. (The chair is currently available in an adult height only.) The curves and contours add to the strength of the chair.

1966

3714 COFFEE TABLE
The table base, designed by Warren Platner, is gracefully formed in steel rods, electrically welded to horizontal tubes, and finished in bright nickel.

1U WV FLOOR LAMP

Cedric Hartman's design consists of a triangular (tent) shade reflector supported by a tubular stem, which is integrated into the rectangular bar-stock base.

PRATONE LOUNGE CHAIR

Designed by Giorgio Cevetti, Piero Derossi, and Ricardo Rosso, the Pratone chair is a key work within the philosophy of Pop Art. The scale of the object is greatly enlarged, and the lounge-chair function is not evident from its form: the form conceals the function. This design was executed in self-skinning polyurethane foam, a finishing technique usually used for car dashboards. The piece comes ready-finished from the mold. This finished surface is derived from a polyurethane film that is put on the sides of the mold before the foaming process.

40 SN STORAGE

The 40 SN has become the standard side-panel storage system in the industry, both in dimensions and detailing. Walter Muller's design was greatly influenced by the 1959 "INwand" system by Herbert Hirche for Christian Holzäpfel of Germany. The design of the system components allowed unlimited expansion.

1967

932 LOUNGE CHAIR

Mario Bellini's design incorporates leather-covered, injection-molded polyurethane foam components, which can be belted together to form a chair or extended into a two- or three-seat sofa. Structure and padding have become one and the same form.

1968

MODULO 3 DESK

The Modulo 3 desk was designed by Bob Noorda and Franco Mirenzi as a knockdown desk, and consists of three panels and a stretcher. The panels are joined along the 45-degree mitered edge with an aluminum extrusion.

SUPERELLIPS DINING TABLE

The Superellips (a modified ellipse) combines the advantages of the square and circular table top. This configuration accommodates easy movement around the table. In addition, the legs spread apart and click into rectangular fittings without the use of tools. The Superellips shape evolved from Piet Hein's solution for a traffic circle for a new square (Sergels Plaza) in Stockholm.

GYRO LOUNGE CHAIR

Eero Aarnio's Gyro chair is a circular bubble with a scooped seat that is molded in two halves. The organic form can be used to float on water or slide on snow.

1969

CARRERA MODULAR SEATING

This gently contoured modular component system, designed by Jonathan De Pas, Donato D'Urbino, and Paolo Lomazzi, is capable of forming single chair units, straight-line conditions, and many totally undulating configurations.

UP 5 LOUNGE CHAIR

Gaetano Pesce's Up series was shipped by the manufacturer compressed in a thermosealed vacuum container. (Polyurethane foam can be compressed so that it requires 90 percent less storage space.) When unsealed, the foam expanded back to its original size and gained full form one hour after the seal was broken.

BOCCA (MARILYN) SOFA

This sofa design by Studio 65 is upholstered in the form of a pair of voluptuous lips (Marilyn Monroe's) and covered in a red knitted textile. It was inspired by Salvador Dali's "Mae West Lips" sofa of 1936 and injects a sense of surrealistic humor into the furniture industry.

1970

PRIMATE KNEELING STOOL

Achille Castiglioni's design represented a new approach to the act of sitting. By kneeling, one reduces stress from the lumbar area of the back by partially redistributing weight to the legs. A later development was the wood version, called Balans, manufactured by the Norwegian firm of Håg.

BOALUM TABLE LAMP

Livio Castiglioni and Gianfranco Frattini designed this soft, totally flexible, luminescent, sculptural lamp of polyvinyl chloride (PVC), reinforced with a segmented coiled spring.

1971

DODONA 300 STORAGE

Ernesto Gismondi was the first to apply the extruded plastic manufacturing process in the furniture industry. A hidden angular linking device is pushed from above into the slots of the side panels.

607 TABLE LAMP

Gino Sarfatti's design was the first lamp on the market with a 12-volt halogen bulb.

1972

SEGMENTED-BASE DINING TABLE

This table was a solution by Charles and Ray Eames for variable-sized conference table configurations. The component table-base system interchanges a hub, a hub/stringer connector, a stringer, and legs to form a continuous structure that accommodates large ellipsoidal tops.

CONTOUR ROCKER LOUNGE CHAIR

Frank Gehry's design is achieved by a technique of laminating corrugated cardboard sheets, with each layer running in opposite directions. The result is a very strong but inexpensive material that can be cut into many shapes.

TIZIO TABLE LAMP

Richard Sapper's Tizio lamp has a concentrated, 55-watt halogen light source and a small reflector. A safety fuse transformer enclosed in the base reduces power from 110 volts to 12 volts, permitting the metal arms to conduct power to the reflector. A counterweight system and a swiveling base make the lamp adjustable to nearly any angle.

1973

FREEFORM DINING TABLE

Jerryll Habegger's organic design provides a variety of sizes of top surfaces to accommodate different-sized objects. The shape of the top allows people to be seated in diverse directions.

WADDELL (713) COFFEE TABLE

The Theodore Waddell table is a "tensegrity" structure: a geometric cable network in which overall tension is imposed by stretching cables in one direction against pulls induced in the opposite direction.

AEO LOUNGE CHAIR

Archizoom Associati are the designers of this piece, which may be used individually or connected in tandem. Strong expression is divided between the distinctively diverse materials of the plastic base, the enameled steel frame, and the upholstery sleeves.

1974

EKC 13 DINING CHAIR

This is Poul Kjaerholm's daring version of Ludwig Mies van der Rohe's Brno chair, in which the back and cantilevered seat structure form a rigid connecting element, thereby eliminating the need for any crossbracing.

SERVOMUTO SIDE TABLE

Achille Castiglioni's design employs a support system consisting of a conical ABS plastic base with a central stem. A table top is placed on the stem to form the service table. Other accessories turn the support system into an umbrella stand, an ashtray, and a display system.

1975

54-102 DINING CHAIR

The concept for this Gae Aulenti chair starts with a bundle of triangular tubes that branch off to form frames, crossbars, and armrests.

DINNERELEMENT DINING TABLE

Joe Colombo's Dinnerelement table accommodates six people and can be moved easily. It contains units for chilling, cutlery and china storage, and an electric hotplate.

1976

BROOKLYN STORAGE

Lodovico Acerbis's storage system consists of a lacquered truss suspended between two pylons. The shelves are hung on thin steel bars from the truss.

1977

VERTEBRA DESK CHAIR

The Vertebra desk chair, designed by Emilio Ambasz and Giancarlo Piretti, is equipped with a mechanism that permits the seat and back to work independently and to move automatically, adapting to relaxed, upright, and forward-tilted positions. The body can thus maintain ideal posture in any seated position.

1978

TUOLI CHAISE LONGUE

The Tuoli, designed by Antti Nurmesniemi, is a very accommodating design in that the back can be shifted easily to alter the sitting angle, without any mechanical connector. (The "connector" is gravity between the seat and back elements of the chaise longue.)

INCAS DINING TABLE

This is further development by Angelo Mangiarotti of the 1971 Eros table. The material plays an instructive part in the design. Flat surfaces and supports come together in a single joint that uses gravity as its attachment.

FRISBI HANGING LAMP

Achille Castiglioni's design consists of an opal, translucent, disc-shaped reflector/diffusor with a center hole. This allows direct and diffused light to pass through it and reflected light to bounce off it.

MAC GEE STORAGE

This easily moved book-shelving system, designed by Philippe Starck, stands firmly as it leans against a wall without attachments.

1979

5/4825 STOOL

Anna Castelli Ferrieri's stool has a seat molded in polyurethane structural foam. It incorporates metal reinforcements for the legs and backrest handle, which are inserted during the molding process.

1980

BURDICK GROUP DESK

Bruce Burdick designed this pedestal-supported system centered on an aluminum-extruded beam. The beams are the basic structural and visual element of the Burdick Group. All components are cantilevered from, suspended below, or supported directly on the beam. Electrical wires can be accommodated beneath the beam. The components and beam configurations can be restructured.

2R DINING TABLE

This table series, designed by Leif Erik Rasmussen and Henrik Rolff, has drop leaves that attach easily without tools. The connector is a bent flat-metal extension, which fits into the top of the hollow table leg. Stabilizer bars extend to support the drop leaf in a raised position.

ALVA STORAGE (c. 1980)

Afra and Tobia Scarpas's glass cases with glass shelves are attached to vertical support posts that serve as uninsulated conductors of electric current for the case lighting.

1981

CARLTON STORAGE

This room divider/storage unit, designed by Ettore Sottsass, is representative of the Memphis fantasy philosophy. This new visual language cultivates a free discontinuity of parts and an enjoyment of shape, texture, and color.

GIBIGIANA TABLE LAMP

Achille Castiglioni's reading lamp has a concealed halogen light source. Light is projected up through the cylinder and is reflected off an adjustable circular mirror, providing a concentrated beam of light.

1982

SECONDA DINING CHAIR

Mario Botta's design makes use of bold textures. Square and round tubular steel frame a ribbed polyurethane back roll against a perforated sheet-metal seat.

PENELOPE DINING CHAIR

Charles Pollock's Penelope chair has a seating shell of great elasticity. This shell is composed of steel wire woven into a tight mesh, cut to size and pressure-molded to maintain its contour. A thermoplastic resin coating is placed over the 54,450 holes.

1983

BELSCHNER GROUP DINING TABLE

Andrew Belschner's table series has a reveal banding separating the top color and the leg color. The color layer is a ⅛-inch cast (not coated) polyester resin in a satin or high-gloss finish. Repair can be completed on site with sandpaper and furniture polish.

ILIOS FLOOR LAMP

Ingo Maurer's kinetic light source is composed of two separate rods with a glass sphere containing a 50-watt/12-volt bulb.

POLIFEMO FLOOR LAMP

Carlo Forcolini's floor lamp has an adjustable metal reflector that incorporates a lens that breaks the light into a colored design on the ceiling.

WOGG I STORAGE

This shelving system, designed by Gerd Lange, consists of horizontal shelving with maximum spans of up to 9 feet 6 inches. The connector is a slotted pyramid of injection-molded polycarbonate, a thermoplastic. The connector accepts both the horizontal shelves and the vertical infill components.

1984

EQUA DESK CHAIR

The introduction of the Equa chair by William Stumpf and Don Chadwick initiated a new generation of office seating. The chair responds naturally to support body movements without the use of mechanical adjustments. This was accomplished through a semirigid/elastic, injection-molded, split shell of glass-fiber-reinforced polyester. The split shell permits the seat and back to operate independently from the thicker side elements.

PENTAX SYSTEM WALL LAMP

Giovanni Bellagamba's lighting unit, pentagonal in section, is constructed of extruded aluminum. Halogen, incandescent, or fluorescent bulbs may be used. Wall mounts include both inside and outside corners. Additional applications include wall tables, wall vases, and wall ashtrays.

1986

TEA-FOR-TWO SIDE TABLE

This small table design by François Scali and Alain Domingo consists of a circular glass top laid in compression against thick and thin steel rods.

1 LOUNGE CHAIRS

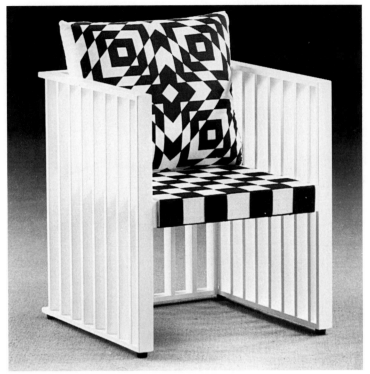

Franz Wittmann   1—1

Cassina   1—2

1–3

1–1 PURKERSDORF

1903
Designer: Josef Hoffmann
Manufacturer: Franz Wittmann
Frame: white lacquered wood
Seat: black and white webbing
Back: loose foam-filled cushion covered in fabric
24" W; 24" D; 33" H; 16½" SH

1–2 WILLOW I

1904
Designer: Charles Rennié Mackintosh
Manufacturer: Cassina
Frame: ashwood with a black ebony stain
Seat: upholstered in Indian fabric
37" W; 16" D; 46.9" H; 15.7" SH

1–3 SITZMACHINE

1905
Designer: Josef Hoffmann
Manufacturer: Kafra
Frame and back: bent beechwood; adjustable back bar is
    pure brass
Seat: Foam cushion covered in velvet
24¼" W; 34⅝" D; 43⁵⁄₁₆" H

1–4 EGG ROCKING CHAIR

1905
Designer: Josef Hoffmann
Manufacturer: Franz Wittmann
Frame: ebonized beechwood
Seat and back: natural cane
28¾" W; 50½" D; 45½" H; 18" SH

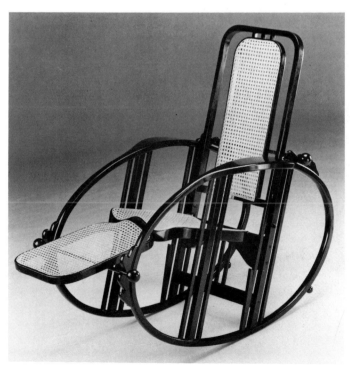

1–4

Franz Wittmann   1–5

Tecta Möbel   1–6

1—5 KUBUS

1910
Designer: Josef Hoffmann
Manufacturer: Franz Wittmann
Frame: hardwood; rubber webbed springing; foam-covered;
  upholstered in leather
Legs: black wood cubes
36" W; 30½" D; 28½" H; 17½" SH

1—6 D 51

1910
Designer: Walter Gropius
Manufacturer: Tecta Möbel
Frame: wood
Seat and back: upholstered in fabric or leather
24" W; 22" D; 31⅛" H; 18⅛" SH

1—7 WHITE CHAIR

c. 1910
Designer: Eliel Saarinen
Manufacturer: Adelta Oy
Frame: handcarved solid birch, lacquered pearl-white
Seat: foam covered in fabric
26¾" W; 21¼" D; 32¾" H; 17¾" SH

1—8 HAUS KOLLER

1911
Designer: Josef Hoffmann
Manufacturer: Franz Wittmann
Frame: hardwood; rubber webbed springing; foam-covered;
  upholstered in fabric or leather; piped edges
35½" W; 32" D; 37" H; 16½" SH; 25½" AH

Cassina   1–9

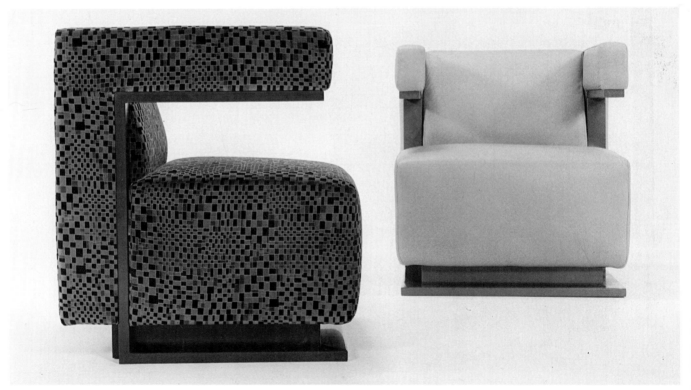

Images of America   1–10

Courtesy of Knoll International   1—11

Cassina   1—12

1—9   RED AND BLUE CHAIR
1918
Designer: Gerrit T. Rietveld
Manufacturer: Cassina
Frame: beech marine plywood; polychrome black- and yellow-
    aniline stained and lacquered beechwood
Seat and back: polychrome red- and blue-aniline stained and
    lacquered beechwood
25.7" W; 32.7" D; 34.6" H; 13" SH

1—10   WALTER (403)
1921
Designer: Walter Gropius
Manufacturer: Images of America
Frame: hardwood and tubular steel
Base: steel
Seat, back, and arms: polyurethane foam and Dacron padding
    covered in fabric or leather
28" W; 27½" D; 29" H; 16½" SH; 29" AH

1—11   WASSILY
1925
Designer: Marcel Breuer
Manufacturer: Knoll International
Frame: tubular steel, polished finish
Seat, back, and arms: leather or canvas
30¾" W; 27" D; 28½" H; 17" SH; 22¾" AH

1—12   SENNA
1925
Designer: Erik Gunnar Asplund
Manufacturer: Cassina
Frame: walnut
Shell: polyester reinforced with Fiberglas; upholstered in saddle
    leather
Headrest: polyester foam padding
36.2" W; 45.3" D; 44" H; 13.4" SH; 21.3" AH

Tecta Möbel   1–13

Galerie Metropol Inc.   1–14

Gebrüder Thonet
1-15

Cassina
1-16

1-13   D 4

1926
Designer: Marcel Breuer
Manufacturer: Tecta Möbel
Frame: tubular steel
Seat, back, and arms: canvas
30 5/8" W; 24" D; 27 1/2" H; 16 1/2" SH

1-14   B 25

1928
Designer: Marcel Breuer
Manufacturer: Gebrüder Thonet
Frame: tubular steel
Seat and back: rattan; coiled spring suspension
Arm pads: wood
25 5/8" W; 33 1/2" D; 43 9/16" H; 13" SH

1-15   S 35

1928
Designer: Marcel Breuer
Manufacturer: Gebrüder Thonet
Frame: chrome-plated steel tubing
Seat and back: natural wicker or leather
Arms: natural beech
25 1/2" W; 31 1/2" D; 32 1/2" H; 14 1/2" SH

1-16   LC/1

1928
Designer: Le Corbusier
Manufacturer: Cassina
Frame: chrome-plated steel
Seat, back, and arms: leather or ponyskin
23.6" W; 25.5" D; 25.2" H; 15.7" SH

Cassina 1–17

Zanotta 1–18

Courtesy of Knoll International   1—19

1—17 LC/2

1928
Designer: Le Corbusier
Manufacturer: Cassina
Frame: chrome-plated steel tubing; reinforced elastic material
    straps; steel hooks
Seat and back: polyurethane and Dacron padding covered
    in fabric, leather, or vinyl
29.9" W; 27.5" D; 26.4" H; 16.9" SH

1—18 LIRA

1929
Designer: Piero Bottoni
Manufacturer: Zanotta
Frame: stainless steel tube
Support: nylon threads
Seat: foam covered in leather
19¾" W; 19" D; 28¼" H; 17¾" SH

1—19 BARCELONA

1929
Designer: Ludwig Mies van der Rohe
Manufacturer: Knoll International
Frame: stainless steel, polished finish
Seat and back: foam cushions covered in leather; constructed
    of welted panels and button tufting; saddle leather straps
30" W; 30" D; 30" H; 17" SH

1—20 TUGENDHAT

1929
Designer: Ludwig Mies van der Rohe
Manufacturer: Knoll International
Frame: stainless steel, polished finish
Seat and back: saddle leather straps with foam rubber cushions
    covered in top-grain leather
29¾" W; 27¼" D; 32¾" H

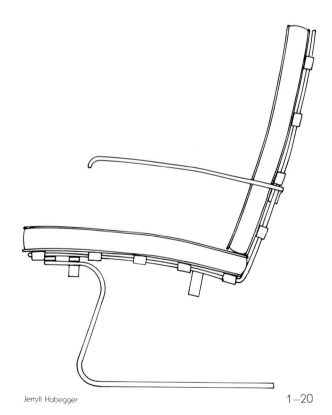

Jerryll Habegger   1—20

11

JG Furniture Systems, Inc.   1—21

Alias   1—22

Adelta Oy   1–23

1–21 H-107

1929
Designer: René Herbst
Manufacturer: JG Furniture Systems
Frame: 14-gauge, 1-inch-diameter steel tubing with a black
    lacquer finish or chrome-plated
Seat and back: rubber spring cords with a nylon covering
    and zinc-plated hooks
21" W; 34"–47" D; 23"–41" H; 12½" SH

1–22 HOMAGE TO THEO VAN DOESBURG

1929
Designer: Theo van Doesburg
Manufacturer: Alias
Frame: chrome-plated tubular steel
Seat and back: polyurethane foam covered in fabric or leather
25½" W; 17¾" D; 25½" H

1–23 BLUE CHAIR

1929
Designer: Eliel Saarinen
Manufacturer: Adelta Oy
Frame: solid birch, blue-gray lacquered with gold leaf
Seat: foam covered in fabric
25" W; 19¾" D; 30" H; 18" SH

1–24 MONZA

1930
Designer: Giuseppe Terragni
Manufacturer: B.D. Ediciones
Frame: beech and curved veneered board in a Corinth-colored
    varnish
Seat and back: polyurethane cushion covered in velvet
27¼" W; 37¾" D; 23½" H; 14¼" SH

B.D. Ediciones   1–24

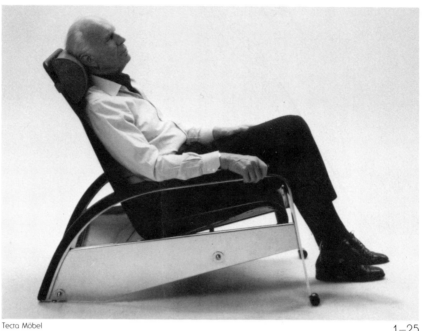

Tecta Möbel   1–25

Arkitektura   1–26

1–27

1–25 D 80

1930
Designer: Jean Prouvé
Manufacturer: Tecta Möbel
Frame: nickel-plated or lacquered folded flat sheet steel
Seat and back: upholstered in fabric or leather
26½" W; 43¼"–55" D; 39" H; 17¾" SH

1–26 SAARINEN HOUSE ARM CHAIR

1930
Designer: Eliel Saarinen
Manufacturer: Arkitektura
Frame: solid hardwood with east Indian rosewood, African
   mahogany, afrormosia, or maple veneers; ebony trim
Seat and back: foam covered in fabric
24¾" W; 21½" D; 31" H; 18" SH

1–27 MR LOUNGE CHAIR

1931
Designer: Ludwig Mies van der Rohe
Manufacturer: Knoll International
Frame: tubular stainless steel, polished finish
Seat and back: channeled foam cushion covered in fabric
   or leather; saddle leather straps
23⅝" W; 36¼" D; 33" H; 17½" SH; 23¼" AH

1–28 PAIMIO (41)

1932
Designer: Alvar Aalto
Manufacturer: Artek
Frame: natural birch
Seat and back: black or white lacquered birch
23⅝" W; 33½" D; 25¼" H; 13" SH

1–28

Artek   1—29

Cadsana, Cadwallader and Sangiorgio Associates   1—30

Rud. Rasmussens Snedkerier   1–31

1–29 AALTO WING (401)

1933
Designer: Alvar Aalto
Manufacturer: Artek
Frame: natural birch
Seat and back: foam-cushioned plywood covered in fabric
  or raffia
24⅝″ W; 31½″ D; 39¼″ H; 13⅜″ SH

1–30 BREUER SEATING COLLECTION (129.212.0)

1933
Designer: Marcel Breuer
Manufacturer: Cadsana, Cadwallader and Sangiorgio Associates
Frame: polished or epoxy-coated aluminum extrusion
Seat, back, and arms: solid wood
23½″ W; 33″ D; 31½″ H; 16½″ SH

1–31 SAFARI

1933
Designer: Kaare Klint
Manufacturer: Rud. Rasmussens Snedkerier
Frame: oiled ash
Seat and back: oxhide, canvas, or linen
Arms: leather straps
22½″ W; 22½″ D; 31½″ H; 13¼″ SH; 22″ AH

1–32 EVA

1934
Designer: Bruno Mathsson
Manufacturer: Dux International
Frame: stratified beech, natural or stained in light mahogany
Seat and back: plaited natural hemp bands or quilted leather
24″ W; 28″ D; 32¼″ H; 15½″ SH; 24″ AH

Dux International   1–32

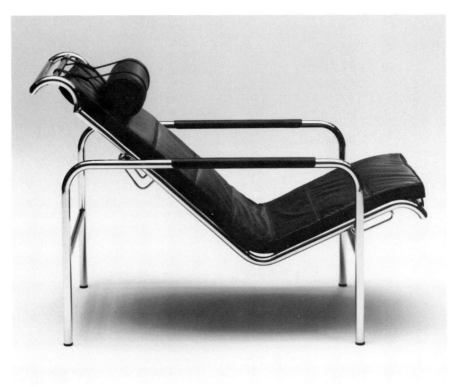

Zanotta

1–33

Zanotta

1–34

1—35

1—33 GENNI

1935
Designer: Gabriele Mucchi
Manufacturer: Zanotta
Frame: chrome-plated steel tubing
Seat, back, and headrest: polyurethane foam covered in
    leather
Springs: steel coil
22½" W; 43" D; 30" H; 16" SH

1—34 SANT'ELIA

1936
Designer: Giuseppe Terragni
Manufacturer: Zanotta
Frame: tubular stainless steel
Seat and back: upholstered leather
Arms: black-stained wood
21¾" W; 26¾" D; 31" H; 16" SH

1—35 BUTTERFLY

1938
Designers: Jorge Hardoy, Antonio Bonet, and Juan Kurchan
Manufacturer: Knoll International
Frame: steel rods
Seat and back: canvas or leather sling
31" W; 27½" D; 34¼" H

1—36 J 16

1944
Designer: Hans J. Wegner
Manufacturer: Nordisk Andels
Frame: beech, natural or lacquered
Seat: handwoven rope
25" W; 34" D; 42" H; 16¼" SH

1—36

Dux International   1–37

Herman Miller, Inc.   1–38

Artek   1–39

1–37   PERNILLA 1

1944
Designer: Bruno Mathsson
Manufacturer: Dux International
Frame: stratified natural beech
Seat and back: plaited hemp bands or quilted leather
28¾" W; 39¾" D; 35¾" H; 15¼" SH; 24½" AH

1–38   LCM

1946
Designers: Charles Eames and Ray Eames
Manufacturer: Herman Miller
Frame: chrome-plated solid steel; nylon self-leveling glides
Seat and back: molded plywood
22¼" W; 25⅜" D; 27⅞" H; 15¼" SH

1–39   406

1947
Designer: Alvar Aalto
Manufacturer: Artek
Frame: natural birch
Seat and back: rattan webbing
23⅝" W; 28¼" D; 34⅝" H; 15¾" SH

1–40   PEACOCK (JH 550)

1947
Designer: Hans J. Wegner
Manufacturer: Johannes Hansens Møbelsnedkeri
Frame: solid ash
Seat: woven twine
Arms: solid teak
30¼" W; 30¼" D; 40½" H; 14¼" SH

Johannes Hansens Møbelsnedkeri, Copenhagen, Denmark   1–40

Jerryll Habegger

1–41

Courtesy of Knoll International

1–42

Courtesy of Knoll International

1—43

1—41   LOUNGE CHAIR
1947
Designers: Hendrik van Keppel and Taylor Green
Manufacturer: Van Keppel-Green
Frame: enameled tubular steel
Seat and back: cotton cord
21 ¼″ W; 31 ½″ D; 25″ H; 10″ SH

1—42   GRASSHOPPER
1948
Designer: Eero Saarinen
Manufacturer: Knoll International
Frame: laminated birch
Seat and back: inner spring construction covered in fabric
26 ½″ W; 31″ D; 35″ H; 16 ½″ SH

1—43   WOMB
1948
Designer: Eero Saarinen
Manufacturer: Knoll International
Frame: foam over a molded plastic shell covered in fabric
Base: steel rod
Seat and back: foam cushions covered in fabric
40″ W; 34″ D; 35 ½″ H; 16″ SH; 20 ½″ AH

1—44   JH 512
1949
Designer: Hans J. Wegner
Manufacturer: Johannes Hansens Møbelsnedkeri
Frame: solid oak
Seat and back: woven cane
24″ W; 29 ½″ D; 30 ¼″ H; 15 ¼″ SH

Johannes Hansens Møbelsnedkeri, Copenhagen, Denmark

1—44

Jerryll Habegger

1–45

Cassina

1–46

Herman Miller, Inc.

1–47

1–45 225

1949
Designer: Hans J. Wegner
Manufacturer: Getama
Frame: matte chrome-plated and lacquered steel
Seat and back: woven flag-line
Headrest: canvas
41″ W; 44½″ D; 31½″ H

1–46 TALIESIN

1949
Designer: Frank Lloyd Wright
Manufacturer: Cassina
Frame: laminated plywood in a natural light cherry veneer
    or cherry-veneer-stained walnut
Seat, back, and interior panels: polyurethane foam and poly-
    ester covered in fabric or leather
37″ W; 35.4″ D; 30.3″ H; 14.9″ SH; 18.5″ AH

1–47 ROCKER

1950
Designers: Charles Eames and Ray Eames
Manufacturer: Herman Miller
Seat and back: molded Fiberglas
Base: steel rod; birch runners
24⅞″ W; 27″ D; 26⅞″ H; 16″ SH

1–48 GM TECH CENTER

c. 1950
Designer: Eero Saarinen
Manufacturer: Unknown
Frame: tubular aluminum, brushed chrome finish
Seat and back: fully upholstered in leather
36½″ W; 33″ D; 26⅜″ H; 18¾″ SH

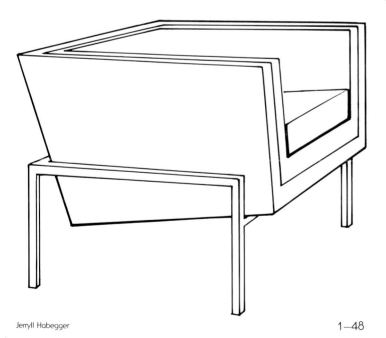

Jerryll Habegger

1–48

Arflex   1–49

Jerryll Habegger   1–50

1–51

1–49 LADY

1951
Designer: Marco Zanuso
Manufacturer: Arflex
Shell: stamped steel
Seat and back: molded foam rubber covered in fabric
Legs: tubular steel
30¼" W; 31½" D; 32¼" H; 15¼" SH

1–50 PK 25

1951
Designer: Poul Kjaerholm
Manufacturer: Fritz Hansen
Frame: matte chrome-plated steel
Seat and back: braided sisal cord
27" W; 28¾" D; 29½" H; 15¾" SH

1–51 DIAMOND CHAIR (421-2)

1951
Designer: Harry Bertoia
Manufacturer: Knoll International
Frame: welded steel wire
Seat pad: polyurethane foam covered in fabric or vinyl
33¾" W; 28" D; 30½" H; 17" SH

1–52 HIGH BACK (423)

1952
Designer: Harry Bertoia
Manufacturer: Knoll International
Frame: welded steel wire; fully upholstered in fabric; detachable foam cover
38½" W; 34½" D; 39" H; 14" SH

1–52

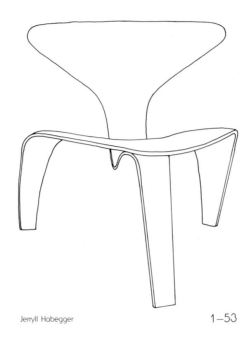

Jerryll Habegger   1–53

Stuttgarter Akademie-Werkstätten   1–54

Tecno   1–55

1–53 CHAIR
1952
Designer: Poul Kjaerholm
Manufacturer: Fritz Hansen
Frame: laminated wood
25" W; 22" D; 29½" H; 17" SH

1–54 EASY CHAIR
1953
Designer: Herbert Hirche
Manufacturer: Stuttgarter Akademie-Werkstätten
Frame: steel tube
Seat and back: polyfoam covered in fabric
22¾" W; 31½" D; 26½" H; 13¾" SH

1–55 P 40
1955
Designer: Osvaldo Borsani
Manufacturer: Tecno
Frame: pressed steel
Seat and back: polyurethane foam covered in fabric or leather
Arms: rubber
28⅜" W; 31½"–59" D; 27½"–35½" H; 15⅜"–16½" SH

1–56 COCONUT
1955
Designer: George Nelson
Manufacturer: Herman Miller
Frame: brake-formed and welded sheet-steel shell
Legs: bright-polished, cast aluminum alloy legs; bright-chrome-plated, round steel rod leg braces
Seat and back: urethane foam covered in fabric, leather, or vinyl
40" W; 33¾" D; 32½" H; 13¾" SH

Herman Miller, Inc.   1–56

Loewenstein   1–57

Herman Miller, Inc.   1–58

Hans J. Wegner

1–59

1–57 REX

c. 1955
Designer: Niko Kralj
Manufacturer: Loewenstein
Seat, back, and arms: laminated natural beech
Legs: natural solid beech
22½" W; 26" D; 29½" H; 15" SH; 23½" AH

1–58 EAMES LOUNGE (ES670)

1956
Designers: Charles Eames and Ray Eames
Manufacturer: Herman Miller
Frame: molded plywood shell
Base: aluminum
Seat and back: foam covered in leather
32½" W; 32¾" D; 33⅜" H; 15" SH

1–59 JH 57

1956
Designer: Hans J. Wegner
Manufacturer: Johannes Hansens Møbelsnedkeri
Legs: steel tubes
Back and seat: upholstered in fabric or oxhide
25¼" W; 24¾" D; 32¼" H; 17¾" SH

1–60 PK 22

1957
Designer: Poul Kjaerholm
Manufacturer: Fritz Hansen
Frame: matte chrome-plated spring steel
Seat and back: leather, canvas, or woven cane
24¾" W; 26½" D; 28" H; 13¾" SH

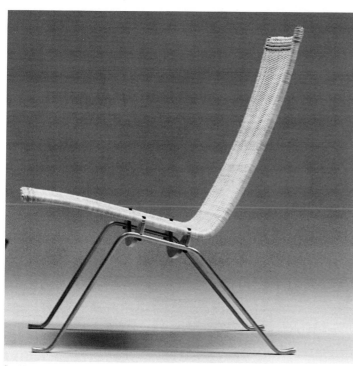

Fritz Hansen

1–60

Herman Miller, Inc.   1-61

Fritz Hansen   1-62

Fritz Hansen   1–63

Fritz Hansen   1–64

1–61   ALUMINUM GROUP

1958
Designers: Charles Eames and Ray Eames
Manufacturer: Herman Miller
Frame: bright-polished cast aluminum alloy; heat-treated steel
    tension bar and swivel shaft; cold-rolled steel seat support
Seat and back: vinyl foam cushioning and nylon covered in
    fabric or leather
Arms: black-nylon- or clear-cellulosic-coated natural aluminum
24¾" W; 28½" D; 33¾" H; 17½" SH

1–62   BOW

1958
Designer: Arne Jacobsen
Manufacturer: Fritz Hansen
Frame: chrome-plated tubular steel
Seat and back: polyfoam over a plastic shell, covered in
    leather
28½" W; 24" D; 27¼" H; 15¾" SH

1–63   SWAN

1959
Designer: Arne Jacobsen
Manufacturer: Fritz Hansen
Shell: molded polyurethane reinforced with Fiberglas and
    molded latex; foam covered in fabric, leather, or vinyl
Base: cast polished aluminum; chromed steel column
29" W; 27" D; 29½" H; 15" SH; 22" AH

1–64   EGG

1959
Designer: Arne Jacobsen
Manufacturer: Fritz Hansen
Shell: molded polyurethane reinforced with Fiberglas and
    molded latex; foam covered in fabric, leather, or vinyl
Base: cast polished aluminum; chromed steel column
34" W; 31" D; 42" H; 14½" SH

Artifort 1—65

Marco Albini and Franca Helg (Architetti Associati) 1—66

Johannes Hansens Møbelsnedkeri
Copenhagen, Denmark

1–67

1–65   437

1959
Designer: Pierre Paulin
Manufacturer: Artifort
Frame: chrome-plated steel tube
Shell: double shell of molded laminated wood upholstered
   in polyfoam and covered in fabric
32" W; 31" D; 29" H; 14" SH

1–66   THREE PIECE

1959
Designers: Franco Albini and Franca Helg
Manufacturer: Carlo Poggi
Frame: steel tubing
Seat and back: foam rubber padding covered in fabric
34" W; 34" D; 40" H; 16" SH

1–67   BULL (JH 46)

1960
Designer: Hans J. Wegner
Manufacturer: Johannes Hansens Møbelsnedkeri
Frame: foam rubber and horsehair over wood, covered in
   leather
Base: tubular brushed chrome steel
39" W; 39" D; 35½" H; 14¼" SH

1–68   602

1960
Designer: Dieter Rams
Manufacturer: Vitsoe
Frame: lacquered or polished aluminum
Shell: Fiberglas-reinforced polyester upholstered in fabric or
   leather
23⅝" W; 25⅝" D; 27½" H; 13⅞" SH

Vitsoe Kollektion

1–68

Jerryll Habegger   1–69

Erik Jørgensen Møbelfabrik   1–70

Vitsoe Kollektion

1–71

Herman Miller, Inc.

1–72

1–69   657

1960
Designer: Charles Pollock
Manufacturer: Knoll International
Legs: tubular steel
Arms and stretchers: cast aluminum
Seat and back: saddle leather sling with foam-rubber cushion
     covered in leather
25″ W; 26″ D; 27¾″ H; 15½″ SH

1–70   CORONA (EJ 605)

1961
Designer: Poul M. Volther
Manufacturer: Erik Jørgensen Møbelfabrik
Frame: chrome-plated spring steel
Seat and back: neoprene foam covered in fabric or leather
35½″ W; 31½″ D; 37⅜″ H

1–71   620

1962
Designer: Dieter Rams
Manufacturer: Vitsoe
Shell: Fiberglas-reinforced polyester with a plastic laminate
     finish
Seat and back: loose down cushions with removable fabric
     or leather covers
34″ W; 31½″ D; 35½″ H; 15½″ SH

1–72   CATENARY

1963
Designer: George Nelson
Manufacturer: Herman Miller
Frame: chrome-plated epoxy-glued steel
Support: rubber-covered steel cables
Seat and back: vinyl-coated steel pans containing latex foam-
     rubber cushioning, covered in fabric or leather
29″ W; 28″ D; 28″ H; 16½″ SH

Fritz Hansen   1-73

Fredericia Stolefabrik   1-74

Courtesy of Knoll International

1–75

Collection Stedelijk Museum, Amsterdam

1–76

1–73   CATHERINE (4335)

1963
Designer: Arne Jacobsen
Manufacturer: Fritz Hansen
Frame: laminated natural beech
Seat and back: polyfoam covered in fabric
25 ½" W; 31 ½" D; 42" H; 15¾" SH; 20¾" AH

1–74   2204

1963
Designer: Børge Mogensen
Manufacturer: Fredericia Stolefabrik
Frame: solid hardwood with foam padding and rubber web-
    bing seat support
Seat and back: loose down-filled cushions covered in leather
Legs: oiled teak
27½" W; 35" D; 41¾" H; 16½" SH

1–75   SUZANNE

1963
Designer: Kazuhide Takahama
Manufacturer: Knoll International
Frame: tubular steel, polished chrome finish
Seat and back: separate foam polyurethane cushions covered
    in fabric
30" W; 34⅝" D; 26¾" H; 14" SH

1–76   STELTMAN

1963
Designer: Gerrit T. Rietveld
Manufacturer: Gerrit T. Rietveld
Frame: solid oak
19¾" W; 17¾" D; 27½" H; 15¾" SH

Alfred Kill   1—77

Comfort   1—78

Beylerian 1–79

1–77 6720 A

1964
Designers: Jørgen Kastholm and Preben Fabricius
Manufacturer: Alfred Kill
Frame: soft-edge, matte chrome steel
Seat and back: foam-down cushions covered in leather
Arms: leather-thong-wrapped
29" W; 31½" D; 31½" H

1–78 ELDA

1964
Designer: Joe Colombo
Manufacturer: Comfort
Frame: Fiberglas shell molded in one piece; swiveling base
Seat and back: detachable molded polyurethane cushions
   covered in fabric or leather
36¼" W; 36¼" D; 36¼" H; 15¼" SH

1–79 KARUSELLI

1964
Designer: Yrjö Kukkapuro
Manufacturer: Avarte Oy
Frame: glass-filled reinforced molded polyester
Base: steel base spring
Shell: foam-rubber padding covered in leather
31" W; 38" D; 35" H; 15" SH

1–80 LOW FIRESIDE CHAIR DJINN

1965
Designer: Olivier Mourgue
Manufacturer: Airborne
Frame: metal with polyfoam upholstery and detachable fabric
   covers
28¼" W; 30" D; 26" H; 13¾" SH

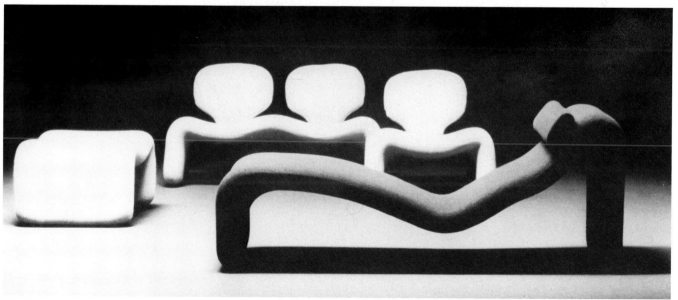

Olivier Mourgue

1–80

Cassina   1–81

Artifort   1–82

Courtesy of Knoll International   1–83

Courtesy of Knoll International   1–84

1–81   925

1965
Designers: Afra Scarpa and Tobia Scarpa
Manufacturer: Cassina
Frame: walnut or rosewood
Seat and back: upholstered in leather
26″ W; 26″ D; 27⅛″ H; 13⅜″ SH

1–82   675

1966
Designer: Pierre Paulin
Manufacturer: Artifort
Frame: chrome-plated steel rods
Seat and back: saddle leather
32¾″ W; 26″ D; 26⅜″ H; 14¼″ SH

1–83   1715

1966
Designer: Warren Platner
Manufacturer: Knoll International
Shell: foam cushion over molded Fiberglas, covered in fabric
Base: steel rod, bright nickel finish
Seat cushion: polyester fiber over molded foam core, covered
    in fabric
36½″ W; 25½″ D; 30½″ H; 18½″ SH; 25″ AH

1–84   EASY CHAIR (1705)

1966
Designer: Warren Platner
Manufacturer: Knoll International
Shell: foam cushion over molded Fiberglas, covered in fabric
Base: steel rod, bright nickel finish
Seat cushion: polyester fiber over molded foam core, covered
    in fabric
40¾″ W; 36½″ D; 39″ H; 17½″ SH; 21″ AH

. Artifort   1—85

Gufram   1—86

Asko Oy   1—87

Courtesy of Knoll International   1—88

1—85   RIBBON

1966
Designer: Pierre Paulin
Manufacturer: Artifort
Frame: tubular steel; rubber mesh seat and tricot canvas back
   upholstered with molded rubber, covered in stretch fabric
Base: high-frequency pressed wood
39⅜″ W; 29¼″ D; 27½″ H; 15″ SH

1—86   PRATONE

1966
Designers: Giorgio Cevetti, Piero Derossi, and Ricardo Rosso
Manufacturer: Gufram
Frame: foam
57½″ W; 53½″ D; 37⅜″ H

1—87   BALL

1966
Designer: Eero Aarnio
Manufacturer: Asko
Frame: glass-reinforced polyester; fully upholstered
Base: steel swivel pedestal
Seat: loose cushion
41¼″ W; 38½″ D; 47¼″ H; 18″ SH

1—88   1425

1966
Designer: Richard Schultz
Manufacturer: Knoll International
Frame: cast and extruded aluminum
Seat and back: woven Dacron mesh with vinyl straps
26″ W; 28¼″ D; 26½″ H; 14″ SH; 20¼″ AH

Artifort   1-89

Artifort   1-90

Brickel Associates   1—91

1—89   301

1967
Designer: Pierre Paulin
Manufacturer: Artifort
Shell: reinforced Fiberglas; removable jersey-covered latex foam
   upholstery
32" W; 27½" D; 24½" H; 15½" SH

1—90   577

1967
Designer: Pierre Paulin
Manufacturer: Artifort
Frame: tubular steel upholstered with polyurethane foam;
   rubber webbing; covered in stretch fabric
33½" W; 35½" D; 24" H; 13⅜" SH

1—91   BANKERS (1423)

1967
Designer: Ward Bennett
Manufacturer: Brickel Associates
Frame: natural oiled cherry or natural oiled ash
Seat and back: upholstered in fabric or leather
30⅜" W; 32½" D; 32" H; 16" SH; 23½" AH

1—92   932

1967
Designer: Mario Bellini
Manufacturer: Cassina
Frame: polyurethane foam rubber and Dacron padding
   covered in fabric, leather, or vinyl
36⅝" W; 33½" D; 24⅜" H; 15¾" SH

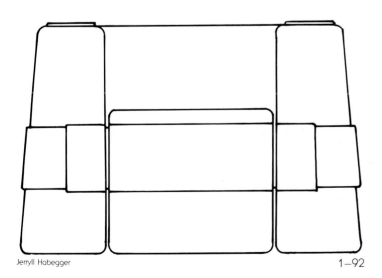

Jerryll Habegger   1—92

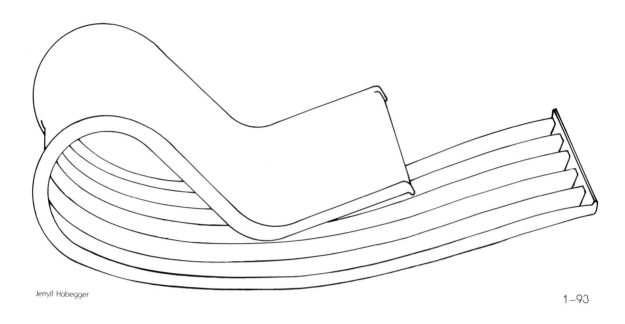

Jerryll Habegger

1–93

Cassina

1–94

Fritz Hansen   1–95

1–93 DONDOLO

1967
Designers: Cesare Leonardi and Franca Stagi
Manufacturer: Elco Bellato
Frame: molded Fiberglas
15¾" W; 69" D; 30¾" H

1–94 CIPREA

1967
Designers: Afra Scarpa and Tobia Scarpa
Manufacturer: Cassina
Frame: injected expanded polyurethane structure; Dacron-
   tufted removable cover in fabric or leather
Base: padding cast on ABS resin
36¼" W; 34⅝" D; 31½" H; 17" SH

1–95 PK 20

1967
Designer: Poul Kjaerholm
Manufacturer: Fritz Hansen
Frame: matte chrome-plated steel
Seat and back: upholstered in oxhide
31½" W; 30" D; 35" H; 14½" SH

1–96 TAIL 13

1967
Designer: Heinz Witthoeft
Manufacturer: Heinz Witthoeft
Structure: cut and molded thermoplastic panel
25½" W; 25½" D; 25½" H; 13¾" SH

Heinz Witthoeft/Richard Schenkirz   1–96a

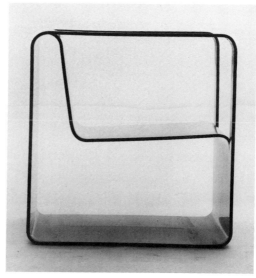

Heinz Witthoeft/Richard Schenkirz   1–96b

Erik Magnussen

1—97

Courtesy of Knoll International

1—98

Asko Oy   1-99

1-97   Z FOLDING
1968
Designer: Erik Magnussen
Manufacturer: Torben Orskov
Frame: chromed or enameled tubular steel
Seat and back: fabric slings
26⅜" W; 18⅞" D; 28⅛" H

1-98   BASTIANO
1968
Designer: Carlo Scarpa
Manufacturer: Knoll International
Frame: solid wood; rubber and steel suspension
Seat, back, and arms: separate cushions of foam with
   convoluted foam wrap covered in leather
36" W; 32" D; 27" H; 16" SH; 24" AH

1-99   GYRO
1968
Designer: Eero Aarnio
Manufacturer: Asko
Shell: Fiberglas
36¾" Diameter; 25" H; 12" SH; 21" AH

1-100   SCISSOR (1098)
1968
Designer: Ward Bennett
Manufacturer: Brickel Associates
Frame: natural oiled ash
Seat and back: upholstered in fabric or leather; right seat
24" W; 29¼" D; 34¾" H; 15½" SH

Brickel Associates   1-100

Herman Miller, Inc.   1–101

B & B Italia   1–102

Alfred Kill   1—103

1—101   SOFT PAD GROUP

1969
Designers: Charles Eames and Ray Eames
Manufacturer: Herman Miller
Frame: bright-polished cast aluminum alloy; heat-treated steel
    tension bar; cold-rolled steel seat support
Seat and back: flexible urethane foam encapsulated by
    polyester fiber batting covered in leather
26" W; 32" D; 40" H; 18" SH

1—102   UP 5

1969
Designer: Gaetano Pesce
Manufacturer: C & B Italia
Frame: expanded polyurethane upholstered in stretch nylon
    and wool jersey
47¼" W; 51¼" D; 40½" H

1—103   SKATING (710)

1969
Designers: Jørgen Kastholm and Preben Fabricius
Manufacturer: Alfred Kill
Frame: molded plastic rimmed in soft-edge matte chrome
    steel
Base: matte chrome steel
Seat and back: upholstered in leather
26½" W; 28½" D; 30" H

1—104   8101

1969
Designer: Jørn Utzon
Manufacturer: Fritz Hansen
Frame: molded laminated wood
Legs: chrome-plated tubular steel
Seat and back: polyfoam covered in fabric
30" W; 38½" D; 36¼" H; 13¾" SH

Fritz Hansen   1—104

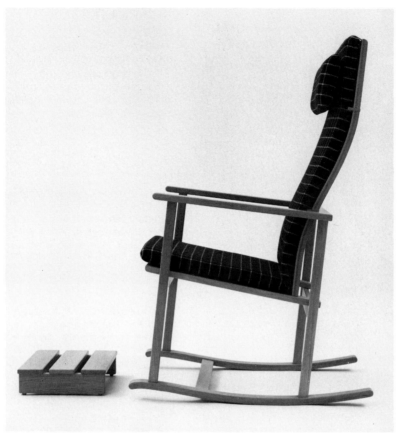

Fredericia Stolefabrik

1–105

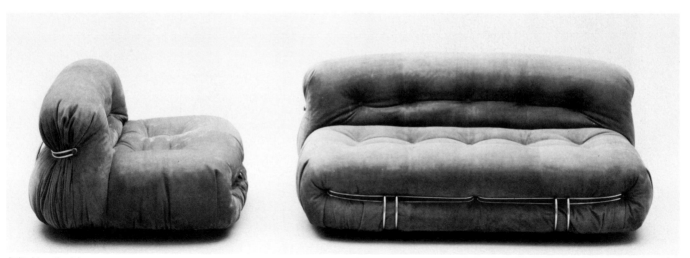

Atelier International, Inc.

1–106

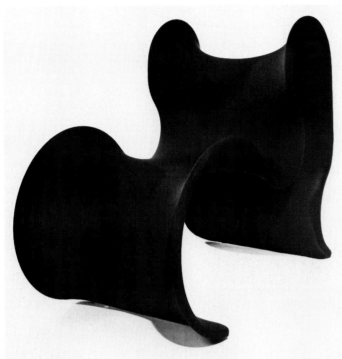

Gruppo Industriale Busnelli   1–107

Johannes Hansens Møbelsnedkeri, Copenhagen, Denmark   1–108

1–105   2268

1970
Designer: Børge Mogensen
Manufacturer: Fredericia Stolefabrik
Frame: mahogany
Seat and back: upholstered in fabric; loose cushion
24½" W; 26⅜" D; 46" H; 17⅜" SH

1–106   SORIANA

1970
Designers: Afra Scarpa and Tobia Scarpa
Manufacturer: Cassina
Frame: high-carbon, chrome-plated spring steel providing shape
    and support
Base: plywood
Seat and back: polyurethane foam and Dacron fiberfill covered
    in fabric, leather, or vinyl
35.1" W; 41.3" D; 28.3" H; 17" SH

1–107   FIOCCO

1970
Designer: Group 14
Manufacturer: Gruppo Industriale Busnelli
Frame: iron tubes covered in stretch fabric
27½" W; 46¾" D; 40½" H

1–108   JH 812

1970
Designer: Hans J. Wegner
Manufacturer: Johannes Hansens Møbelsnedkeri
Frame: matte stainless steel
Seat and back: saddle leather
24¾" W; 25¼" D; 30¾" H; 14¾" SH

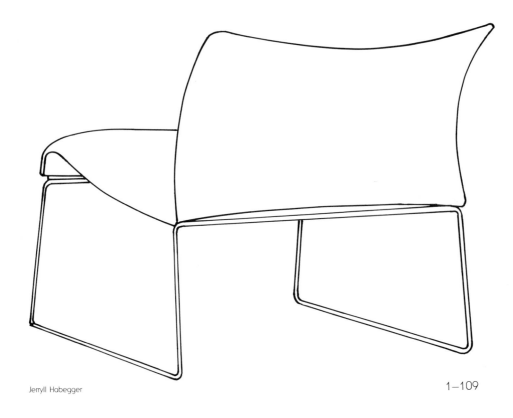

Jerryll Habegger

1–109

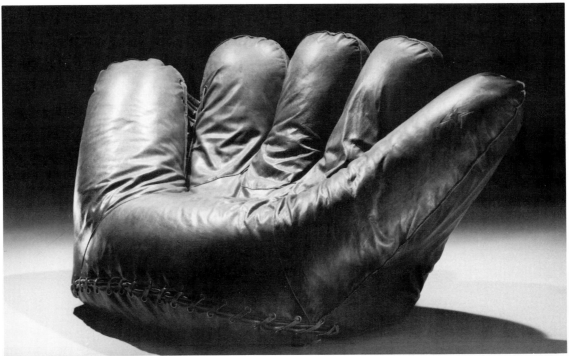

Poltronova

1–110

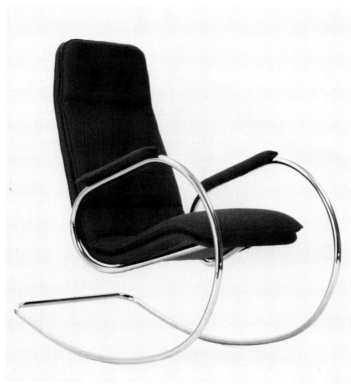

Gebrüder Thonet   1–111

Walter Knoll   1–112

1–109   SAGHI

1970
Designer: Kazuhide Takahama
Manufacturer: Simon International
Frame: chromed drawn steel rod
Seat and back: foam and synthetic wood padding covered
    in fabric
30¼″ W; 25¼″ D; 26″ H; 16″ SH

1–110   JOE

1971
Designers: Jonathan De Pas, Donato D'Urbino, and Paolo
    Lomazzi
Manufacturer: Poltronova
Frame: molded expanded foam over sprung steel, covered
    in fabric or leather
65¾″ W; 41¼″ D; 34″ H; 15¾″ SH

1–111   S 826

1971
Designer: Ulrich Böhme
Manufacturer: Gebrüder Thonet
Frame: chrome-plated tubular steel
Seat and back: polyurethane foam over plywood, covered
    in fabric or leather
23½″ W; 40½″ D; 43¼″ H; 18″ SH

1–112   701

1972
Designer: Preben Fabricius
Manufacturer: Walter Knoll
Frame: profile steel
Seat and back: saddle leather
26″ W; 27¼″ D; 30¼″ H; 14¼″ SH

Frank Gehry   1—113

B.B.B. Over   1—114

Kartell   1–115

1–113 CONTOUR ROCKER
1972
Designer: Frank Gehry
Manufacturer: Chiru
Frame: laminated corrugated cardboard
24" W; 40" D; 46" H

1–114 FLAP
1972
Designers: Jonathan De Pas, Donato D'Urbino, and Paolo
   Lomazzi
Manufacturer: B.B.B. Over
Frame: elastic structure
Seat, back, and arms: polyurethane and quilted Dacron pad-
   ding covered in fabric; removable covers
Bottom: rubber
41" W; 35½" D; 26" H; 16" SH

1–115 5/4794
1972
Designer: Gae Aulenti
Manufacturer: Kartell
Frame: rigid expanded polyurethane
27½" W; 29" D; 28" H; 13" SH

1–116 REMMI
1972
Designer: Yrjö Kukkapuro
Manufacturer: Avarte Oy
Frame: 1-inch polished chrome-plated tubular steel; plastic-
   covered spiral steel wire cushion support
Seat and back: plastic foam and Noven padding covered in
   fabric or leather
Arms: plastic-sheathed steel or laminated birch
31" W; 36" D; 33" H; 15" SH; 21" AH

Beylerian   1–116

Artifort

1–117

Cassina

1–118

Cassina   1–119

Hans J. Wegner   1–120

1–117   598

1973
Designer: Pierre Paulin
Manufacturer: Artifort
Frame: tubular steel interlaced with a network of springs in
    the seat and back; frame encased in soft polyurethane
    foam covered in stretch fabric
Foot glides: aluminum with plastic coating
33½" W; 26" D; 25½" H; 14¼" SH

1–118   AEO

1973
Designer: Archizoom Associati
Manufacturer: Cassina
Frame: baked enamel tubular and strap steel
Base: rigid, weighted, enameled urethane
Seat: polyurethane foam and Dacron cushioning covered in
    fabric
Back and arms: sling/sleeve upholstery units
31⅛" W; 29⅛" D; 42⅛" H; 18⅛" SH

1–119   WISKEY (402)

1976
Designer: Mario Bellini
Manufacturer: Cassina
Frame: welded steel armatures and spring steel structures
    individually upholstered and covered in leather
Seat: Dacron fiberfill and/or natural down feathers covered
    in leather
24.8" W; 24" D; 26.3" H; 18" SH

1–120   PP 112

1978
Designer: Hans J. Wegner
Manufacturer: P.P. Møbler
Frame: solid ash
Seat: woven twine
27½" W; 24½" D; 30" H; 15" SH

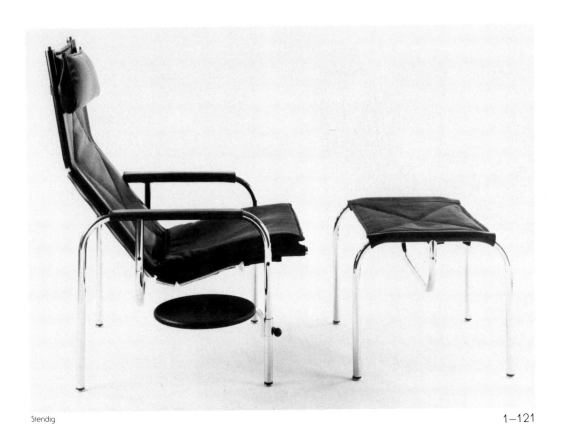

Srendig   1–121

Sunar Hauserman   1–122

Walter Knoll   1—123

1—121   EICHENBERGER (316-L)

1978
Designer: Hans Eichenberger
Manufacturer: Strässle Collection
Frame: tubular bent steel with a mirror-polished chrome finish;
    ebonized wood stretcher under front of seat for angle
    adjustment
Seat and back support: adjustable black webbed straps and
    chrome-finished buckles
Seat and back: fiberfill covered in leather
Headrest: foam wrapped with fiberfill and covered in leather
Arms: wrapped in saddle leather
27½" W; 31½" D; 38·¼" H; 15" SH; 20" AH

1—122   ROTONDA

1979
Designer: Massimo Vignelli
Manufacturer: Sunar Hauserman
Frame: polyurethane foam injected over a tubular steel frame
    and covered in fabric or leather
32¾" W; 26" D; 32" H; 16" SH

1—123   710

1979
Designer: Preben Fabricius
Manufacturer: Walter Knoll
Frame: matte-chrome flat steel
Seat and back: foam covered in leather
25¼" W; 27½" D; 36½" H; 18" SH

1—124   WINK

1980
Designer: Toshiyuki Kita
Manufacturer: Cassina
Frame: expanded polyurethane foam injected over a welded
    steel armature; padded with Dacron fiberfill and covered
    in fabric, leather, or vinyl
30.7" W; 35.4"–78.7" D; 31.5"–37.4" H; 15" SH

Cassina   1—124

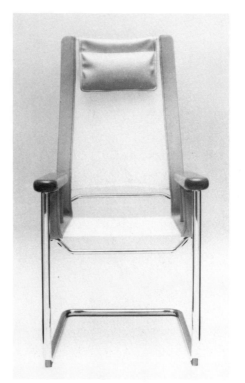

Add Interior Systems   1–125a

Add Interior Systems   1–125b

Antti Nurmesniemi   1–126

Bo-Ex   1—127

Fritz Hansen   1—128

1—125 WARREN

1980
Designer: Roger Leib
Manufacturer: Add Interior Systems
Frame: heavy-wall (14-gauge) mild lustre-grade steel tubing
    base and crossbars; frame support of flat hot-formed alloy
    truck-spring steel
Seat and back: breathable mesh of knitted or woven polyester
Arms: flexible molded vinyl
Trim: Naugahyde vinyl upholstery
25" W; 26" D; 47½" H; 18" SH

1—126   004

1980
Designer: Antti Nurmesniemi
Manufacturer: Vuokko
Frame: steel tubing
Shell: foam rubber covered in cotton canvas
33½" W; 33½" D; 28¾" H; 16½" SH

1—127   BO 1711

1980
Designers: Jørgen Lund and Ole Larsen
Manufacturer: Bo-Ex
Frame: matte chrome-plated steel
Seat and back: cane
29⅛" W; 28¼" D; 30¼" H; 14¼" SH

1—128   3810

c. 1980
Designer: Jens Ammundsen
Manufacturer: Fritz Hansen
Frame: chromed steel
Seat and back: foam over a steel frame, covered in fabric
    or leather
23½" W; 29½" D; 35¾" H; 15¼" SH; 22½" AH

Vecta   1–129

Driade   1–130

Cassina   1–131

1–129   OHL 180

1982
Designer: Herbert Ohl
Manufacturer: Vecta
Frame and base: mirror-chromed aluminum
Seat and back: black polyester mesh; black leather trim
23¼" W; 24½" D; 27" H; 15¾" SH

1–130   PRATFALL

1982
Designer: Philippe Starck
Manufacturer: Driade
Frame: varnished iron tubing
Back: lacquered bent plywood
Seat: polyurethane-resin-stuffed and black-leather-covered
    cushion
24¼" W; 30¾" D; 34" H

1–131   TORSO

1982
Designer: Paolo Deganello
Manufacturer: Cassina
Frame: tubular steel with elastic webbing, cast within poly-
    urethane foam and padded with Dacron polyester; covered
    in fabric, leather, or vinyl
Legs: tubular steel
42.9" W; 35.4" D; 45.6" H; 17.7" SH

1–132   QUANTUM

1982
Designer: Richard Frinier
Manufacturer: Brown Jordan
Frame: extruded aluminum
Seat and back: vinyl mesh
24¾" W; 29¾" D; 28¼" H; 16" SH

Brown Jordan/Richard Frinier   1–132

ICF, Inc.   1—133

Avarte Oy   1—134

Courtesy of Knoll International   1–135

1–133   RICHARD III

1982
Designer: Philippe Starck
Manufacturer: Baleri Italia
Frame: silver or black molded rigid polyurethane
Seat: cushion covered in black leather
36¼" W; 32¼" D; 36" H

1–134   EXPERIMENT

1983
Designer: Yrjö Kukkapuro
Manufacturer: Avarte Oy
Frame: chrome-plated tubular steel
Seat and back: plastic laminate over press-formed birch veneer;
   polyurethane foam and Dacron padding detachable cush-
   ions, covered in fabric or leather
Arms: press-formed birch plywood
21" W; 29" D; 29" H; 15" SH; 23" AH

1–135   RIART ROCKING CHAIR (790)

1983
Designer: Carlos Riart
Manufacturer: Knoll International
Frame: ebony with horizontal crossmembers of Brazilian
   amaranthe; mother-of-pearl inlays
Seat and back: layered foam over plywood panels, covered
   in fabric
24¾" W; 42½" D; 39¼" H; 19½" SH; 24" AH

1–136   PP 124

1983
Designer: Hans J. Wegner
Manufacturer: P.P. Møbler
Frame: solid ash with seat and back support of woven cord
Seat: cushion covered in canvas
29½" W; 34½" D; 42½" H; 15¾" SH

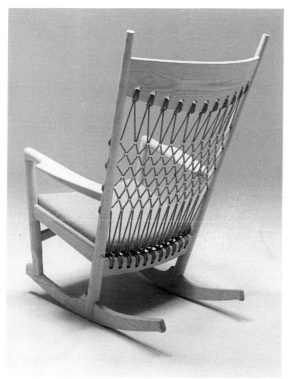

Hans J. Wegner   1–136

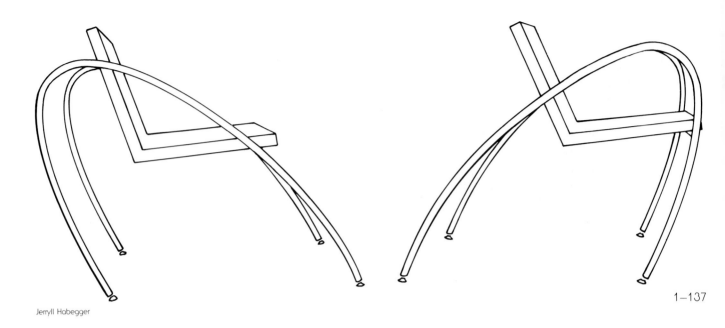

Jerryll Habegger

1–137

Tecta Möbel

1–138

Poltrona Frau   1-139

1-137 MORENO + MARINI

1983
Designers: François Scali and Alain Domingo
Manufacturer: Nemo
Frame: chrome-plated steel
Seat and back: polyurethane foam covered in leather
21 ¼" W; 35 ½" D; 30" H

1-138 D 35

c. 1984
Designer: Antti Nurmesniemi
Manufacturer: Tecta Möbel
Frame: tubular steel
Seat and back: wicker
27 ¼" W; 34 ¼" D; 37" H; 15" SH

1-139 ANTROPOVARIUS

1984
Designer: F.A. Porsche
Manufacturer: Poltrona Frau
Frame: steel sheets containing carbon fiber and covered in
    leather
Base: steel covered in full-grain leather
Seat and back: foam covered in full-grain leather
28" W; 37"–64" D; 25"–48" H

1-140 JEFFERSON CHAIR

1984
Designer: Niels Diffrient
Manufacturer: Sunar Hauserman
Frame: cast aluminum side members; tubular steel crossbars;
    formed steel spine; die-cast headrest support and armrest
    supports
Seat, back, headrest, and arm cushions: plastic shell with
    metal bracketry; separate polyurethane cushions covered
    in fabric or leather
34" W; 34" D; 43" H

Sunar Hauserman   1-140

2 CHAISE LONGUES

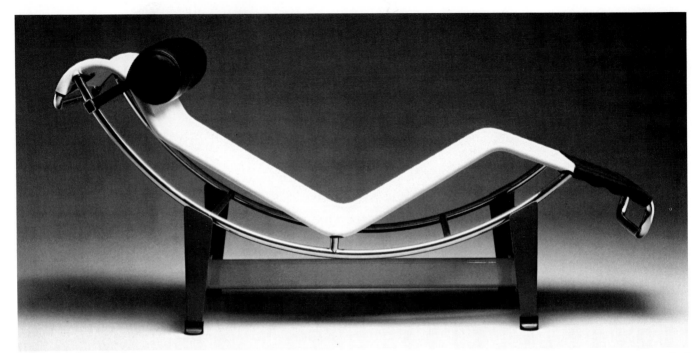

Cassina 2–1

Tecta Möbel 2–2

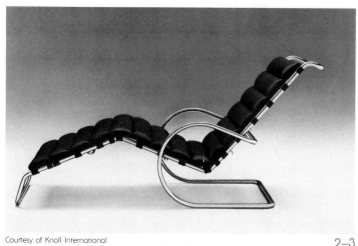

Courtesy of Knoll International   2–3

2–1 LC/4

1928
Designer: Le Corbusier
Manufacturer: Cassina
Frame: chrome-plated steel
Support: reinforced elastic material straps and steel hooks
Mat: polyester padding and muslin covered in leather or
    hairyskin
Base: black-lacquered steel; rubber-wrapped cylindrical tubes
    attached to base to support frame
Headrest: Dacron padding covered in leather
22 ¼" W; 63" D; 28 ¾" H

2–2 F 41

1930
Designer: Marcel Breuer
Manufacturer: Tecta Möbel
Frame: tubular steel; five rubber wheels
Seat and back: leather or cane
17 ½" W; 67" D; 26 ½" H

2–3 ADJUSTABLE CHAISE (242)

1931
Designer: Ludwig Mies van der Rohe
Manufacturer: Knoll International
Frame: tubular stainless steel, polished finish
Support: saddle leather straps
Mat: channeled foam cushions covered in leather
26" W; 70 ¼" D; 30 ½"–35 ¼" H; 19 ⅝" AH

2–4 CHAISE LONGUE (241)

1931
Designer: Ludwig Mies van der Rohe
Manufacturer: Knoll International
Frame: tubular stainless steel, polished finish
Support: saddle leather straps
Mat: channeled foam cushions covered in leather
23 ⅝" W; 47 ¼" D; 37 ½" H; 19" SH

Courtesy of Knoll International   2–4

Rud. Rasmussens Snedkerier   2—5

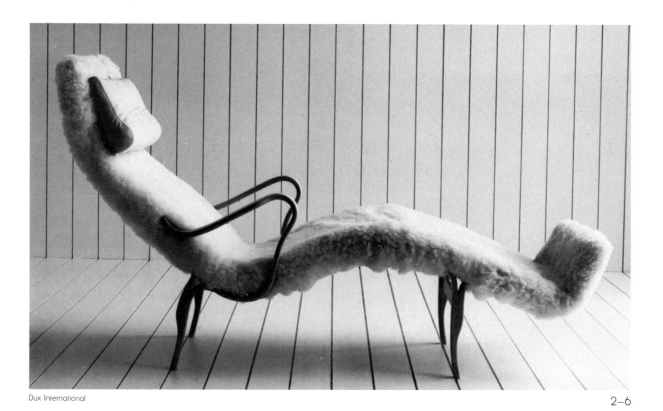

Dux International   2—6

Furniture of the Twentieth Century, Inc.   2—7

2—5 DECK CHAIR (4699)

1933
Designer: Kaare Klint
Manufacturer: Rud. Rasmussens Snedkerier
Frame: teak with canework in seat, back, and foot rest
Mat: foam covered in natural canvas
22¾" W; 59" D; 34¾" H; 13¾" SH

2—6 PERNILLA 3

1935
Designer: Bruno Mathsson
Manufacturer: Dux International
Frame: stratified beech, natural or light-mahogany stained
Seat and back: plaited hemp bands or upholstered in sheepskin
25½" W; 66¼" D; 35½" H; 17" SH; 24½" AH

2—7 ISOKON LONG CHAIR

1935
Designer: Marcel Breuer
Manufacturer: Windmill Furniture
Frame: laminated Finnish birch in a black or natural finish
Seat and back: foam rubber over plywood and covered in
    fabric
24" W; 56" D; 34" H; 9¾" SH

2—8 ARMCHAIR 39

1937
Designer: Alvar Aalto
Manufacturer: Artek
Frame: laminated birch
Seat and back: cross-woven in natural linen webbing
25½" W; 64½" D; 27" H

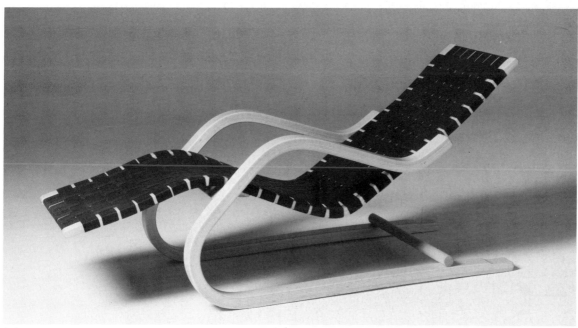

Artek   2—8

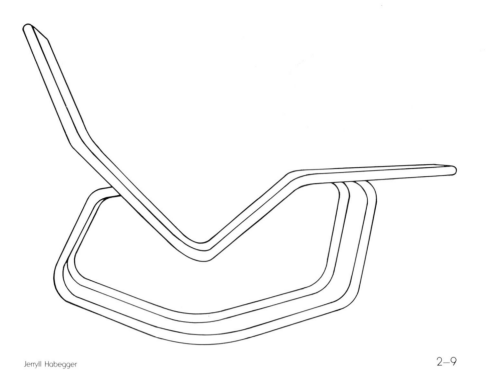

Jerryll Habegger   2–9

Jerryll Habegger   2–10

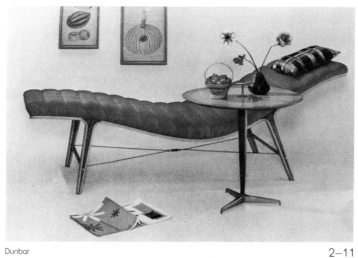

Dunbar   2–11

2–9   BARWA

1947
Designers: Jack Waldheim and Edgar Bartolucci
Manufacturer: Patio Shop
Frame: aluminum tube
Sling: slipcovered in canvas
20½" W; 70" D; 27" H; 12" SH

2–10   CHAISE

1947
Designers: Hendrik van Keppel and Taylor Green
Manufacturer: Van Keppel-Green
Frame: enameled tubular steel
Seat and back: cotton cord
32" W; 68" D; 17" H; 8½" SH

2–11   LISTEN-TO-ME (4873)

1948
Designer: Edward Wormley
Manufacturer: Dunbar
Frame: laminated cherry and birch; metal crossbrace at bottom
Seat and back: rubber-filled channels covered in fabric or
    leather
26½" W; 73½" D; 26" H; 14" SH

2–12   P.3S

1962
Designer: Tito Agnoli
Manufacturer: Pierantonio Bonacina
Frame: tubular steel
Seat and back: natural rattan; polyurethane foam cushion
    covered in fabric
26¾" W; 65" D; 23½" H

Pierantonio Bonacina   2–12

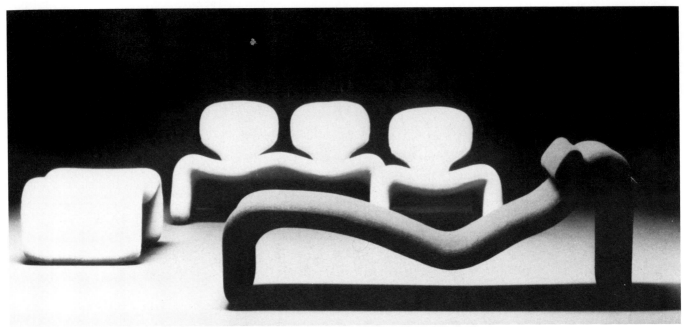

Olivier Mourgue

2—13

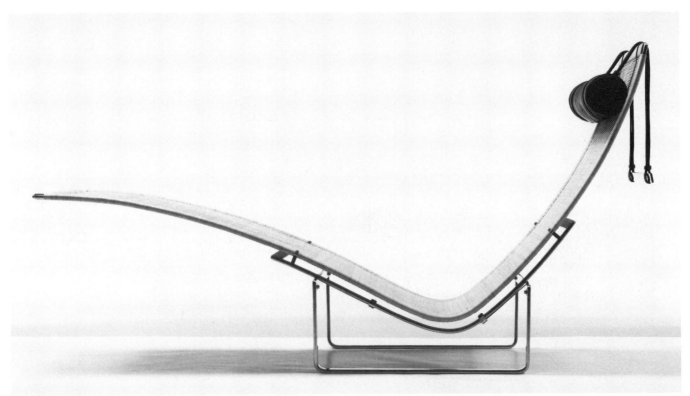

Fritz Hansen

2—14

2–15

2–13 DJINN

1964
Designer: Olivier Mourgue
Manufacturer: Airborne
Frame: tubular steel
Seat and back: polyether foam covered in removable nylon
    jersey
24¼" W; 67" D; 25½" H; 9" SH

2–14 PK 24

1965
Designer: Poul Kjaerholm
Manufacturer: Fritz Hansen
Frame: stainless steel
Seat and back: woven cane
Headrest: cushion covered in leather
26½" W; 61" D; 34" H; 5½" SH

2–15 7442/41

1966
Designer: Richard Schultz
Manufacturer: Knoll International
Frame: cast and extruded aluminum; adjustable back
Seat and back: woven Dacron mesh with vinyl straps
Wheels: plastic with rubber ring
25½" W; 76" D; 14½"–35½" H (Model 7442); 24½" W;
    58" D; 33¾" H; 13" SH (Model 7441)

2–16 EAMES CHAISE (ES 106)

1968
Designers: Charles Eames and Ray Eames
Manufacturer: Herman Miller
Frame: cast aluminum alloy
Support: nonstretch nylon fabric sling
Mat: flexible urethane foam encapsulated with polyester fiber
    and covered in leather
17½" W; 75" D; 28¾" H; 20½" SH

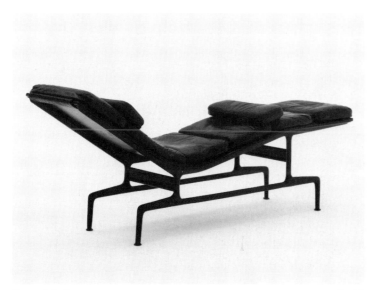

2–16

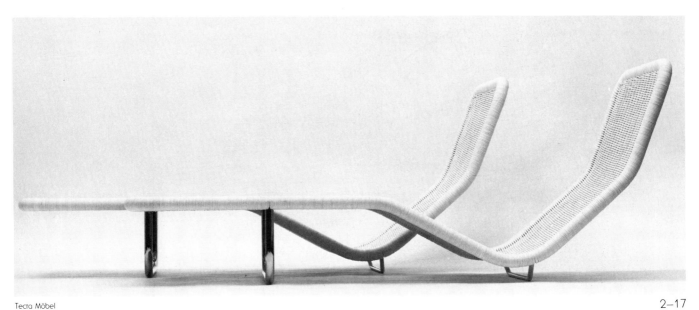

Tecta Möbel 2–17

Alfred Kill 2–18

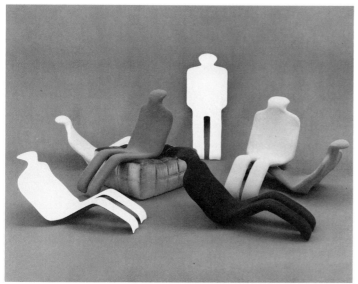

Arconas Corporation

2–19

2–17 F 10
1968
Designer: Antti Nurmesniemi
Manufacturer: Tecta Möbel
Frame: Fiberglas shell
Seat and back: rubber padding covered in fabric
Leg: chrome-plated steel
Supporting base: aluminum
23½" W; 63" D; 26" H; 12½" SH

2–18 GRASSHOPPER
1968
Designers: Jørgen Kastholm and Preben Fabricius
Manufacturer: Alfred Kill
Frame: matte-chrome spring steel
Support: raw linen sling
Mat and headrest: padded leather
Arms: wound with leather thongs
28" W; 57" D; 32" H

2–19 BOULOUM
1969
Designer: Olivier Mourgue
Manufacturer: Arconas
Structure: reinforced molded Fiberglas covered in urethane
    foam and upholstered in Avignon fabric
Outside version: white gel-coat surface and black underside
26" W; 57" D; 23" H

2–20 FENIX 76
1976
Designer: Sam Larsson
Manufacturer: Dux International
Frame: tubular steel
Support: fabric
Mat: polyether and fiberfill covered in fabric or leather
Base: stratified natural beech
30¼" W; 57"–61" D; 30¾"–36½" H; 17¾" SH; 21¾" AH

Dux International

2–20

Antti Nurmesniemi   2–21

Saporiti Italia   2–22

Saporiti Italia

2–23

Dux International

2–24

2–21   TUOLI

1978
Designer: Antti Nurmesniemi
Manufacturer: Cassina
Frame: polished chrome-plated steel
Seat and back: polyurethane foam padding covered in fabric
    or leather
25" W; 54¼" D; 28¾" H; 13¾" SH

2–22   LONGWAVE

1978
Designer: Giovanni Offredi
Manufacturer: Saporiti Italia
Frame: indeformable urethane rubber with a steel inner frame
Leg supports: chromed or burnished steel
Mat: foam covered in fabric or leather
39" W; 67" D; 26" H

2–23   SWING

1980
Designer: Giovanni Offredi
Manufacturer: Saporiti Italia
Frame: bent plywood
Mat: Dacron polyurethane stuffing covered in fabric or leather
Base: chrome-plated steel tubing
24" W; 71" D; 29" H

2–24   CICERO

c. 1980
Designer: Kenneth Bergenblad
Manufacturer: Dux International
Frame: chrome-plated tubular steel
Support: leather sling
Mat: polyether and fiberfill cushion covered in leather
26¾" W; 57"–61" D; 35½"–41¼" H; 17¾" SH; 21¾" AH

DSI (Design Selections International)

2–25

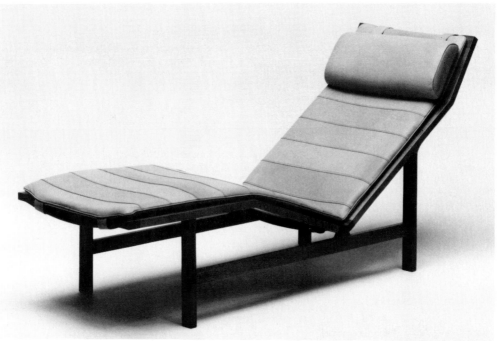

Rudd International

2–26

Brown Jordan/Richard Frinier

2—27

2—25 CHAISE
1982
Designer: Erik Krogh
Manufacturer: Altaform
Seat and back: layered battens of birch plywood
Mat: foam covered in linen canvas
Base: galvanized black steel
25" W; 58" D; 35" H

2—26 KINGS CHAISE
1983
Designers: Rud Thygesen and Johnny Sorensen
Manufacturer: Botium
Frame: beech or mahogany
Support: French cane
Mat and headrest: cushion covered in leather
22" W; 62" D; 30" H; 8" SH

2—27 LEGEND CONTOUR
1986
Designer: Richard Frinier
Manufacturer: Brown Jordan
Frame: welded flat-oval extruded aluminum
Seat and back: vinyl mesh or acrylic fabric
27" W; 70" D; 30" H; 17 1/4" SH

3 DINING/ CONFERENCE CHAIRS

Stendig   3–1

Cassina   3–2

Jack Lenor Larsen

3–3

3–1   CORBUSIER

1870
Designer: Gebrüder Thonet
Manufacturer: Drevounia
Frame: beech in natural, walnut, or red aniline finishes
Seat and back: natural cane
21 ½″ W; 22 ½″ D; 31″ H; 18 ¾″ SH; 27 ¾″ AH

3–2   ARGYLE

1897
Designer: Charles Rennie Mackintosh
Manufacturer: Cassina
Frame: ebonized ashwood
Seat: upholstered in fabric
20″ W; 18″ D; 53 ½″ H; 18 ½″ SH

3–3   MUSIC ROOM

1899
Designer: Richard Riemerschmid
Manufacturer: Jack Lenor Larsen
Frame: golden natural or ebonized beechwood
Seat: studded cushion covered in fabric or leather
19 ½″ W; 23 ¾″ D; 31 ¾″ H; 18″ SH

3–4   18

1902
Designer: Otto Wagner
Manufacturer: Nienkämper
Frame: stained beechwood
Seat: upholstered
Legs and armrest: available with brass or chrome trim
22 ¼″ W; 22 ¼″ D; 29 ½″ H; 18 ½″ SH; 29 ½″ AH

Nienkämper

3–4

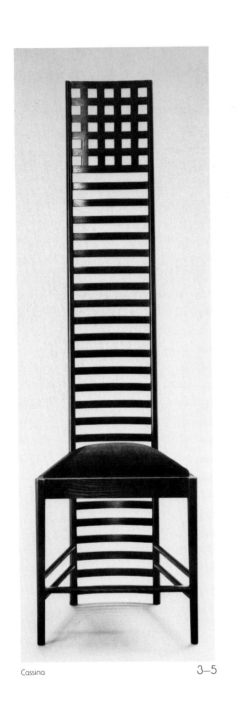

Cassina   3–5

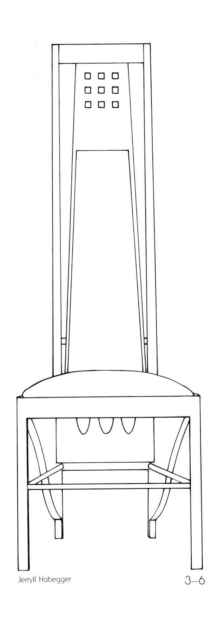

Jerryll Habegger   3–6

Cassina   3–7

B.D. Ediciones

3–8

3–5 HILL HOUSE I

1903
Designer: Charles Rennie Mackintosh
Manufacturer: Cassina
Frame: ebonized ashwood
Seat: upholstered in fabric
16" W; 13.2" D; 55.5" H; 16.8" SH

3–6 1903.20

1903
Designer: Charles Rennie Mackintosh
Manufacturer: B.D. Ediciones
Frame: silver-painted oak
Seat and back: foam covered in lilac velvet; upper back inlaid
  with purple-colored glass
19⅓" W; 18⅞" D; 53⅛" H

3–7 WILLOW 2

1904
Designer: Charles Rennie Mackintosh
Manufacturer: Cassina
Frame: ashwood in an ebony or walnut stain
Seat: woven sea grass
17¾" W; 15¼" D; 41" H; 16½" SH

3–8 1904.17

1904
Designer: Charles Rennie Mackintosh
Manufacturer: B.D. Ediciones
Frame: black-stained and varnished sycamore
Seat: foam covered in white linen
18" W; 16½" D; 43¾" H

Thonet Industries   3–9

Franz Wittmann   3–10

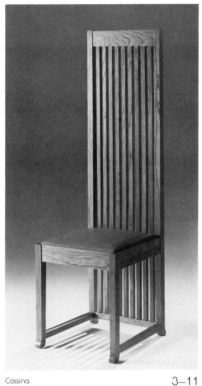

Cassina   3–11

3–9   FLEDERMAUS

1905
Designer: Josef Hoffmann
Manufacturer: Thonet Industries
Frame: steam-bent elm
Seat: upholstered over steel springs and fabric straps; rubberized
   fiber pad; urethane foam
22½" W; 18" D; 29½" H; 18" SH

3–10   ARMLÖFFEL

1908
Designer: Josef Hoffmann
Manufacturer: Franz Wittmann
Frame: limed black-stained ash
Seat: loose foam-filled cushion covered in black leather
26" W; 20" D; 38" H; 17½" SH; 27⅝" AH

3–11   ROBIE

1908
Designer: Frank Lloyd Wright
Manufacturer: Cassina
Frame: solid, natural light cherrywood
Seat: polyurethane foam covered in fabric or leather
15.7" W; 18" D; 52.5" H; 18.1" SH

3–12   GARMISCH

1911
Designer: Otto Blumel
Manufacturer: Montina
Frame: solid ash
Seat: foam on plywood, covered in fabric or leather
18¼" W; 21¾" D; 27½" H; 17½" SH

Stendig   3–12

Rud. Rasmussens Snedkerier   3—13

Cassina   3—14

Cassina

3-15

Werner Blaser

3-16

3-13 FAABORG

1914
Designer: Kaare Klint
Manufacturer: Rud. Rasmussens Snedkerier
Frame: mahogany
Back: canework
Seat: covered with oxhide
27 ¼" W; 25 ¼" D; 28 ¼" H; 17 ¾" SH

3-14 MIDWAY 1

1914
Designer: Frank Lloyd Wright
Manufacturer: Cassina
Frame: solid, natural light cherrywood or cherrywood-stained
    ebony or walnut
Seat and back: polyurethane foam covered in fabric or leather
20.3" W; 18.9" D; 34.3" H; 18" SH

3-15 MIDWAY 2

1914
Designer: Frank Lloyd Wright
Manufacturer: Cassina
Frame: welded structural steel-rod with a high-gloss enamel
    finish
Seat and/or back: polyurethane foam pads covered in fabric
15.7" W; 18.1" D; 34.6" H; 18.3" SH

3-16 DINING

c. 1920
Designer: Ludwig Mies van der Rohe
Manufacturer: Unknown
Frame: rosewood
Seat and back: foam covered with pigskin
20 ½" W; 17 ¼" D; 32 ¾" H; 17 ¾" SH

Collection Stredelijk Museum, Amsterdam   3–17

Tecta Möbel   3–18

Furniture of the Twentieth Century, Inc.

3–19

3–17   BERLIN CHAIR

1923
Designer: Gerrit T. Rietveld
Manufacturer: Gerrit T. Rietveld
Frame, seat, and back: wood
27 ½" W; 21 ¾" D; 41 ¼" H; 19 ¾" SH

3–18   B 80

1924
Designer: Jean Prouvé
Manufacturer: Tecta Möbel
Frame: flat steel with polished nickel finish
Seat: loose cushion upholstered in fabric
Back: stretched fabric
17 ¼" W; 20" D; 40 ½" H; 17 ¼" SH

3–19   CHAIR

1924
Designer: Sybold van Ravesteyn
Manufacturer: Ecart International
Frame: black- and white-lacquered wood
17 ¼" W; 19 ¾" D; 34 ¾" H

3–20   PRAGUE

1925
Designer: Josef Hoffmann
Manufacturer: Thonet Industries
Frame: steam-bent elm
Seat and back: natural cane
19 ¾" W; 20 ¾" D; 31 ½" H; 18 ½" SH; 27 ½" AH

Thonet Industries

3–20

Thonet Industries   3–21

Gebrüder Thonet   3–22

Courtesy of Knoll International

3–23

Gordon International

3–24

3–21 4300

1926
Designer: Mart Stam
Manufacturer: Thonet Industries
Frame: 14-gauge polished chrome-plated tubular steel
Seat and back: oak-veneer molded plywood
Armrests: solid oak
20½" W; 19½" D; 30⅜" H; 17½" SH; 25¼" AH

3–22 S 33

1926
Designer: Mart Stam
Manufacturer: Gebrüder Thonet
Frame: chrome nickel-plated tubular steel
Seat and back: leather
19¾" W; 26½" D; 33½" H; 18" SH

3–23 MR

1927
Designer: Ludwig Mies van der Rohe
Manufacturer: Knoll International
Frame: tubular stainless steel, polished finish
Seat and back: saddle leather with rawhide lacing
21" W; 32½" D; 31" H; 17½" SH; 25½" AH

3–24 TATLIN ARM CHAIR (860)

1927
Designer: Vladimir Tatlin
Manufacturer: Gordon International
Frame: polished chrome steel tube
Seat: molded foam covered in leather
26" W; 26¾" D; 29¾" H; 19" SH

Pallucco   3—25

Courtesy of Knoll International   3—26

Cassina

3–27

Artek

3–28

3–25 CHAIR

1927
Designer: J.J.P. Oud
Manufacturer: Ecart International
Frame: steel with blue lacquer finish
Seat: black-finished wood
16¾" W; 16¾" D; 35¾" H; 17" SH

3–26 CESCA

1928
Designer: Marcel Breuer
Manufacturer: Knoll International
Frame: polished chrome tubular steel
Seat and back: cane with solid wood frame
Arms: solid wood
22⅝" W; 22⅝" D; 31¾" H; 18¼" SH; 27¼" AH

3–27 LC/7

1928
Designer: Le Corbusier
Manufacturer: Cassina
Frame: polished chrome tubing or glossy urethane finish
Seat: cushions covered in fabric, leather, or vinyl
22.8" W; 23.6" D; 28.7" H; 19.7" SH

3–28 15

1929
Designer: Alvar Aalto
Manufacturer: Artek
Frame: beech with lacquered black finish
20" W; 21" D; 27" H

Gebrüder Thonet

3—29

Artek

3—30

Tecta Möbel 3–31

Courtesy of Knoll International 3–32

3–29   S 37

1929
Designer: Anton Lorenz
Manufacturer: Gebrüder Thonet
Frame: tubular steel
Seat and back: foam covered in fabric or leather
22¾" W; 21¼" D; 29¼" H; 18" SH

3–30   611

1930
Designer: Alvar Aalto
Manufacturer: Artek
Frame: natural birch
Seat and back: cross-woven webbing
19" W; 19¼" D; 31½" H; 17¾" SH

3–31   D 61

1930
Designer: El Lissitzky
Manufacturer: Tecta Möbel
Frame: Plexiglas
Seat: cushion covered in fabric
22½" W; 19¼" D; 28¾" H; 17¼" SH

3–32   BRNO (255)

1930
Designer: Ludwig Mies van der Rohe
Manufacturer: Knoll International
Frame: flat stainless steel, polished finish
Seat and back: hardwood frame with foam over spring
   suspension seat covered in fabric or leather
23" W; 23" D; 31½" H; 17½" SH; 25¾" AH

Courtesy of Knoll International   3–33

Images of America   3–34

Ecart International
Copyright: Deidi von Schaewen   3—35

Arkitektura   3—36

3—33   BRNO (245)

1930
Designer: Ludwig Mies van der Rohe
Manufacturer: Knoll International
Frame: tubular stainless steel, polished finish
Seat and back: hardwood frame with foam over spring sus-
   pension seat covered in fabric or leather
22″ W; 23¼″ D; 32½″ H; 17¼″ SH; 25¾″ AH

3—34   DESSAU (203)

1930
Designers: Bauhaus students
Manufacturer: Images of America
Frame: ¾-inch round, heavy-gauge chrome-plated steel tube
Seat and back: black, rigid, sandblasted polyurethane
17¾″ W; 18½″ D; 30″ H; 18″ SH

3—35   DINING CHAIR

1930
Designer: Robert Mallet-Stevens
Manufacturer: Ecart International
Frame: tubular and sheet steel welded construction
17″ W; 16⅝″ D; 32″ H; 17¾″ SH

3—36   SAARINEN HOUSE SIDE CHAIR

1930
Designer: Eliel Saarinen
Manufacturer: Arkitektura
Frame: solid hard maple; ebony and ochre enamel stripes;
   clear lacquer finish
Seat: upholstered in fabric
17″ W; 19″ D; 37½″ H; 18″ SH

Larry Whireley   3–37

Gebrüder Thonet   3–38

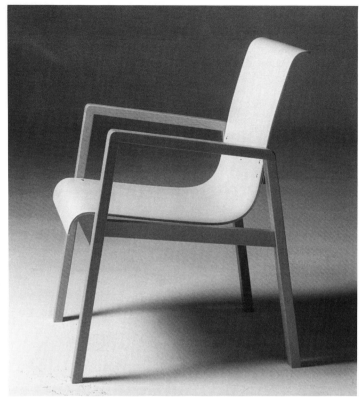

Artek

3—39

3—37   SIDE CHAIR

c. 1930
Designer: Gilbert Rohde
Manufacturer: Heywood-Wakefield Company
Seat and back: contoured wood covered in fabric
Base: bent laminated wood
16¼" W; 21½" D; 31½" H

3—38   S 36

1931
Designers: Wassili Luckhardt and Hans Luckhardt
Manufacturer: Gebrüder Thonet
Frame: tubular steel
Seat and back: molded plywood
21" W; 23¼" D; 34¼" H; 18" SH

3—39   403

1932
Designer: Alvar Aalto
Manufacturer: Artek
Frame: birch
Seat and back: molded plywood
21" W; 24" D; 31" H; 16" SH

3—40   MK FOLDING

1932
Designer: Mogens Koch
Manufacturer: Rud. Rasmussens Snedkerier
Frame: beechwood
Seat and back: Scottish canvas or natural-colored oxhide
Arms: natural-colored oxhide
22" W; 22" D; 34¼" H

Rud. Rasmussens Snedkerier

3—40

Images of America   3—41

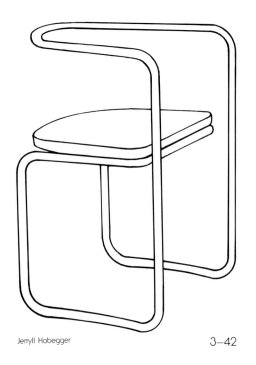

Jerryll Habegger   3—42

Cassina   3-43

3-41 ROQUEBRUNE

1932
Designer: Eileen Gray
Manufacturer: Images of America
Frame: chrome-plated tubular steel
Seat and back: leather
17¾" W; 22¾" D; 31" H; 18½" SH

3-42 CHAIR

1933
Designer: Agnoldomenico Pica
Manufacturer: Daniele Tagliabue
Frame: steel tubing
Seat: wood
17¾" W; 18" D; 27½" H; 15" SH

3-43 ZIG-ZAG

1934
Designer: Gerrit T. Rietveld
Manufacturer: Cassina
Frame: edge-grain, laminated, kiln-dried elm
14¾" W; 17" D; 28¾" H; 16½" SH

3-44 FOLLIA

1934
Designer: Giuseppe Terragni
Manufacturer: Zanotta
Seat and back: black, molded polyurethane
Back support: chrome-plated steel
19¾" W; 23½" D; 31½" H; 16" SH

Zanotta   3-44

111

Fritz Hansen   3–45

Artek   3–46

Zanotta   3–47

3–45　LADDER BACK

1934
Designer: Kaare Klint
Manufacturer: Fritz Hansen
Frame: oak finished in matte lacquer
Seat: woven paper-cord
20½" W; 19¾" D; 33" H; 17" SH

3–46　65

1935
Designer: Alvar Aalto
Manufacturer: Artek
Frame: birch
Back: molded plywood
13¾" W; 15" D; 26" H; 17¼" SH

3–47　S 5

1935
Designer: Gabriele Mucchi
Manufacturer: Zanotta
Frame: chrome-plated tubular steel
Seat and back: woven wicker
15½" W; 22" D; 29" H

3–48　LARIANA

1936
Designer: Giuseppe Terragni
Manufacturer: Zanotta
Frame: tubular stainless steel
Seat and back: molded beech plywood
16½" W; 22" D; 31" H; 17" SH

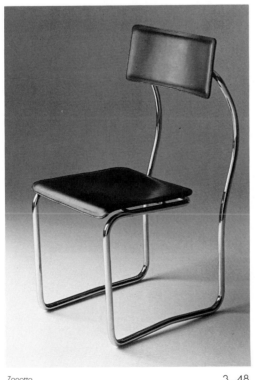

Zanotta   3–48

Cassina   3—49

Cassina   3—50

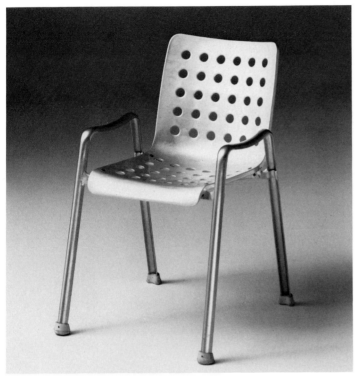

Zanotta   3–51

3–49   GOTEBORG

1937
Designer: Erik Gunnar Asplund
Manufacturer: Cassina
Frame: walnut or ashwood
Seat: molded ABS; polyurethane foam padding; leather
Back: steel frame; polyurethane foam padding; leather
15.7" W; 20.5" D; 31.5" H; 17.7" SH

3–50   BARREL

1937
Designer: Frank Lloyd Wright
Manufacturer: Cassina
Frame: solid, natural light cherrywood or cherry-stained walnut
Seat: polyurethane foam pad covered in fabric or leather
21.5" W; 21.9" D; 31.8" H; 19.7" SH; 24.8" AH

3–51   SPARTANA

1938
Designer: Hans Coray
Manufacturer: Zanotta
Frame: aluminum alloy
21 ¼" W; 25 ½" D; 29 ¾" H; 17" SH

3–52   WORK CHAIR

1938
Designer: Herman A. Sperlich
Manufacturer: Ironrite Inc.
Frame: steel
Seat and back: lacquered wood
17" W; 18 ½" D; 26" H; 17" SH

Larry Whiteley   3–52

Fritz Hansen

3–53

Nordisk Andels

3–54

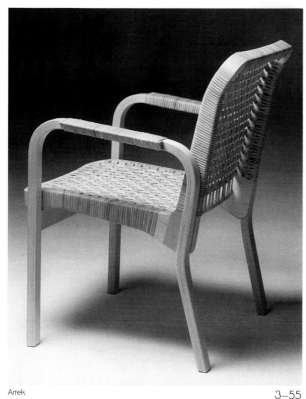

Artek   3–55

3–53   CHINESE CHAIR (4283)

1944
Designer: Hans J. Wegner
Manufacturer: Fritz Hansen
Frame: cherrywood
Seat: loose leather pad
21¾" W; 21¾" D; 32¼" H; 17¾" SH; 26¾" AH

3–54   J 39

1947
Designer: Børge Mogensen
Manufacturer: Nordisk Andels
Frame: beech or oak, natural or lacquered
Seat: woven cane
19" W; 16½" D; 30" H; 17½" SH

3–55   ARMCHAIR 45

1947
Designer: Alvar Aalto
Manufacturer: Artek
Frame: natural birch
Seat and back: webbing, rattan, quilted leather, or canvas
Armrests: bound in rattan or leather
24" W; 23⅝" D; 31½" H; 16½" SH; 24½" AH

3–56   THE CLASSIC CHAIR (JH 501)

1947
Designer: Hans J. Wegner
Manufacturer: Johannes Hansens Møbelsnedkeri
Frame: solid oak
Seat: natural woven cane
24¾" W; 20½" D; 30" H; 17" SH

Johannes Hansens Møbelsnedkeri   3–56

Zanotta

3–57

JG Furniture Systems, Inc.

3–58

Carl Hansen   3–59

3–57   TAPIOLA

1949
Designer: Ilmari Tapiovaara
Manufacturer: Zanotta
Frame: fire-lacquered tubular steel
Seat and back: formed beech plywood
Armrests: pressed ABS
21¼″ W; 20″ D; 30″ H; 18″ SH

3–58   KOMAI CHAIR (939)

1949
Designer: Ray Komai
Manufacturer: JG Furniture Systems
Seat and back: plywood shell formed from hand-matched,
   symmetrically centered walnut faces
Base: ⅝-inch-diameter steel rod with a black baked-enamel
   finish or chrome-plated
21″ W; 21″ D; 30¾″ H; 18⅝″ SH

3–59   CH 24

1950
Designer: Hans J. Wegner
Manufacturer: Carl Hansen
Frame: natural oak, teak-stained beech, or black and red
   lacquered finish
Seat: handwoven cord
21½″ W; 20½″ D; 28¾″ H; 16¾″ SH

3–60   ANTELOPE

1950
Designer: Ernest Race
Manufacturer: Race Furniture
Frame: steel rod
Seat: plywood
22″ W; 22½″ D; 31″ H; 16¾″ SH

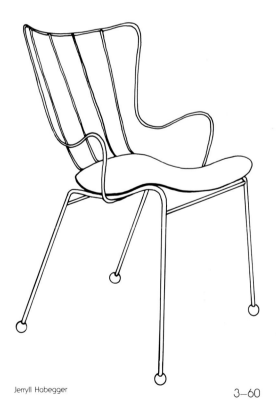

Jerryll Habegger   3–60

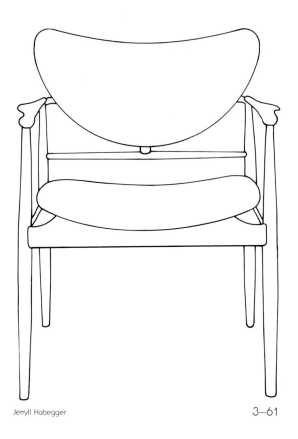

Jerryll Habegger   3–61

Courtesy of Knoll International   3–62

Cadsana, Cadwallader and Sangiorgio Associates

3–63

Herman Miller, Inc.

3–64

3–61   CHAIR

1951
Designer: Finn Juhl
Manufacturer: Ivan Schlechter
Frame: teak
Seat and back: upholstered leather
27 ¼" W; 25" D; 30" H

3–62   SIDE CHAIR (420-2)

1951
Designer: Harry Bertoia
Manufacturer: Knoll International
Frame: welded steel wire
Seat pad: upholstered
21" W; 22 ½" D; 30" H; 18" SH

3–63   NEW YORK SEATING (161.000.0)

1952
Designers: Ross Littell, William Katavolos, and Douglas Kelley
Manufacturer: Cadsana, Cadwallader and Sangiorgio Associates
Frame: rectangular steel, black finish
Legs: chrome-plated round steel
Seat and back: harness leather
23 ⅝" W; 23 ⅛" D; 32 ¼" H; 17 ¼" SH

3–64   DKR

1952
Designers: Charles Eames and Ray Eames
Manufacturer: Herman Miller
Frame: wire rod; removable cushion
19" W; 21" D; 32" H; 18 ¾" SH

Jerryll Habegger   3–65

Fritz Hansen   3–66

Marco Albini and Franca Helg (Architetti Associati)   3—67

3—65   ANT (3101)

1952
Designer: Arne Jacobsen
Manufacturer: Fritz Hansen
Base: chrome-plated steel tubing
Seat and back: molded plywood
19″ W; 19″ D; 30¼″ H; 17¼″ SH

3—66   SERIE 7

1955
Designer: Arne Jacobsen
Manufacturer: Fritz Hansen
Base: chrome-plated steel tubing
Seat and back: molded plywood or upholstered in fabric
25″ W; 20½″ D; 30½″ H; 17½″ SH; 26″ AH

3—67   LUISA

1955
Designers: Franco Albini and Franca Helg
Manufacturer: Carlo Poggi
Frame: walnut or rosewood
Seat and back: rubber padded with fabric or leather cover
22″ W; 22″ D; 30″ H; 17″ SH

3—68   SAFFA

1955
Designer: Hans Eichenberger
Manufacturer: Teo Jakob
Frame: chrome-plated tubular steel
Back: leather or cane-wrapped
Seat: polyfoam covered in leather
21¼″ W; 20″ D; 29⅛″ H

Hans Eichenberger   3—68

Courtesy of Knoll International   3–69

Tecno   3–70

Cadsana, Cadwallader and Sangiorgio Associates   3–71

Cassina   3–72

3–69   PEDESTAL CHAIR (151)

1956
Designer: Eero Saarinen
Manufacturer: Knoll International
Shell: molded, Fiberglas-reinforced plastic, lacquer finish
Swivel base: cast aluminum, fused epoxy finish
Seat: removable foam cushion covered in fabric
19½" W; 22" D; 32½" H; 18½" SH

3–70   S 88

1956
Designer: Osvaldo Borsani
Manufacturer: Tecno
Frame: varnished tubular steel
Seat and back: molded plywood
19¾" W; 19¾" D; 29½" H; 16½" SH

3–71   PRETZEL

1957
Designer: George Nelson
Manufacturer: Cadsana, Cadwallader and Sangiorgio Associates
Frame: laminated oak
Seat pad: polyurethane foam covered in fabric or leather
24" W; 19¼" D; 31½" H

3–72   SUPERLEGERRA

1957
Designer: Gio Ponti
Manufacturer: Cassina
Frame: ashwood with natural or stained walnut, rosewood,
  or ebony
Seat: India cane
16⅛" W; 18½" D; 32¾" H; 17¾" SH

Fritz Hansen   3–73

Herman Miller, Inc.   3–74

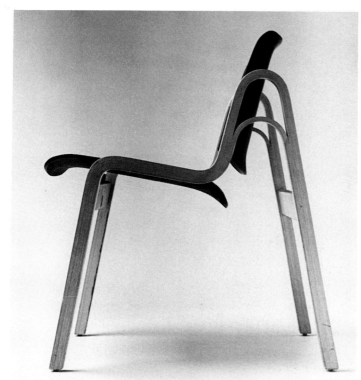

Museum of Applied Arts, Helsinki

3—75

3—73   PK 11

1957
Designer: Poul Kjaerholm
Manufacturer: Fritz Hansen
Frame: matte chrome-plated steel
Arm: matte lacquered ash or oak
Seat: leather
22" W; 23½" D; 29" H; 16" SH

3—74   DAA

1958
Designer: George Nelson
Manufacturer: Herman Miller
Seat and back: Fiberglas
Legs: chrome-plated tubular steel
27⅝" W; 25" D; 34" H; 18" SH

3—75   WILHELMINA

1959
Designer: Ilmari Tapiovaara
Manufacturer: Wilhelm Schauman
Frame: bent plywood
Seat and back: bent plywood, pressure-molded
21" W; 21½" D; 27¼" H; 16½" SH

3—76   FENIS

1959
Designer: Carlo Mollino
Manufacturer: Zanotta
Structure: natural cherrywood
16" W; 19¾" D; 37½" H; 17¼" SH

Zanotta

3—76

Carl Auböck   3–77

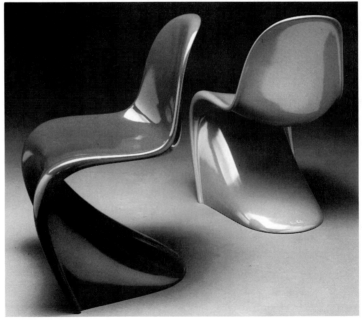

Nienkämper   3–78

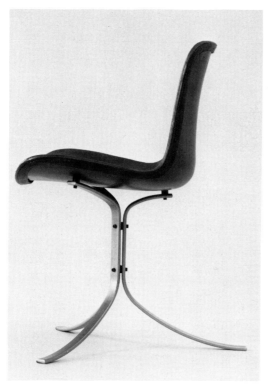

Fritz Hansen   ·3—79

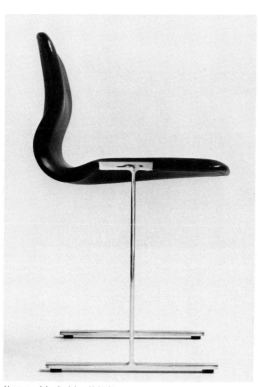

Museum of Applied Arts, Helsinki   3—80

3—77 4906
1960
Designer: Carl Auböck
Manufacturer: Meidlinger Pollack
Frame: oak
Seat and back: teak
16" W; 17" D; 32" H; 17¼" SH

3—78 PANTON STACKING
1960
Designer: Verner Panton
Manufacturer: Nienkämper
Frame: polyurethane
19" W; 21½" D; 33¼" H; 17" SH

3—79 PK 9
1960
Designer: Poul Kjaerholm
Manufacturer: Fritz Hansen
Base: matte chrome-plated steel
Seat and back: leather
22" W; 23½" D; 29" H; 16" SH

3—80 TRIENNALE
1960
Designer: Antti Nurmesniemi
Manufacturer: J. Merivaara
Frame: steel
Seat and back: polyfoam covered in leather
16½" W; 17¾"; 28¾" H; 17¾" SH

Herman Miller, Inc.   3—81

Stendig   3—82

John Stuart International   3–83

3–81 LA FONDA

1961
Designers: Charles Eames and Ray Eames
Manufacturer: Herman Miller
Shell: Fiberglas-reinforced plastic
Base: bright-polished, chrome-plated cast aluminum
Seat and back: foam covered in fabric or vinyl
25" W; 22" D; 29½" H; 18½" SH

3–82 ZURICH

1961
Designer: Willi Guhl
Manufacturer: Emil Guhl
Frame: beech
Seat and back: woven natural cane
20½" W; 19" D; 30½" H; 16¾" SH

3–83 POLYPROP

1963
Designer: Robin Day
Manufacturer: S. Hille and Co. Ltd.
Seat and back: injection-molded polypropylene
Legs: chrome-plated tubular steel
20¾" W; 20½" D; 29½" H; 15½" SH

3–84 NELSON II

1963
Designers: Borge Lindau and Bo Lindekrantz
Manufacturer: Lammhults Mobel AB
Frame: laminated oak plywood
Seat and back: foam covered in fabric
21" W; 22" D; 30½" H; 18" SH; 25¼" AH

Stendig   3–84

131

Larry Whiteley   3—85

GF Furniture Systems   3—86

Bo-Ex

3—88

3—85   PK 12

1964
Designer: Poul Kjaerholm
Manufacturer: E. Kold Christensen
Frame: chrome-plated tubular steel
Seat and arms: natural canvas or oxhide
24¾" W; 20½" D; 26¾" H; 17¼" SH

3—86   40/4

1964
Designer: David Rowland
Manufacturer: GF Furniture Systems
Frame: chrome-plated steel rod
Seat and back: stamped-out PVC-coated sheet metal
20" W; 21¼" D; 30" H; 15½" SH

3—87   BO 591

1964
Designers: Preben Fabricius and Jørgen Kastholm
Manufacturer: Bo-Ex
Frame: matte chrome-plated steel
Seat: foam covered in fabric or leather
26¾" W; 18½" D; 25¼" H; 16½" SH

3—88   APRIL

1964
Designer: Gae Aulenti
Manufacturer: Zanotta
Frame: stainless steel; aluminum alloy joints
Seat and back: fabric or leather sling
20½" W; 20¾" D; 31½" H; 16½" SH

Zanotta

3—87

Brickel Associates   3–89

Carl Hansen   3–90

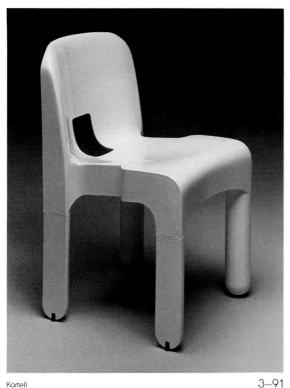

Kartell   3–91

3–89 LANDMARK SERIES (1074)

c. 1964
Designer: Ward Bennett
Manufacturer: Brickel Associates
Frame: natural oiled ash
Seat and back: French-upholstered style; tight seat
23" W; 24" D; 32½" H; 18½" SH; 24½" AH

3–90 CH 47

1965
Designer: Hans J. Wegner
Manufacturer: Carl Hansen
Frame: beech or oak
Seat: cord
21½" W; 20" D; 30¼" H; 16½" SH

3–91 5/4867

1965
Designer: Joe Colombo
Manufacturer: Kartell
Frame: polypropylene
16¾" W; 19⅔" D; 28" H; 17" SH

3–92 STEPHENS

1965
Designer: William Stephens
Manufacturer: Knoll International
Frame: laminations of wood veneers
Seat and back: foam over molded shell covered in fabric
23" W; 22½" D; 32" H; 18" SH; 25½" AH

Courtesy of Knoll International   3–92

Fritz Hansen   3—93

Hans J. Wegner   3—94

Zographos Designs

3–95

3–93 OXFORD (3271)

1965
Designer: Arne Jacobsen
Manufacturer: Fritz Hansen
Seat and back: foam over oxhide
Base: swivel pedestal of aluminum
25¼" W; 21¼" D; 35½" H; 17¼" SH; 26" AH

3–94 JH 701

1965
Designer: Hans J. Wegner
Manufacturer: Johannes Hansens Møbelsnedkeri
Frame: matte stainless steel
Back: solid maple
Seat: upholstered in leather
24¾" W; 18" D; 26¾" H; 17¼" SH

3–95 CH 66

1966
Designer: Nicos Zographos
Manufacturer: Zographos Designs Ltd.
Frame: polished stainless steel tube
Seat and back: leather
19" W; 22" D; 31" H; 18" SH

3–96 1725

1966
Designer: Warren Platner
Manufacturer: Knoll International
Frame: steel rod in a bright nickel finish
Seat cushion and back: polyester fiber over a molded foam
    core, covered in fabric
26½" W; 22" D; 29" H; 19" SH; 25½" AH

Courtesy of Knoll International

3–96

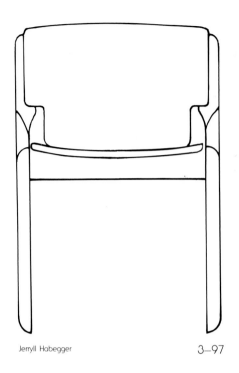

Jerryll Habegger   3—97

Brickel Associates   3—98

Brickel Associates

3—99

Alfred Kill

3—100

3—97   122

1967
Designer: Vico Magistretti
Manufacturer: Cassina
Frame: walnut, matte dark-brown aniline, or ebony-stained
  beechwood
Seat: upholstered in velvet or leather
19¾" W; 20½" D; 29½" H; 17⅞" SH

3—98   1107

c. 1967
Designer: Ward Bennett
Manufacturer: Brickel Associates
Frame: natural oiled walnut
Seat and back: upholstery
24" W; 24" D; 30½" H; 19¼" SH; 25" AH

3—99   DOWEL (1068)

1968
Designer: Ward Bennett
Manufacturer: Brickel Associates
Frame: natural oiled cherry
Seat and back: upholstered in fabric
21½" W; 23" D; 34½" H; 18¼" SH; 26½" AH

3—100   FK 90

1968
Designers: Jørgen Kastholm and Preben Fabricius
Manufacturer: Alfred Kill
Frame: steel rod, chrome-plated or covered with PVC enamel
  finish
Seat and back: contoured latex foam over molded plywood,
  covered in leather
21" W; 18" D; 30" H; 18" SH

ICF, Inc.   3—101

Rudd International   3—102

Hans J. Wegner

3–103

Artemide

3–104

3–101 FRANCESCA SPANISH

1968
Designer: Philippe Starck
Manufacturer: Baleri Italia
Frame: steel tubing in a silver or black baked-epoxy finish
Seat: black rigid polyurethane
Back: metal or polyurethane
20½" W; 17¼" D; 30¾" H; 17" SH; 26½" AH

3–102 MO 6111

1969
Designers: Rud Thygesen and Johnny Sorensen
Manufacturer: Magnus Olesen
Frame: laminated beech, white oak veneer
Seat and back: urethane foam covered in fabric, leather, or vinyl
19½" W; 23" D; 29¼" H; 17½" SH; 25" AH

3–103 OXBOW (PP 203)

1969
Designer: Hans J. Wegner
Manufacturer: P.P. Møbler
Frame: solid mahogany
Seat: upholstered in fabric
23" W; 19¼" D; 27½" H; 17" SH

3–104 SELENE

1969
Designer: Vico Magistretti
Manufacturer: Artemide
Frame: Fiberglas-reinforced plastic (Reglar)
18½" W; 19¾" D; 29½" H; 17⅝" SH

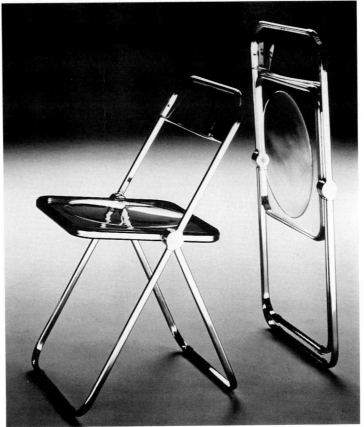

Castelli   3–105

Jerryll Habegger   3–106

Rudd International   3–107

3–105   PLIA

1969
Designer: Giancarlo Piretti
Manufacturer: Castelli
Frame: chromed or plastic-coated tubular steel
Seat and back: polypropylene or Indian cane
18½" W; 19¾" D; 29½" H

3–106   STACKING (MO 4554)

1969
Designers: Rud Thygesen and Johnny Sorensen
Manufacturer: Magnus Olesen
Frame: laminated beech, white oak veneer
Seat and back: urethane foam covered in fabric, leather, or
    vinyl
21½" W; 22" D; 31" H; 18" SH

3–107   KINGS CHAIR

1969
Designers: Rud Thygesen and Johnny Sorensen
Manufacturer: Botium
Frame: solid white oak or Khaya mahogany
Back: natural French cane
Seat: cold-cure urethane covered in vegetable-tanned leather
21" W; 20" D; 33" H; 17" SH

3–108   KAZUKI

1969
Designer: Kazuhide Takahama
Manufacturer: Simon International
Frame: lacquered wood
18" W; 18" D; 41¾" H

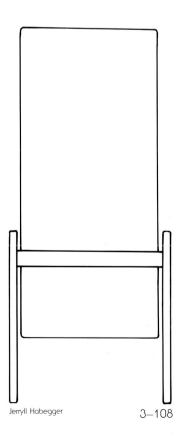

Jerryll Habegger   3–108

Marco Zanuso   3–109

Courtesy of Knoll International   3–110

Jerryll Habegger   3–111

3–109   MINISEAT

1970
Designer: Marco Zanuso
Manufacturer: Elam
Shell: Fiberglas-reinforced polyester
Base: chrome-plated steel tube
19″ W; 21″ D; 27½″ H; 16″ SH

3–110   PETITT CHAIR (1105)

1970
Designer: Don Petitt
Manufacturer: Knoll International
Frame: oak, walnut, or mahogany veneer
Seat and back: foam rubber bonded to formed metal, covered
    in fabric or leather
22½″ W; 24″ D; 32″ H; 18″ SH; 26″ AH

3–111   ENNO UNO

1970
Designer: Studio DeMartini, Falconi, & Fois
Manufacturer: C & B Italia
Frame: compression-molded Fiberglas-reinforced polyester
21¼″ W; 18¾″ D; 28″ H; 17″ SH

3–112   GAUDI

1971
Designer: Vico Magistretti
Manufacturer: Artemide
Frame: Fiberglas-reinforced plastic (Reglar)
23⅝″ W; 21⅝″ D; 28¾″ H; 17¼″ SH

Artemide   3–112

145

Kusch + Co.   3–113

Castelijn Collection   3–114

Gebrüder Thonet   3–115

3–113   7200
1971
Designer: Jørgen Kastholm
Manufacturer: Kusch + Co.
Frame: chrome steel
Seat and back: upholstered in fabric or leather
21" W; 20" D; 30" H

3–114   STRIP CHAIR
1974
Designer: Gijs Bakker
Manufacturer: Castelijn Collection
Frame: laminated wood
17¼" W; 30¼" H

3–115   FLEX
1974
Designer: Gerd Lange
Manufacturer: Gebrüder Thonet
Shell: injection-molded polypropylene
Legs and stretchers: beech
Arms: glass-filled nylon
Glides: nylon
19¾" W; 19¼" D; 31½" H; 17¾" SH

3–116   EKC 13
1974
Designer: Poul Kjaerholm
Manufacturer: Fritz Hansen
Frame: chrome-plated spring steel
Seat and back: upholstered in oxhide
24" W; 19¾" D; 30¼" H; 16" SH

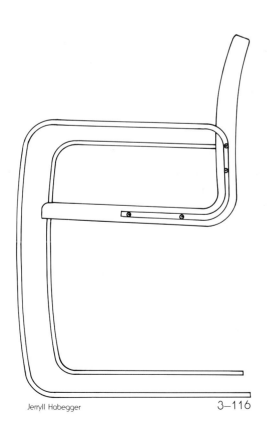

Jerryll Habegger   3–116

Courtesy of Knoll International

3–117

Scope Furniture

3–118

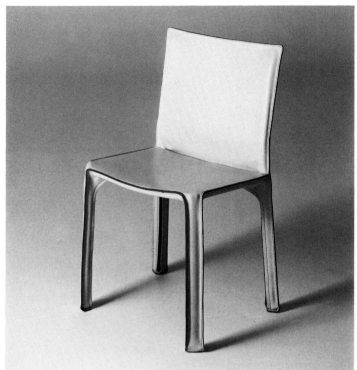

Cassina   3–119

3–117   54-102

1975
Designer: Gae Aulenti
Manufacturer: Knoll International
Frame: metal extrusion, fused finish
Seat and back: foam cushion bent to curved, laminated
    plywood
22½″ W; 20½″ D; 32¼″ H; 17¾″ SH; 23½″ AH

3–118   OUTLINE #2

1975
Designer: David Weinstock
Manufacturer: Scope Furniture
Frame: stainless steel
Seat and back: foam covered in fabric or leather
21″ W; 22″ D; 31″ H; 18″ SH; 24½″ AH

3–119   CAB

1977
Designer: Mario Bellini
Manufacturer: Cassina
Frame: welded tubular steel; heavy-gauge leather, zippered
    cover
20.5″ W; 18.5″ D; 32.3″ H; 17.7″ SH

3–120   TURTLE BACK (1502)

1977
Designer: Ward Bennett
Manufacturer: Brickel Associates
Frame: natural oiled ash
Seat and back: upholstered in fabric
24¼″ W; 24½″ D; 34½″ H; 18½″ SH; 24″ AH

Brickel Associates   3–120

Hans J. Wegner   3—121

Brickel Associates   3—122

Alberto Bazzani   3–123

Dux International   3–124

3–121   PP 55

1977
Designer: Hans J. Wegner
Manufacturer: P.P. Møbler
Frame: solid maple
Seat: upholstered in leather
24½″ W; 19″ D; 28¼″ H; 17½″ SH

3–122   UNIVERSITY (1550)

1978
Designer: Ward Bennett
Manufacturer: Brickel Associates
Frame: natural oiled ash
22¼″ W; 24″ D; 32½″ H; 18″ SH; 25¼″ AH

3–123   LOTUS

1978
Designer: Naoki Matsunaga
Manufacturer: Alberto Bazzani
Frame: lacquered curved wood
Seat: polyurethane foam covered in leather
17¾″ W; 17¾″ D; 29½″ H

3–124   KERSTIN

1979
Designer: Bruno Mathsson
Manufacturer: Dux International
Frame: stratified beech
Seat: molded plywood; polyether-fabric-covered, tufted seat
  cushion
Back: cane filling
17¾″ W; 23¾″ D; 30¾″ H; 18¼″ SH

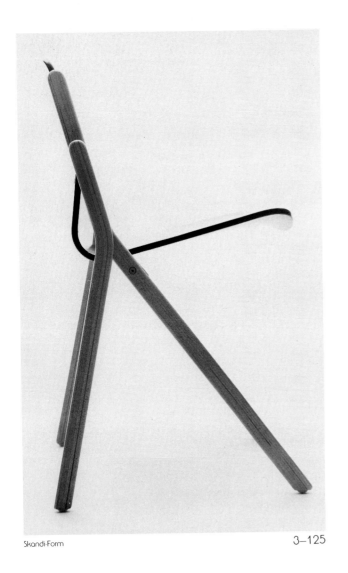

Skandi-Form

3–125

Tecta Möbel

3–126

B & B Italia

3–127

Alias

3–128

3–125   JET

1979
Designers: Soren Nissen and Ebbe Gehl
Manufacturer: Skandi-Form
Frame and back: natural or stained laminated beech with
   a plastic lacquer finish
Seat: beech or upholstered
21¼" W; 19¾" D; 30¾" H; 17¾" SH

3–126   "THE CHAIR"

1979
Designer: Stefan Wewerka
Manufacturer: Tecta Möbel
Frame: lacquered wood
Seat: upholstered in fabric
27½" W; 19" D; 29¼" H; 18" SH

3–127   IALEA

1980
Designers: Antonio Citterio and Paolo Nava
Manufacturer: B & B Italia
Frame: chrome-plated steel; anodized aluminum
Seat: plywood upholstered with leather
Back: metal upholstered with leather
22⅞" W; 18½" D; 27½" H; 18½" SH

3–128   SPAGHETTI

1980
Designer: Giandomenico Belotti
Manufacturer: Alias
Frame: steel tubing, chrome-plated or baked epoxy finish
Seat and back: PVC spaghetti winding
27" W; 25" D; 28" H; 15" SH; 23½" AH

Rudd International   3–129

Monel Contract Furniture   3–130

Zanotta   3–131

3–129   CABARET (MO 8003)

1981
Designers: Rud Thygesen and Johnny Sorensen
Manufacturer: Magnus Olesen
Frame: laminated beech veneers; wedge-lock joining (expanding wedge into conical hole)
Seat: cross-laminated beech veneers; top with linoleum or upholstered
Back: laminated beech veneers
21″ W; 16″ D; 27½″ H; 17½″ SH

3–130   SPARTA

1981
Designer: Bruno Rey
Manufacturer: Monel Contract Furniture
Frame: solid beech in natural, light, or dark walnut-stained finish
Seat and back: molded plywood with polyurethane foam, covered in fabric or leather
Support: aluminum bracket assembly glued to legs and seat panel
22″ W; 22″ D; 33″ H; 17½″ SH; 26″ AH

3–131   TONIETTA

1981
Designer: Enzo Mari
Manufacturer: Zanotta
Frame: natural or fire-lacquered aluminum alloy
Seat and back: cowhide-covered
15¼″ W; 18½″ D; 32¾″ H; 18¼″ SH

3–132   810

1982
Designer: Richard Meier
Manufacturer: Knoll International
Frame: laminated hard maple veneers; solid hard maple
21″ W; 20″ D; 27½″ H; 17½″ SH; 27½″ AH

Courtesy of Knoll International   3–132

Gemla Möbler
3—133

Castelli
3—134

Alias   3–135

3–133   SCANDINAVIAN

1982
Designer: Ake Axelsson
Manufacturer: Gemla Möbler
Frame: beech
Seat and back: cane or upholstered in fabric
21 ½" W; 20 ½" D; 31 ½" H; 17 ¼" SH; 25 ½" AH

3–134   PENELOPE

1982
Designer: Charles Pollock
Manufacturer: Castelli
Frame: 13-mm-diameter, alloy-hardened steel rod
Shell: woven steel wire net with thermoplastic resins
Arms: integral polyurethane
22 ¹³/₁₆" W; 24 ⅝" D; 31 ⅞" H; 17 ¾" SH

3–135   SECONDA

1982
Designer: Mario Botta
Manufacturer: Alias
Frame: galvanized tubular steel, epoxy-coated black or silver
Seat: perforated sheet steel, enamel-coated black or silver
Back: self-skinned, charcoal-colored expanded polyurethane
20 ½" W; 22 ¾" D; 28 ¼" H; 18 ½" SH; 26" AH

3–136   SERIES 8600

1982
Designer: Hans U. Bitsch
Manufacturer: Kusch + Co.
Frame: steel tube
Seat and back: woven steel
26 ¼" W; 22" D; 31" H; 17 ¾" SH

Kusch + Co.   3–136a

Kusch + Co.   3–136b

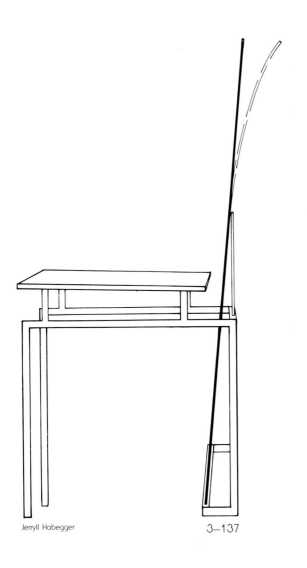

Jerryll Habegger   3–137

Driade   3–138

Stendig

3–139

3–137 FAIZZZ

1982
Designers: François Scali and Alain Domingo
Manufacturer: Nemo
Frame: black epoxy metal
Back: flexible PVC
Seat: foam covered in jersey
14¼" W; 16½" D; 39¼" H

3–138 COSTES

1982
Designer: Philippe Starck
Manufacturer: Driade
Frame: varnished iron tubing
Back: lacquered bent plywood
Seat: polyurethane-resin-stuffed cushion covered in black
    leather
18½" W; 21½" D; 31" H

3–139 ANDOVER

1983
Designer: Davis Allen
Manufacturer: Montina
Frame: beech
Seat: foam on webbed plywood frame covered in fabric,
    leather, or vinyl
22" W; 22½" D; 36" H; 18" SH; 26¼" AH

3–140 RUBBER CHAIR

1983
Designer: Brian Kane
Manufacturer: Metropolitan Furniture
Frame: black steel with polypropylene back straps encased
    in EPDM rubber tubing
Seat: exposed hardwood plywood or upholstered padded
    plywood
22" W; 22" D; 30" H; 18" SH; 26" AH

Metropolitan Furniture Corporation

3–140

Pallucco   3–141

ICF, Inc.   3–142

Brickel Associates

3–143

3–141   LIZIE

1983
Designer: Regis Protiere
Manufacturer: Pallucco
Frame: tubular steel with drawn-steel rods
Seat: natural beech or aluminum
19¾" W; 20" D; 28¼" H; 16¼" SH

3–142   STARCK

1983
Designer: Philippe Starck
Manufacturer: Baleri Italia
Frame: steel tubing in a silver or black baked epoxy finish
Seat: black diamond-tip rubber or black leather
Feet: rubber
21" W; 21¼" D; 30" H; 18½" SH

3–143   GRID (1515)

c. 1983
Designer: Ward Bennett
Manufacturer: Brickel Associates
Frame: natural oiled ash
Seat: upholstered in fabric or leather
20¾" W; 19" D; 31¼" H; 17½" SH; 24" AH

3–144   DALLAS STACKING

1984
Designer: Paolo Favoretto
Manufacturer: Kinetics
Frame: tubular steel
Seat and back: metal
22¼" W; 20" D; 31" H; 18" SH; 26¾" AH

Kinetics

3–144

Kusch + Co.   3–145a

Kusch + Co.   3–145b

Brickel Associates   3–146

Rosenthal

3–147

3–145 SOLEY

1984
Designer: Valdimar Hardarson
Manufacturer: Kusch + Co.
Frame: steel rod
Seat and back: wood or upholstered with fabric
20" W; 19¼" D; 29½" H; 17¾" SH

3–146 YOKE (1584)

1984
Designer: Ward Bennett
Manufacturer: Brickel Associates
Frame: natural oiled ash
Seat and back: fully upholstered in fabric or leather
23¾" W; 22½" D; 29" H; 18" SH; 25" AH

3–147 SWING

1984
Designers: Herbert Ohl and Jutta Ohl
Manufacturer: Rosenthal
Structure: white, red, black, or chrome-plated steel
23½" W; 19¼" D; 30¾" H; 15¾" SH

3–148 VON VOGELSANG

1984
Designer: Philippe Starck
Manufacturer: Driade
Frame: steel tubing
Seat: perforated metal
21" W; 20" D; 28" H

Driade

3–148

Fixtures Furniture   3–149

3–149   RHOMBUS (40100)

1985
Designer: Gerd Lange
Manufacturer: Fixtures Furniture
Frame: rhombus-shaped steel tube
Seat: molded urethane foam cushion over a molded structural
    polypropylene seat support, covered in fabric
Backs: 5/16-inch urethane foam covered in fabric
Arms: die-cast aluminum in a rhombus shape
24″ W; 24″ D; 36″ H; 17″ SH; 25″ AH

3–150   HANDKERCHIEF

1986
Designers: Lella Vignelli and Massimo Vignelli
Manufacturer: Knoll International
Frame: steel wire, in a painted or polished chrome finish
Seat and back: molded Fiberglas and polyester
23″ W; 22½″ D; 29″ H

Courtesy of Knoll International   3–150

4 DESK CHAIRS

Barry Friedman Ltd., New York   4—1

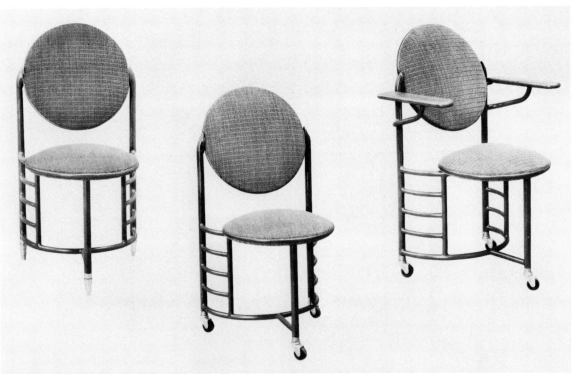

Steelcase   4—2

Jerryll Habegger   4–3

Herman Miller, Inc   4–4

4–1   LARKIN SWIVEL BASE

1904
Designer: Frank Lloyd Wright
Manufacturer: Van Dorn Iron Works
Frame and base: painted metal
Seat and back: oak
24¹¹⁄₁₆" W; 21 ⅛" D; 37 ½" H

4–2   JOHNSON WAX ADJUSTABLE

1937
Designer: Frank Lloyd Wright
Manufacturer: Steelcase
Frame and base: cast aluminum and magnesite
Seat and back: foam covered in fabric
Arms: walnut
21 ½" W; 20" D; 34" H; 21" SH

4–3   ADJUSTABLE SWIVEL

c. 1953
Designer: Works Design
Manufacturer: Nordiska Kompanient
Frame, base, and back: metal
Seat: molded laminated wood, with or without upholstery
20" W; 20" D; 27"–34" H; 18" SH

4–4   ALUMINUM GROUP

1958
Designers: Charles Eames and Ray Eames
Manufacturer: Herman Miller
Frame, base, and arms: bright-polished cast aluminum alloy
Column: steel
Seat support: cold-rolled steel
Seat and back: vinyl foam cushions and nylon suspension
    members covered in fabric or vinyl
22½" W; 23" D; 39½"–41 ½" H; 16½"–18½" SH

Herman Miller, Inc. 4–5

Alfred Kill 4–6

Herman Miller, Inc.   4–7

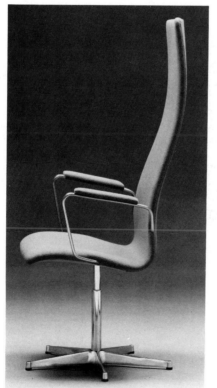

Fritz Hansen   4–8

4–5   KD 128 (KEVI)

1960
Designer: Jørgen Rud. Rasmussen
Manufacturer: Herman Miller
Base and column: polished aluminum or black umber
Seat and back: foam covered in fabric or vinyl; outside shell
    is black polypropylene
18½″ W; 18½″ D; 25″–36″ H; 17″–22″ SH

4–6   TULIP

1964
Designers: Jørgen Kastholm and Preben Fabricius
Manufacturer: Alfred Kill
Frame: Fiberglas with contoured latex padding covered in
    leather; removable padded leather jacket
Base: steel
31″ W; 27½″ D; 41″ H

4–7   PERCH

1964
Designer: Robert Propst
Manufacturer: Herman Miller
Base: polished aluminum
Column: steel
Seat support and ring: chrome-plated steel
Seat and back: foam covered in fabric, leather, or vinyl
27½″ W; 27½″ D; 41¼″–43″ H; 30¼″–33″ SH

4–8   OXFORD (3292)

1965
Designer: Arne Jacobsen
Manufacturer: Fritz Hansen
Base and arms: cast aluminum
Seat and back: molded laminated wood upholstered in
    molded foam and covered in leather
25¼″ W; 21¼″ D; 50½″–53½″ H; 17¼″–20½″ SH;
    26″–29″ AH

Herman Miller, Inc.   4-9

Olivetti   4-10

Steelcase

4–11

Brayton International

4–12

4–9 SOFT PAD GROUP

1969
Designers: Charles Eames and Ray Eames
Manufacturer: Herman Miller
Frame, base, and arms: bright-polished cast aluminum alloy
Column: steel
Seat support: cold-rolled steel
Seat and back: flexible urethane foam encapsulated by pol-
    yester fiber batting, covered in fabric
22½" W; 23¾" D; 40"–42" H; 18½"–20½" SH

4–10 Z 9/3

1973
Designer: Ettore Sottsass
Manufacturer: Olivetti
Frame and base: die-cast coated aluminum alloy
Seat and back: foam covered in fabric
22½" W; 22½" D; 32¼" H; 18½" SH

4–11 430 SERIES

1974
Designer: Peter Bunk
Manufacturer: Steelcase
Frame: tubular steel
Base: nylon-coated die-cast aluminum or chrome-plated oval
    tube steel
Column: zinc-plated steel
Seat and back: polyurethane foam covered in fabric or leather;
    outside shell is injection-molded polypropylene
Arms: nylon-coated upholstered polyurethane or polished
    chrome
24" W; 23" D; 33½"–37½" H; 17"–21" SH

4–12 LOGOS

1975
Designer: Bernd Munzebrock
Manufacturer: Brayton International
Frame: molded hand-laid Fiberglas
Base: aluminum
Seat and back: high-density urethane foam and Dacron fiber
    covered in fabric or leather
25½" W; 25½" D; 41" H; 18" SH; 26" AH

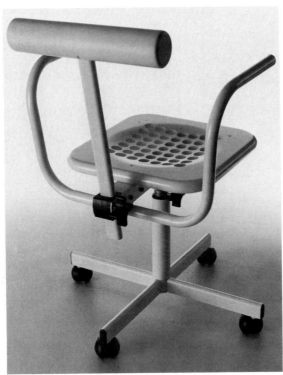

Heron Parigi   4–13

Herman Miller, Inc.   4–14

4–13   POLO

1975
Designer: Paolo Parigi
Manufacturer: Heron Parigi
Frame and base: welded steel
Seat: structural foam
Roll back: self-skinning soft polyurethane
16½" W; 16½" D; 33½" H; 17¾"–23¾" SH; 28"–34"
    AH

4–14   ERGON

1976
Designer: William Stumpf
Manufacturer: Herman Miller
Frame and base: bright-polished aluminum
Seat and back: foam covered in fabric or leather; outside
    shell is polypropylene
Arms: vinyl
26½" W; 23¼" D; 36½"–42" H; 17"–20" SH

4–15   VERTEBRA

1977
Designers: Emilio Ambasz and Giancarlo Piretti
Manufacturer: Krueger
Frame and column: seam-welded tubular steel
Base: die-cast aluminum with a steel understructure and self-
    skinning urethane surface
Seat and back: foam cushions covered in fabric or leather;
    outer shell is molded plastic
Arms: steel covered in self-skinning urethane
23" W; 24¾" D; 38⅜"–40⅞" H; 17"–19½" SH (Executive)

4–16   FYSIO

1978
Designer: Yrjö Kukkapuro
Manufacturer: Avarte Oy
Base: pressure-cast aluminum or chrome-plated tubular steel
Seat and back: form-pressed birch veneer with plastic laminate
    seat upholstered with foam padding and covered in fabric
    or leather
Arms: plastic-clad metal
25" W; 27"–33" D; 42"–45" H; 16"–20" SH; 25" AH

Krueger   4–15

Beylerian   4–16

Walter Knoll   4-17

Economic-Kaluste Oy   4-18

4–19

4–20

4–17   711

1979
Designer: Preben Fabricius
Manufacturer: Walter Knoll
Seat and back: foam covered in leather
Arms: flat steel covered in leather
Base: aluminum
25¼″ W; 27½″ D; 36½″ H; 18″ SH

4–18   VERDE-700N

1979
Designers: Yrjö Wiherheimo and Simo Heikkilä
Manufacturer: Economic-Kaluste Oy
Frame and base: tubular steel
Seat and back: natural or black-stained birch; foam cushions
    covered in fabric or leather
Support: metal springs attached to the frame
22¾″ W; 23½″ D

4–19   BASIC OPERATIONAL

1979
Designer: Niels Diffrient
Manufacturer: Knoll International
Frame: stamped steel, textured finish
Base and column: die-cast aluminum
Seat and back: polyurethane foam covered in fabric
Arms: tubular steel with Plastisol or upholstered
25½″ W; 21″ D; 32½″–36½″ H; 16″–18½″ SH; 24″–
    26½″ AH

4–20   SAPPER COLLECTION

1979
Designer: Richard Sapper
Manufacturer: Knoll International
Frame: rubber-covered nylon mesh
Base: aluminum
Seat and back: foam covered in fabric or leather
28⅜″ W; 27½″ D; 38½″–41⅜″ H; 17¾″–20½″ SH;
    24¼″–27¼″ AH

Courtesy of Knoll International   4–21

Castelli   4–22

4–21 DIFFRIENT EXECUTIVE

1980
Designer: Niels Diffrient
Manufacturer: Knoll International
Frame: stamped steel
Base and column: die-cast aluminum
Seat and back: polyurethane foam covered in fabric, leather, or vinyl
Arms: steel
26⅜″ W; 28¼″ D; 38¼″–41⅞″ H; 17½″–21⅛″ SH; 25⅞″–29½″ AH

4–22 SIMBIO

1982
Designer: Castelli Design Center
Manufacturer: Castelli
Frame: structural steel
Base, column, and arms: steel with self-skinning polyurethane finish
Seat and back: molded polyurethane upholstered in polyurethane foam and covered in fabric
23¼″ W; 26½″ D; 32″–35¾″ H; 16¾″–20½″ SH; 25¼″ AH

4–23 BALANS VITAL 6035

1983
Designers: Peter Opsvik and Hans Chr. Mengshoel
Manufacturer: Håg
Base and column: aluminum
Seat and knee pad: plywood upholstered in foam and covered in fabric
25½″ W; 25½″ D; 25¼″ H; 17¾″–23¼″ SH

4–24 HELENA

1983
Designer: Niels Diffrient
Manufacturer: Sunar Hauserman
Frame and column: 1-inch, heavy-gauge steel tubing
Base: glass-reinforced Zytel
Seat: molded polyurethane foam over contoured laminated hardwood shell, covered in fabric or leather
Back: molded polyurethane foam over a stamped steel armature, covered in fabric or leather
Arms: 1-inch, heavy-gauge steel tubing with textured, integral skin polyurethane foam pads
24⅝″ W; 24″ D; 32⅜″–35⅜″ H; 17½″–20½″ SH

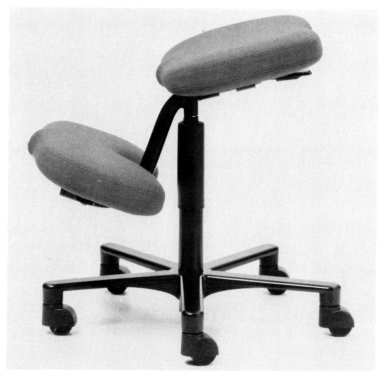

Håg

4–23a

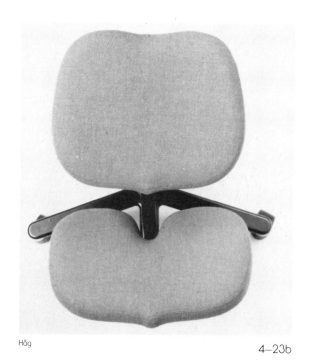

Håg

4–23b

Sunar Hauserman

4–24

Comforto 4–25

Herman Miller, Inc. 4–26

Comforto   4–27

4–25 SYSTEM 15 (1507)

c. 1983
Designer: Unknown
Manufacturer: Comforto
Frame: polypropylene
Base and column: steel with a molded scuff plate
Seat and back: polyurethane foam covered in fabric or leather
Arms: steel armature covered with molded urethane
25¼" W; 25¼" D; 42"–46" H; 16"–19½" SH

4–26 EQUA

1984
Designers: William Stumpf and Don Chadwick
Manufacturer: Herman Miller
Frame, base, and column: aluminum
Seat and back: thermoplastic shell upholstered in polyurethane
    foam and covered in fabric or leather
Arms: aluminum; pads in vinyl or upholstered
25½" W; 22½" D; 32"–36" H; 16"–20" SH

4–27 SYSTEM 25 (2532)

1985
Designer: Richard Sapper
Manufacturer: Comforto
Frame, base, and column: steel
Seat and back: polyurethane foam covered in fabric or leather;
    outer shell is polypropylene
Arms: polypropylene
31" W; 31" D; 37"–41" H; 16½"–20½" SH

4–28 LAUREN

1986
Designer: Richard Schultz
Manufacturer: Cadsana, Cadwallader and Sangiorgio Associates
Frame and base: die-cast aluminum
Seat and back: foam padding over plywood, covered in fabric
    or leather
23½" W; 23½" D; 34½" H; 18" SH

Cadsana, Cadwallader and Sangiorgio Associates

4–28

Airon

4–29

4–29 MONOPOLI

1986
Designer: Pietro Arosio
Manufacturer: Airon
Frame: chrome-plated or black-painted steel tubing
Seat and back: perforated sheet steel with a black epoxy-
    painted finish
Base: aluminum
21¾" W; 23¾" D; 30¾" H; 17¾"–23¾" SH

5 SOFAS

Cassina

5–1

Franz Wittmann

5–2

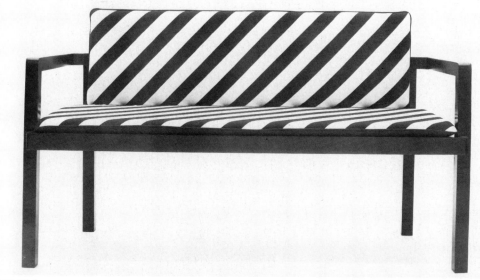

Tecta Möbel

5–3

5–1 ARGYLE (310/02)

1897
Designer: Charles Rennie Mackintosh
Manufacturer: Cassina
Frame: ashwood, stained walnut, or ebony; steel; plywood
Seat and back: polyurethane foam and polyester fiber padding
   covered in fabric or leather
Arm panels: polyurethane foam covered in fabric or leather
46" W; 26.4" D; 27.5" H; 16.3" SH

5–2 FLEDERMAUS SPINDLE-BACK SETTEE

1905
Designer: Josef Hoffmann
Manufacturer: Franz Wittmann
Frame: natural, ebonized, or rosewood-stained beech
Seat: foam-padded and covered in Hoffmann-designed fabrics
47½" W; 18" D; 30" H; 18½" SH

5–3 D 51/2

1910
Designer: Walter Gropius
Manufacturer: Tecta Möbel
Frame: wood
Seat and back: foam covered in fabric
55½" W; 22" D; 31" H; 18" SH

5–4 CABINETT

c. 1910
Designer: Josef Hoffmann
Manufacturer: Franz Wittmann
Frame: solid mahogany
Seat and back: rubber-webbed springing; foam covered in
   fabric
49½" W; 27" D; 30" H; 17½" SH

Franz Wittmann

5–4

Images of America
5–5

Cassina
5–6

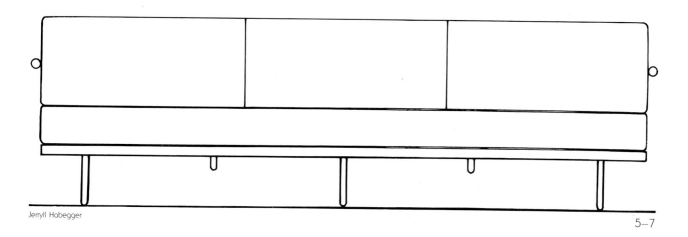

Jerryll Habegger

5—7

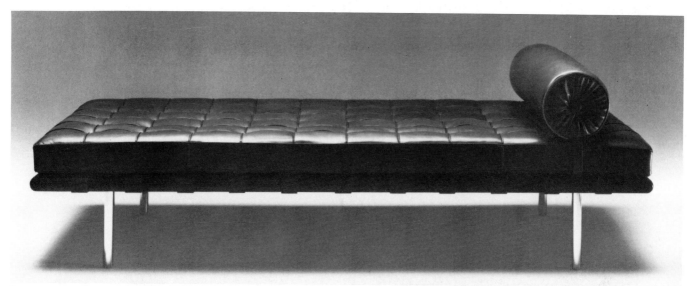

Courtesy of Knoll International

5—8

5—5 LOTA

1924
Designer: Eileen Gray
Manufacturer: Images of America
Frame: upholstered base and back support; down- and fiber-
    filled seat mattress and cushions; end boxes on casters
Legs: wood
95" W; 34½" D; 32½" H; 16" SH

5—6 LC/3/2

1928
Designer: Le Corbusier
Manufacturer: Cassina
Frame: highly polished chrome tubing and angle steel; rubber
    straps surrounding high-tensile-strength coiled steel springs
    for seat support
Seat, back, and arms: polyurethane and Dacron covered in
    fabric, leather, or vinyl
66.2" W; 28.8" D; 24.4" H; 13.8" SH

5—7 LC/5

1929
Designer: Le Corbusier
Manufacturer: Cassina
Frame: bent polished-chrome tubular steel; Pirelli rubber
    webbing support
Seat and back: polyurethane and Dacron fiberfill, covered in
    fabric, leather, or vinyl
101¼" W; 30¾" D; 31½" H

5—8 MIES COUCH (258)

1930
Designer: Ludwig Mies van der Rohe
Manufacturer: Knoll International
Frame: hardwood; saddle leather straps
Seat: foam mattress with polyester padding, covered in leather
Legs: tubular stainless steel, polished finish
78" W; 39" D; 15½" H

Thonet Industries

5—9

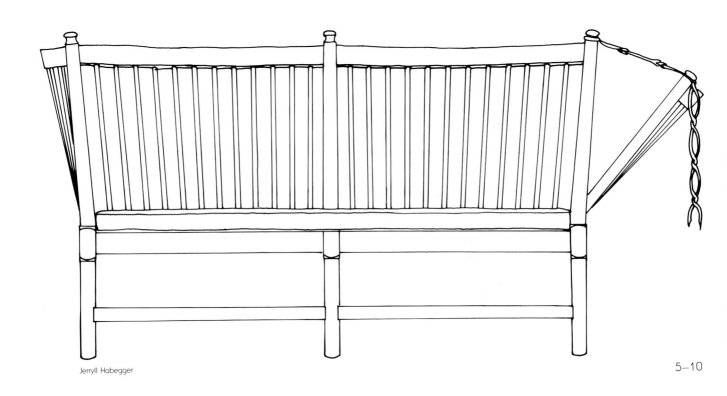

Jerryll Habegger

5—10

Cadsana, Cadwallader and Sangiorgio Associates   5-11

5-9 7000

1931
Designer: Marcel Breuer
Manufacturer: Thonet Industries
Frame: polished stainless steel, 1-inch diameter 11 x 16-gauge
    tube and ⅜-inch × 1-inch bar-stock frame
Seat and back: urethane filled; covered in leather
55″ W; 29″ D; 38¼″ H; 18″ SH

5-10 1789

1945
Designer: Børge Mogensen
Manufacturer: Fritz Hansen
Frame: beech, matte lacquer; leather straps
Seat, back, and arms: foam covered in fabric
63″–74¾″ W; 28¾″ D; 32″ H; 15¾″ SH

5-11 NEW YORK SOFA

1953
Designers: Ross Littrell, William Katavolos, and Douglas Kelley
Manufacturer: Cadsana, Cadwallader and Sangiorgio Associates
Frame: chrome-plated or epoxy-finished rectangular steel
Legs: chrome-plated round steel
Seat and back: polyurethane foam covered in fabric or leather
48″, 68″, or 97″ W; 27½″ D; 27½″ H; 15¾″ SH

5-12 SOFA COMPACT

1954
Designers: Charles Eames and Ray Eames
Manufacturer: Herman Miller
Frame: cold-rolled steel bar legs, spreaders, and back-support
    members; steel angle front and rear seat supports; medium-
    density particle-board supports for back; fabric-reinforced
    rubber webbing for seat support over curly flat steel springs
Seat and back: firm urethane foam cushioning covered in
    fabric
Legs: bright chrome-plated steel
72½″ W; 29⅞″ D; 34⅞″ H; 15⅞″ SH

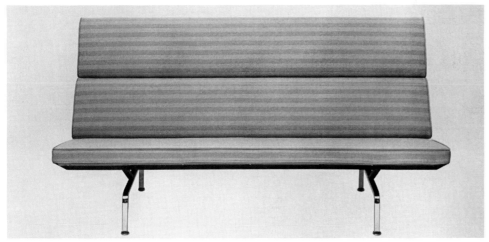

Herman Miller, Inc.   5-12

Tecno   5–13

5–13   D 70

1954
Designer: Osvaldo Borsani
Manufacturer: Tecno
Frame: black-enameled metal
Seat and back: polyurethane foam covered in fabric or leather
76¾″ W; 35½″–45¼″ D; 33½″ H; 15¾″ SH

5–14   2/PK 26

1956
Designer: Poul Kjaerholm
Manufacturer: Fritz Hansen
Frame: matte chrome-plated spring steel; canvas-covered
    support
Seat and back: loose leather cushions
30″ W; 30″ D; 30″ H; 14″ SH

5–15   JH 35/3

1956
Designer: Hans J. Wegner
Manufacturer: Johannes Hansens Møbelsnedkeri
Frame: wood
Seat and back: polyfoam covered in fabric
Legs: round steel
76″ W; 30″ D; 28¼″ H; 15″ SH

5–16   MARSHMALLOW LOVE SEAT (5670)

1956
Designer: George Nelson
Manufacturer: Herman Miller
Frame: satin chrome or black-painted metal
Seat and back: eighteen individual cushions covered in fabric,
    vinyl, or leather
52″ W; 33″ D; 32½″ H; 16″ SH

Fritz Hansen

5–14

Hans J. Wegner   5–15

Herman Miller, Inc.   5–16

Fritz Hansen   5—17

5—17 BENCH
1957
Designer: Poul Kjaerholm
Manufacturer: Fritz Hansen
Frame: matte chrome-plated steel
Seat: foam covered in leather
71" W; 31½" D; 12" H

5—18 3003
1957
Designer: Arne Jacobsen
Manufacturer: Fritz Hansen
Frame: chrome-plated tubular steel
Seat and back: foam covered in fabric or leather
71½" W; 31" D; 28½" H; 14¼" SH; 19¼"—21¼" AH

5—19 PK 31/3
1958
Designer: Poul Kjaerholm
Manufacturer: Fritz Hansen
Frame: matte chrome-plated spring steel
Seat and back: foam covered in leather; loose cushions
78" W; 30" D; 30" H; 15" SH

5—20 SETTEE (2212)
1963
Designer: Børge Mogensen
Manufacturer: Fredericia Stolefabrik
Frame: solid hardwood with foam padding and rubber webbing seat support
Seat and back: loose down-filled cushions covered in leather
Legs: white oak
62¼" W; 32¼" D; 31½" H; 17" SH

Fritz Hansen   5—18

Fritz Hansen

5—19

Fredericia Stolefabrik

5—20

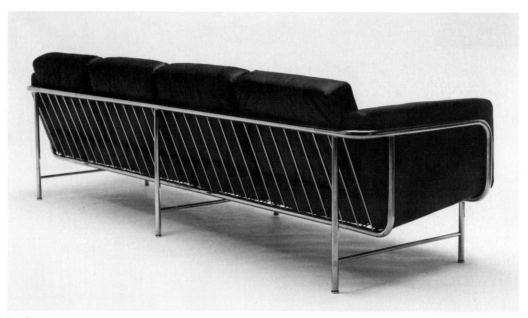

Hans Eichenberger   5–21

Herman Miller, Inc.   5–22

Poltronova

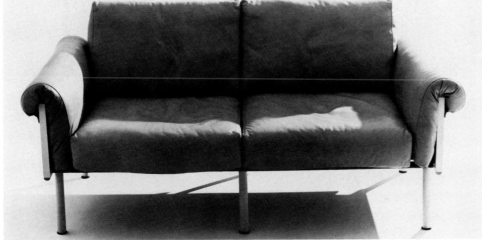

5–23

5–21   HE 84

1963
Designer: Hans Eichenberger
Manufacturer: Strässle Collection
Frame: mirror-chromed tubular steel; no-sag spring supports
Seat, back, and arms: loose cushions of polyurethane foam with Dacron overlay and covered in leather
100¼" W; 31½" D; 29½" H; 17¾" SH

5–22   SLING SOFA

1964
Designer: George Nelson
Manufacturer: Herman Miller
Frame: bright chrome-plated round tubular steel; heavyweight cattlehide sling supported by fabric-reinforced rubber webbing at back and neoprene platforms across seat
Seat and back: cushions of soft urethane foam encapsulated with polyester fiber and covered in leather
87" W; 32¼" D; 29¾" H; 15½" SH

5–23   SARATOGA

1964
Designers: Lella Vignelli and Massimo Vignelli
Manufacturer: Poltronova
Frame: wood lacquered in glossy black or gray
Seat and back: polyurethane foam and goose feather cushions covered in fabric or leather
59", 82½", or 106¼" W; 35½" D; 24" H

5–24   ATELJEE

1964
Designer: Yrjö Kukkapuro
Manufacturer: Avarte Oy
Frame and legs: tubular steel
Arms, back, and headrest panels: birch veneer
Seat: foam cushions; Dacron padding; upholstered in fabric or leather; interlaced rubber-strap seat cushion support
62" W; 32" D; 27" H; 15" SH; 24" AH

Beylerian

5–24

Brickel Associates

5—25

Zanotta

5—26

Poltronova

5—27

5—25 STRAIGHT LINE SERIES
c. 1964
Designer: Ward Bennett
Manufacturer: Brickel Associates
Frame: wood upholstered in fabric or leather
Cushions: polyurethane foam or down covered in fabric or leather
Legs: recessed, natural oiled walnut
72", 84", or 96" W; 33" D; 28¼" H; 16½" SH; 25" AH

5—26 THROWAWAY
1965
Designer: Willie Landels
Manufacturer: Zanotta
Frame: expanded polyurethane covered in fabric, leather, or vinyl
Base: vacuum-formed polystyrene
59" W; 29½" D; 22" H; 13" SH

5—27 SUPERONDA
1966
Designer: Archizoom Associati
Manufacturer: Poltronova
Structure: expanded resin covered in white, blue, or red plastic jet, or in fabric
94½" W; 39½" D; 30" H; 15" SH

5—28 BOCCA (MARILYN)
1969
Designer: Studio 65
Manufacturer: Gufram
Frame: molded foam over steel frame covered in stretch nylon
81" W; 33" D; 34¾" H; 16" SH

Gufram

5—28

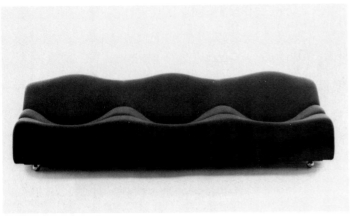

Artifort   5–29

Giovanetti   5–30a

Giovanetti   5–30b

5–29   261

1969
Designer: Pierre Paulin
Manufacturer: Artifort
Frame: fully upholstered injection-molded polyurethane foam
    secured to a tubular steel frame with rubber webbing seat
    and canvas back; covered in stretch fabric
64½" W; 32⅝" D; 24⅜" H; 14¼" SH

5–30   ANFIBIO

1970
Designer: Alessandro Becchi
Manufacturer: Giovanetti
Frame: steel, filled with expanded polyurethane and Dacron;
    upholstered mattress cover in synthetic sheepskin
94½" W; 38½" D; 25½" H

5–31   BOERI SYSTEM

1971
Designer: Cini Boeri
Manufacturer: Knoll International
Frame: shock-resistant polystyrene; casters
Seat, back, and arms: cushions of polyester foam covered in
    leather
90½" W; 37⅜" D; 26⅜" H; 14" SH ·

5–32   CLEOPATRA

1973
Designer: Geoffrey Harcourt
Manufacturer: Artifort
Frame: tubular steel upholstered with polyether and covered
    in stretch fabric; mounted on casters
75½" W; 35¾" D; 25¼" H; 11" SH

Courtesy of Knoll International

5–31

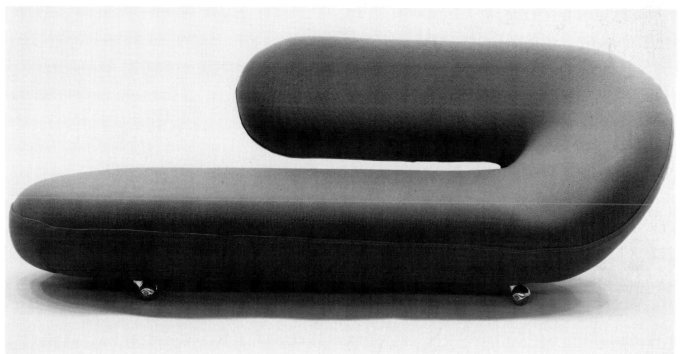

Artifort

5–32

B & B Italia   5—33

Arflex   5—34

Jerryll Habegger

5—35

5—33 LE STELLE

1974
Designer: Mario Bellini
Manufacturer: B & B Italia
Frame: three-part hinged steel support combined with polyurethane; seat structure is bent steel tube, embedded in
  polyurethane foam padding
Seat, back, and arms: polyurethane wrapped in Dacron fiberfill,
  covered in fabric or leather
92 ⅛" W; 34 ¼" D; 29 ½" H

5—34 BENGODI

1974
Designer: Cini Boeri
Manufacturer: Arflex
Frame: structural frame clad in polyurethane foam; Dacron
  padding covered in fabric or leather
Base: industrial wood
69 ¼" W; 39 ¼" D; 30 ¾" H; 15" SH; 18" AH

5—35 BUTCHER BLOCK

1974
Designer: Jerryll Habegger
Manufacturer: Arthur Habegger
Frame: laminated wood
Seat and back: foam covered in fabric
78" W; 34" D; 27 ½" H; 17" SH

5—36 LAURIANA

1976
Designers: Afra Scarpa and Tobia Scarpa
Manufacturer: B & B Italia
Frame: structural sheet embedded in molded polyurethane
  with seat springs
Seat, back, and arms: cushions upholstered in fabric or leather
64" W; 33 ½" D; 33 ⅛" H; 18 ⅛" SH; 22 ⅞" AH

B & B Italia

5—36

Courtesy of Knoll International

Cadsana, Cadwallader and Sangiorgio Associates 5—38

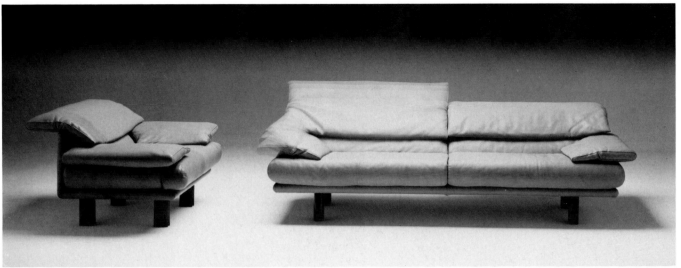

B & B Italia   5–39

5–37 BRIGADIER

1977
Designer: Cini Boeri
Manufacturer: Knoll International
Frame: wood with a lacquerlike polyester finish
Seat, back, and armrests: cushions of polyester foam covered
   in leather over elastic suspension straps
70″ W; 35½″ D; 21¼″ H; 15¾″ SH

5–38 SORO

1979
Designer: Francesco Soro
Manufacturer: Cadsana, Cadwallader and Sangiorgio Associates
Frame: tubular steel with an epoxy finish
Seat and back: polyurethane foam covered in fabric or leather
109⅛″ W; 41¾″ D; 30¼″ H

5–39 ALANDA

1980
Designer: Paolo Piva
Manufacturer: B & B Italia
Frame: steel structure embedded in cold-formed polyurethane
Seat, back, and arms: Dacron and polyurethane padding
   covered in fabric or leather
103⁹⁄₁₀″ W; 33⁷⁄₁₆″–41″ D; 28¾″–35⁷⁄₁₆″ H; 17⅜″ SH

5–40 CARTOUCHE (2532)

c. 1980
Designer: Ward Bennett
Manufacturer: Brickel Associates
Frame: foam over wood
Seat, back, and arms: tight upholstered, covered in fabric
85″ W; 32¼″ D; 25″ H; 15″ SH; 25″ AH

Brickel Associates   5–40

201

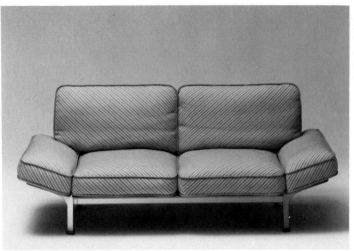

Zanotta   5—41

Driade   5—42

5—41   DINAMO

1981
Designers: Jonathan De Pas, Donato D'Urbino, and Paolo
   Lomazzi
Manufacturer: Zanotta
Frame: lacquered aluminum
Seat, back, and arms: cushions of Dacron and down covered
   in fabric or leather
90½" W; 32¾" D; 31½" H; 15¾" SH

5—42   SQUASH

1981
Designer: Paolo Deganello
Manufacturer: Driade
Frame: wood back and seat support with foam covered in
   fabric; metal back support
Seat: polyurethane foam covered in fabric
Legs: metal
72½" or 96" W; 31½" D; 39" H

5—43   1060

c. 1982
Designer: Joe D'Urso
Manufacturer: Knoll International
Frame: constructed hardwood covered in fabric or leather
Seat: foam-wrapped Dacron cushions covered in fabric or
   leather
Back: waterfowl feather pillows covered in fabric or leather
96" W; 48" D; 24" H; 15½" SH; 24" AH

5—44   TEATRO

c. 1983
Designers: Aldo Rossi and Luca Meda
Manufacturer: Domus Italia
Frame: exposed wood
Seat and back: polyurethane covered in fabric or leather
43" W; 20" D; 30" H

Courtesy of Knoll International

5-43

Domus Italia

5-44

Herman Miller, Inc.

5—45

Cassina

5—46

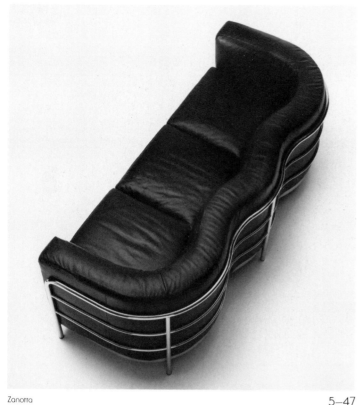

Zanotta   5–47

5–45 EAMES SOFA

1984
Designers: Charles Eames and Ray Eames
Manufacturer: Herman Miller
Frame: oiled teak or walnut
Base: cast aluminum in a polished or espresso finish
Seat and back: foam covered in leather
80″ W; 21″ D; 33″ H; 16½″ SH

5–46 VERANDA 3

1984
Designer: Vico Magistretti
Manufacturer: Cassina
Frame: molded steel
Seat and back: polyurethane foam and polyester padding
    covered in fabric or leather
Base: lacquered wood
102¼″ W; 33½″ D; 29½″–43¼″ H; 16″ SH

5–47 ONDA (1030)

1984
Designers: Jonathan De Pas, Donato D'Urbino, and Paolo
    Lomazzi
Manufacturer: Zanotta
Frame: 18/8 tubular stainless steel
Seat and back: Dacron and polyurethane foam covered in
    fabric or leather
76¾″ W; 30¾″ D; 28½″ H; 17¾″ SH

5–48 EJ 20

1984
Designer: Jørgen Gammelgaard
Manufacturer: Erik Jørgensen Møbelfabrik
Frame: leather-covered wood
Seat and back: polyurethane foam cushions covered in leather
Legs: beech or chrome-plated metal
55⅞″ or 78¾″ W; 31″ D; 28⅜″ H; 16½″ SH

Erik Jørgensen Møbelfabrik   5–48a

Erik Jørgensen Møbelfabrik   5–48b

6 MODULAR SEATING

Tecta Möbel   6-1

Herman Miller, Inc.   6-2 a

Herman Miller, Inc.   6-2 b

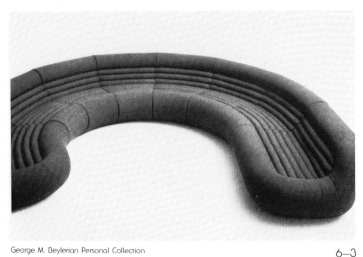

George M. Beylerian Personal Collection

6–3

6–1   THEATER CHAIRS

1926
Designer: Marcel Breuer
Manufacturer: Tecta Möbel
Frame: tubular steel
Seat and back: canvas
Arms: wood
68″ W; 17¾″ D; 34¼″ H; 18½″ SH

6–2   TANDEM SEATING

1962
Designers: Charles Eames and Ray Eames
Manufacturer: Herman Miller
Frame: polished aluminum
Seat and back: flat pillows of Naugahyde consisting of vinyl
    foam and Fiberthin
23¼″ W; 28″ D; 33¾″ H; 17⅝″ SH

6–3   CARRERA

1969
Designers: Jonathan De Pas, Donato D'Urbino, and Paolo
    Lomazzi
Manufacturer: B.B.B. Over
Frame: injection-molded polyurethane foam covered in stretch
    fabric or leather
23½″ W; 35½″ D; 25″ H; 16″ SH

6–4   NOVEMILA

1969
Designer: Tito Agnoli
Manufacturer: Arflex
Frame: dense polyurethane foam
Base: industrial wood
Seat and back: polyurethane foam covered in fabric; re-
    movable covers
Feet: PVC
25½″ W; 31½″ D; 23½″ H; 13¾″ SH

Arflex

6–4

B & B Italia   6-5

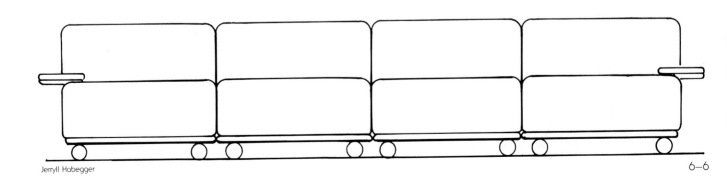

Jerryll Habegger   6-6

De Sede   6–7

B & B Italia   6–8

6–5   AMANTA 24

1971
Designer: Mario Bellini
Manufacturer: B & B Italia
Shell: molded metal, high-density reinforced Fiberglas
Seat and back: injection-molded polyurethane cushions cov-
    ered in fabric, leather, or vinyl
Feet: hard rubber ball feet
25¼" W; 33½" D; 28⅜" H; 16½" SH

6–6   PIANURA

1971
Designer: Mario Bellini
Manufacturer: Cassina
Frame and arms: solid walnut
Seat and back: loose polyurethane and Dacron cushions cov-
    ered in fabric, leather, or vinyl
31½" W; 36⅝" D; 27⅝" H; 15¾" SH

6–7   DS-600

1972
Designers: Eleonore Peduzzi-Riva, Ueli Berger, and Heinz Ulrich
Manufacturer: De Sede
Frame: metal and wood-reinforced, molded, rigid foam with
    plywood deck; covered in nonwoven carpeting
Seat and back: foam wrapped with fiberfill, covered in canvas
    or leather
9½" W; 39½" D; 30¾" H; 16" SH

6–8   LE BAMBOLE

1972
Designer: Mario Bellini
Manufacturer: B & B Italia
Frame: polyurethane foam body encased in pillows of foam
    and Dacron fiberfill covered in fabric or leather
31½" W; 37¼" D; 28⅜" H; 18⅛" SH

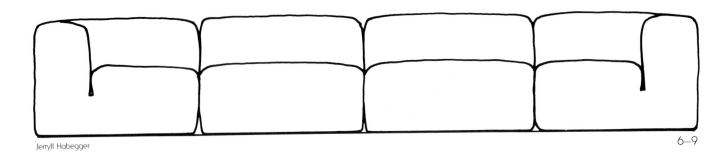

Jerryll Habegger

6–9

Srendig

6–10

Vecta   6–11

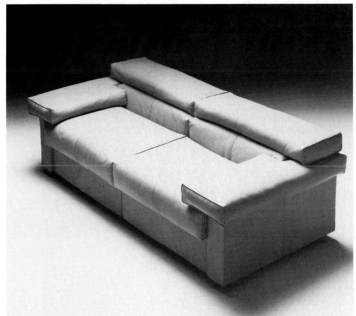

B & B Italia   6–12

6–9   LE MURA

1972
Designer: Mario Bellini
Manufacturer: Cassina
Frame: urethane foam injection upholstered in fabric, leather, or vinyl
Base: injected-molded black ABS pan
36¼″ W; 36¼″ D; 24⅜″ H; 16½″ SH

6–10   COSMOS (DS-28)

c. 1972
Designer: Ubald Klug
Manufacturer: De Sede
Frame: hardwood with rubber webbing; urethane foam and Dacron fiberfill covered in fabric or leather
26¼″ W; 33″ D; 28¼″ H; 15″ SH

6–11   TAPPO

1973
Designer: John Mascheroni
Manufacturer: Vecta
Frame: high-compression foam; soft urethane foam; ¾-inch fiberboard seat and back panels for support, strength, and durability; heavy steel welded T-bars connect seat and back; covered in fabric
Base: ABS
30″ W; 34″ D; 27″ H; 16″ SH

6–12   ERASMO

1973
Designers: Afra Scarpa and Tobia Scarpa
Manufacturer: B & B Italia
Frame: polyurethane foam over a steel armature covered in fabric, leather, or vinyl
35⅛″ W; 38⅝″ D; 27⅛″ H; 18⅛″ SH

Zanotta

6—13

Strendig

6—14

B & B Italia

6–15

Herman Miller, Inc.

6–16

6–13   OTTAWA

1973
Designers: Jonathan De Pas, Donato D'Urbino, and Paolo
    Lomazzi
Manufacturer: Zanotta
Frame: steel structure; flexible steel springs; polyurethane foam
    covered in fabric or leather
Seat, back, and arms: Dacron filled and covered in fabric or
    leather
Base: vacuum-formed polystyrene
31½" W; 33½" D; 30¼" H; 17" SH

6–14   ENVIRON ONE (610-C/P)

c. 1973
Designer: Ennio Chiggio
Manufacturer: Nikol International
Frame: heavyweight solid urethane foam covered in fabric
180" W; 116" D; 24" H; 13¾" SH

6–15   ELOGIO

1974
Designers: Afra Scarpa and Tobia Scarpa
Manufacturer: B & B Italia
Frame: steel armature and injected polyurethane foam cov-
    ered in fabric, leather, or vinyl
Seat and back: cushions of polyurethane foam and Dacron
    filling covered in fabric, leather, or vinyl
41" W; 42⅝" D; 26" H; 14½" SH

6–16   CHADWICK

1974
Designer: Don Chadwick
Manufacturer: Herman Miller
Frame: molded urethane foam covered in fabric or vinyl
Base: black molded polystyrene
28" W; 31" D; 27" H; 15¼" SH

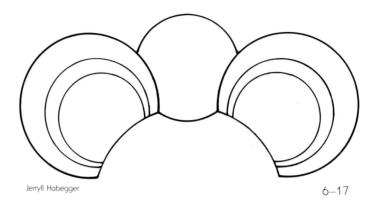

Jerryll Habegger

6—17

Herman Miller, Inc.

6—18

Brayton International

6—19

Brayton International

6–20a

Brayton International

6–20b

6–17   CIRCLE SEATING

c. 1975
Designer: Leif Blodee
Manufacturer: American Seating
Frame: foam covered in fabric
34½" W; 34½" D; 25¼" H; 15¾" SH

6–18   MODULAR SOFA GROUP

1976
Designer: Ray Wilkes
Manufacturer: Herman Miller
Frame: all-birch plywood; cold-rolled steel tubing support beam;
    urethane foam cushioning covered in fabric
25" W; 29" D; 24¾" H; 15" SH

6–19   DOMANE

1976
Designer: Bernd Munzebrock
Manufacturer: Brayton International
Frame: multiple laminations of foam densities on a wood
    frame covered in fabric
Base: recessed hardwood in a black ebony finish
28½" W; 36" D; 26" H; 16" SH

6–20   PLUS

1976
Designer: Friedrich Hill
Manufacturer: Brayton International
Frame: hardwood with multiple laminations of foam densities
    covered in fabric or leather
Seat and back: cushions of polyester fiberfill and foam covered
    in fabric or leather
30" W; 33" D; 28" H; 16" SH

Hanne Kjaerholm   6—21

Brayton International   6—22

Brayton International

6–23

Brayton International

6–24

6–21 THEATER SEAT
1976
Designer: Poul Kjaerholm
Manufacturer: P.P. Møbler
Frame: maple
Seat and back: woven wood slats
23 ½" W

6–22 PICCOLINO
1977
Designer: Jochen Hoffmann
Manufacturer: Brayton International
Frame: hardwood with multiple laminations of rigid and flexible foam densities covered in fabric or leather
16" W; 31 ½" D; 27 ½" H; 15" SH

6–23 FEELING
1977
Designer: Walter Knoll Design Team
Manufacturer: Brayton International
Frame: hardwood with multiple laminations of foam densities
  covered in fabric or leather
Seat and back: cushions of polyester fiberfill and foam covered
  in fabric or leather
24 ½" W; 34 ¼" D; 35" H; 16" SH

6–24 WINGS
1978
Designer: Michael Knoll
Manufacturer: Brayton International
Frame: hardwood and molded wood veneer with multiple
  laminations of foam densities covered in fabric or leather
Seat and back: polyester fiberfill cushions covered in fabric
  or leather
25" W; 31" D; 38 ½" H; 17" SH

Hanne Kjaerholm   6–25

Fixtures Furniture   6–26

Vecta

6–27

6–25   THEATER SEAT

1979
Designer: Poul Kjaerholm
Manufacturer: P.P. Møbler
Frame: mahogany
Base: stainless steel
23½" W

6–26   FLIP SEAT

1979
Designer: David Goodwin
Manufacturer: Fixtures Furniture
Frame: steel
Seat: molded structural polypropylene
22" W; 8"–13" D; 26" H; 24" SH (module)

6–27   MIKO

1980
Designer: Vecta in-house
Manufacturer: Vecta
Frame: polyurethane foam covered in fabric
Seat and back: ¾-inch-thick fiberboard panels joined with
    heavy-duty steel brackets
Base: seamless molded ABS plastic
24" W; 28" D; 29" H; 18" SH

6–28   SERIE 4

c. 1980
Designers: Ole Gjerlov-Knudsen and Torben Lind
Manufacturer: Fritz Hansen
Frame: beech, oak, or teak
Seat and back: foam covered in fabric, leather, or vinyl
22¾" W; 26" D; 29½" H; 16¼" SH

Fritz Hansen

6–28

August   6—29

Rudd International   6—30

6—29   AUGUST SERIES

1982
Designer: Lee Fister, Jr.
Manufacturer: August
Frame: foam covered in fabric or leather
32″ W; 32″ D; 29″ H; 18″ SH

6—30   PIPELINE

1984
Designers: Johannes Foersom and Peter Hiort-Lorentzen
Manufacturer: Eric Jørgensen Møbelfabrik
Frame: 2.5-mm steel tube
Seat: injection-molded foam over a laminated wood seat
   pan covered in fabric
Back: injection-molded foam over a steel armature covered
   in fabric
76″ W; 29″ D; 29″ H; 18″ SH

7 DINING/ CONFERENCE TABLES

Cassina

7–1

B.D. Ediciones

7–2

Heinz & Co.   7-3a

Heinz & Co.   7-3b

7-1   G.S.A.

1900
Designer: Charles Rennie Mackintosh
Manufacturer: Cassina
Top: veneered particle-board stained in walnut or black ebony
Base: beechwood dowels
74.8" Diameter; 29" H

7-2   1903.25

1903
Designer: Charles Rennie Mackintosh
Manufacturer: B.D. Ediciones
Top and legs: silver-painted wood; legs inlaid with purple-
   colored glass
29" W; 29" D; 28⅞" H

7-3   PRINT TABLE

1903
Designer: Frank Lloyd Wright
Manufacturer: Heinz & Co.
Structure: oak
48" W; 44" D; 25½" Top Height; 46" Total Height

7-4   MIDWAY 3

1914
Designer: Frank Lloyd Wright
Manufacturer: Cassina
Top: 0.6-inch-thick clear plate glass with a polished edge
Base: welded steel rod with a high-gloss enamel finish
47.2" Diameter; 27.2" H

Cassina   7-4

Cassina

7–5

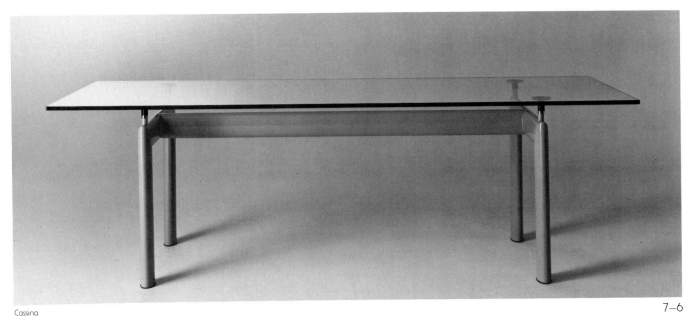

Cassina

7–6

Cassina   7–7

Images of America   7–8

7–5   ALLEN

1917
Designer: Frank Lloyd Wright
Manufacturer: Cassina
Structure: natural light cherrywood
101.3" or 110.2" W; 41.7" D; 27.7" H

7–6   LC/6

1928
Designer: Le Corbusier
Manufacturer: Cassina
Top: 0.7-inch clear polished glass
Base: welded oval aircraft-type steel tubing; nylon support
   cushions
90" W; 33½" D; 27⅛" H

7–7   LC/10-P

1928
Designer: Le Corbusier
Manufacturer: Cassina
Top: 0.59-inch clear polished glass with 45-degree chamfered
   edges
Frame: steel T-shaped frame members; black rubber cushion
Legs: polished chrome steel
55" W; 31½" D; 27½" H

7–8   JEAN

1929
Designer: Eileen Gray
Manufacturer: Images of America
Top: white-colored formica
Legs: polished chrome tubular steel
25¼" W; 25¼" D; 28¼" H (closed); 50¼" W; 25¼" D;
   28¼" H (open)

Artek   7—9

Artek   7—10

7—9   ROUND TABLE (91)

1933
Designer: Alvar Aalto
Manufacturer: Artek
Top: birch veneer; linoleum or plastic laminate with birch
    band
Legs: solid natural birch
49¼" Diameter; 28" H

7—10   MULTI-SECTIONAL (4-905)

1933
Designer: Alvar Aalto
Manufacturer: Artek
Top: birch veneer; linoleum or plastic laminate with birch
    band
Legs: solid natural birch
90¾" W; 47¼" D; 28" H

7—11   MARIA

1936
Designer: Bruno Mathsson
Manufacturer: Dux International
Top: natural beech or curly grained birch
Base: natural beech
94½" or 110¼" W; 43¼" D; 28½" H

7—12   NEW YORK CONFERENCE TABLE

1953
Designers: Ross Littell, William Katavolos, and Douglas Kelley
Manufacturer: Cadsana, Cadwallader and Sangiorgio Associates
Top: granite or glass
Base: polished stainless steel
78¾" W; 39⅜" D; 28¼" H

Dux International

7-11

Cadsana, Cadwallader and Sangiorgio Associates

7-12

Artek   7–13

Artek   7–14

7–15

7–13   FAN-LEGGED (X800)

1954
Designer: Alvar Aalto
Manufacturer: Artek
Top: natural ash
Legs: natural birch
53⅛" W; 31½" D; 28" H

7–14   H-LEGGED (H90)

1955
Designer: Alvar Aalto
Manufacturer: Artek
Top: veneered ash or oak
Legs: veneered ash or oak with white-lacquered cast steel
     connectors
72½" W; 50½" D; 28¾" H

7–15   OVAL (174)

1956
Designer: Eero Saarinen
Manufacturer: Knoll International
Top: marble, plastic laminate, oak, or walnut veneer
Base: cast metal pedestal, white-fused finish
78" W; 48" D; 28½" H

7–16   OMEGA

1956
Designer: Hans Eichenberger
Manufacturer: Teo Jakob
Top: plastic laminate, wood veneers, glass, or marble
Base: round steel tube, mirror-polished chrome finish
60" W; 30" D; 29¼" H

Hans Eichenberger   7–16

231

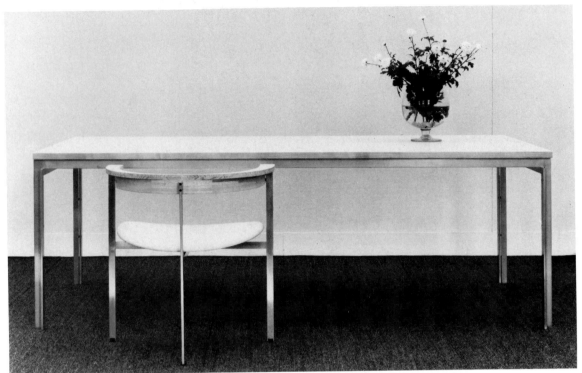

Fritz Hansen   7–17

Fritz Hansen   7–18

Fritz Hansen

7-19

7-17   PK 55

1957
Designer: Poul Kjaerholm
Manufacturer: Fritz Hansen
Top: lacquered ash
Base: matte chrome-plated steel
71" W; 35½" D; 27" H

7-18   A 725

1958
Designer: Arne Jacobsen
Manufacturer: Fritz Hansen
Top: plastic laminate, teak, or beech
Base: aluminum; chrome-plated column
47¼" Diameter; 27½" H

7-19   PK 54

1963
Designer: Poul Kjaerholm
Manufacturer: Fritz Hansen
Top: flint-rolled blanc clair marble; solid maple extensions
Base: matte chrome-plated steel
55" Diameter; 82¾" Diameter (with extensions); 25½" H

7-20   NIBAY

1963
Designer: Tobia Scarpa
Manufacturer: Knoll International
Top: veneer over solid wood core; solid wood edge
Base: solid wood
57⅞" W; 39⅜" D; 28⅜" H

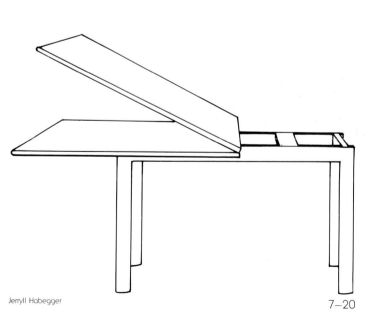

Jerryll Habegger

7-20

Fredericia Stolefabrik

7–21

Poltronova

7–22

7–21   6288

1965
Designer: Børge Mogensen
Manufacturer: Fredericia Stolefabrik
Top and base: teak or oak
38½" W; 38½" D; 27½" H

7–22   LOTOROSSO

1965
Designer: Ettore Sottsass
Manufacturer: Poltronova
Top and base: red Verona marble, white Carrara marble, or
    black Marquine marble
Support stem: black or white-pearl stove enameled, or chrome-
    plated metal
51¼" Diameter; 28" H

7–23   DOGE

1967
Designer: Carlo Scarpa
Manufacturer: Simon International
Top: clear plate glass
Base: satin-polished bar steel
120", 136", or 170" W; 40" D; 28" H

7–24   470

c. 1967
Designer: Warren Platner
Manufacturer: CI Designs
Top: glass or marble with ash, oak, or mahogany underframe
Base: marble
80", 96", 120", 144", 180", or 210" W; 40", 48", or 60" D;
    29" H

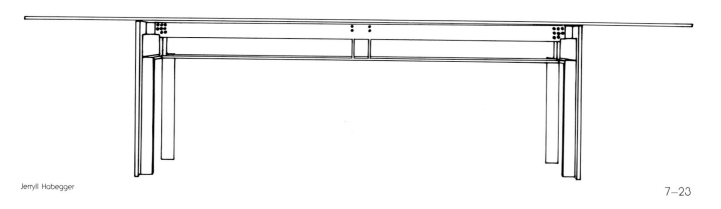

Jerryll Habegger

7–23

CI Designs

7–24

Zanotta

7–25

Fritz Hansen

7–26

Alberto Bazzani 7—27

Angelo Mangiarotti 7—28

7—25 POKER

1968
Designer: Joe Colombo
Manufacturer: Zanotta
Top: white plastic laminate; snap-on green wool cover bound
   in black leather
Legs: 4-inch stainless steel
38½" W; 38½" D; 28¼" H

7—26 SUPERELLIPS

1968
Designers: Piet Hein and Bruno Mathsson
Manufacturer: Fritz Hansen
Top: plastic laminate with matte-polished aluminum edge
   banding, or solid wood with matching edge banding
Legs: chrome-plated steel
71" W; 47¼" D; 27½" H

7—27 CAROLA

1968
Designer: Giovanni Offredi
Manufacturer: Alberto Bazzani
Top and legs: lacquered curved wood
49¼" Diameter; 26½" H

7—28 M 1

1969
Designer: Angelo Mangiarotti
Manufacturer: Tisettanta
Top and base: marble
53¼" Diameter; 28¼" H

Rudd International

7—29

Zanotta

7—30

Angelo Mangiarotti

7–31

7–29 KINGS TABLE

1969
Designers: Rud Thygesen and Johnny Sorensen
Manufacturer: Botium
Top and legs: oak or mahogany
53" or 73" W; 36" D; 29" H (rectangular); 53" or 73" Diameter; 29" H (half-round)

7–30 GAETANO

1971
Designer: Gae Aulenti
Manufacturer: Zanotta
Top: tempered plate glass or white plastic laminate
Base: removable trestles in aluminum alloy; rubber knobs
59" W; 29 ½" D; 27 ½" H

7–31 EROS

1971
Designer: Angelo Mangiarotti
Manufacturer: Skipper
Top and legs: marble
94 ½" W; 55" D; 28 ¼" H

7–32 I-BEAM (3106)

c. 1971
Designer: Ward Bennett
Manufacturer: Brickel Associates
Top: ¾-inch marble with polished edge
Base: black steel pedestal
48" W; 48" D; 28 ½" H

Brickel Associates

7–32

Herman Miller, Inc.   7–33

Vitsoe Kollektion   7–34

Simon International

7–35

7–33 SEGMENTED BASE

1972
Designers: Charles Eames and Ray Eames
Manufacturer: Herman Miller
Top: ⅞-inch-thick Italian white marble with rounded edge
Base: chrome-plated and polished aluminum
78″ W; 42″ D; 29½″ H

7–34 720

1972
Designer: Dieter Rams
Manufacturer: Vitsoe
Top: polystyrol with synthetic lacquer finish
Legs: seamless PVC tubing
76¾″ W; 43¼″ D; 28″ H

7–35 VALMARANA

1972
Designer: Carlo Scarpa
Manufacturer: Simon International
Top: ash veneer
Base: solid wood
98½″ W; 30¼″ D; 28¼″ H

7–36 FREE FORM

1973
Designer: Jerryll Habegger
Manufacturer: Arthur Habegger
Top: lacquered wood
Legs: wood covered in fabric
104″ W; 69″ D; 28″ H

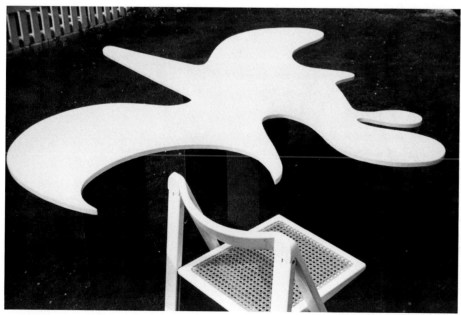

Jerryll Habegger

7–36

B & B Italia   7–37

Driade   7–38

Rosenthal   7–39

7–37   TOBIO ALTO

1974
Designers: Afra Scarpa and Tobia Scarpa
Manufacturer: B & B Italia
Top: glass, marble, or leather-lined wood
Base: cylindrical shape covered in leather; stem filled with
    pressed cement ballast
59" W; 51 ¼" D; 28 ¾" H

7–38   FRATE

1974
Designer: Enzo Mari
Manufacturer: Driade
Top: glass
Base: burnished metal legs; natural oak stretcher
51 ¼", 78 ¾", or 106 ¼" W; 30 ¾" D; 28 ¼" H

7–39   DINNERELEMENT

1975
Designer: Joe Colombo
Manufacturer: Rosenthal
Structure: plastic-coated wood
67" W; 42 ½" D; 28" H

7–40   54-126

1975
Designer: Gae Aulenti
Manufacturer: Knoll International
Top: plastic laminate or glass
Base: steel extrusion, fused finish
57 ⅛" W; 57 ⅛" D; 28 ¾" H

Courtesy of Knoll International   7–40

GF Furniture Systems

7–41

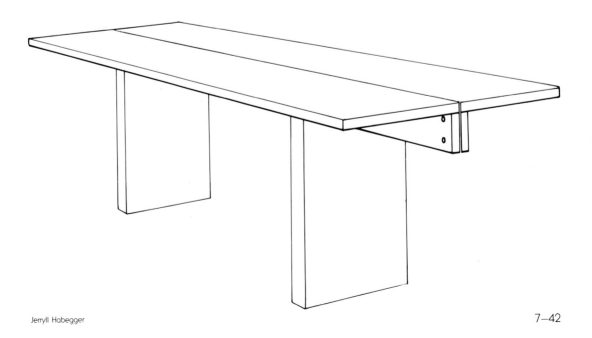

Jerryll Habegger

7–42

Cassina

7–43

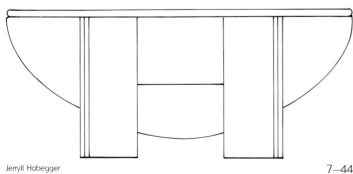

Jerryll Habegger

7–44

7–41   710

1975
Designer: Andrew Belschner
Manufacturer: GF Furniture Systems
Top: wood veneer or Hila-Tex
Legs: chrome-plated steel rod
30″ or 36″ W; 30″ or 36″ D; 28″ H

7–42   LAMBDA

1975
Designer: Superstudio
Manufacturer: Giovanetti
Top and base: wood ingot
98½″ W; 33½″ D; 28¼″ H

7–43   IL COLONNATO

1977
Designer: Mario Bellini
Manufacturer: Cassina
Top: travertine, marble, or glass
Legs: travertine or marble
55⅛″ W; 55⅛″ D; 28¾″ H

7–44   ANTELLA

1977
Designer: Kazuhide Takahama
Manufacturer: Simon International
Top and base: plywood in enamel or glossy pigmented
    polyester
66½″ W; 24¼″–48″ D; 28¼″ H

Courtesy of Knoll International

7–45

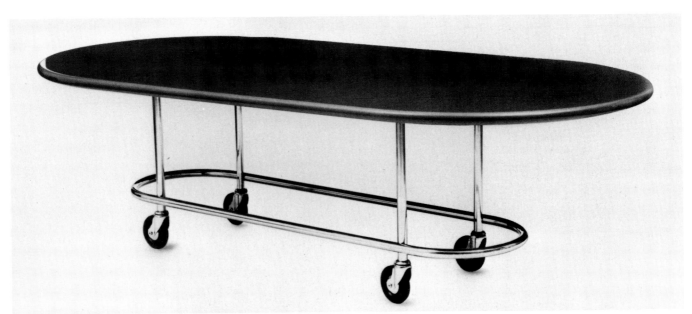

Brickel Associates

7–46

Angelo Mangiarotti   7–47

7–45 3017

1977
Designer: Charles Pfister
Manufacturer: Knoll International
Top: oak veneer, Honduras mahogany, or high-gloss polyester finish
Base: polished chrome or high-gloss polyester finish
94½" W; 59" D; 28¾" H

7–46 ROLLING CAPSULE (3163)

c. 1977
Designer: Ward Bennett
Manufacturer: Brickel Associates
Top: 1½-inch wood with polyurethane enamel finish, bull-nosed edge
Base: stainless steel tubing; rubber wheel casters
96" W; 48" D; 26" H

7–47 INCAS

1978
Designer: Angelo Mangiarotti
Manufacturer: Skipper
Top and base: sandstone
78¾" W; 21¾" D; 28¼" H

7–48 CENTRO CUSTOM

1978
Designer: Giancarlo Piretti
Manufacturer: Krueger
Top: hardwood veneer or plastic laminate
Base: polished aluminum legs; chrome or black enameled columns and stringers
120" W; 54" D; 29" H

Krueger   7–48

247

B & B Italia   7–49

Unifor   7–50

Alberto Bazzani

7–51

7–49   TAVOLI DIALOGO

1978
Designers: Afra Scarpa and Tobia Scarpa
Manufacturer: B & B Italia
Top: crystal
Legs and top frame: black-polyester-lacquered wood or walnut
Cross bars: stove-enameled metal
78¾" W; 37⅞" D; 28¾" H

7–50   MASTER

1978
Designers: Afra Scarpa and Tobia Scarpa
Manufacturer: Unifor
Top: 2½-inch-thick oak, walnut, or rosewood veneer with
   open-pore catalyzed finish; edges wrapped with black leather
Base: die-cast aluminum legs; extruded aluminum stretchers
201" W; 67" D; 29½" H

7–51   LOTUS

1978
Designer: Naoki Matsunaga
Manufacturer: Alberto Bazzani
Structure: lacquered wood
53" W; 53" D; 28¼" H

7–52   PLANO

1978
Designer: Giancarlo Piretti
Manufacturer: Castelli
Top: rigid polyester
Base: polished die-cast aluminum alloy
Glides: nylon
33½" W; 33½" D; 28¼" H

Castelli

7–52

Tecta Möbel   7–53

Angelo Mangiarotti   7–54

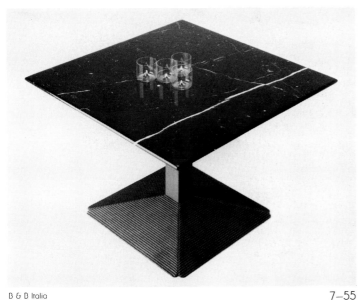

B & B Italia

7–55

7–53 M 1

1979
Designer: Stefan Wewerka
Manufacturer: Tecta Möbel
Top and base: black-stained ash
74″ W; 58¼″ D; 29″ H

7–54 ASOLO

1979
Designer: Angelo Mangiarotti
Manufacturer: Skipper
Top and legs: granite
94½″ W; 31½″ D; 28¼″ H

7–55 PIEDIFERRO

1979
Designers: Afra Scarpa and Tobia Scarpa
Manufacturer: B & B Italia
Top: marble or fabric-covered wood
Base: cast iron with enamel or lacquer finish
47¼″ W; 47¼″ D; 28¾″ H

7–56 BO 983

1979
Designers: Jørgen Lund and Ole Larsen
Manufacturer: Bo-Ex
Top: wood
Base: matte chrome-plated steel
126″ W; 39¼″ D; 28″ H

Bo-Ex

7–56

Fritz Hansen 7–57

7–57   2R

1980
Designers: Leif Erik Rasmussen and Henrik Rolff
Manufacturer: Fritz Hansen
Top: 1-inch-thick wood veneer
Base: 2-inch steel support rail finished in black powder coat
   enamel
Legs: 1 ½-inch polished chrome
32″, 48″, or 64″ W; 32″ D; 29 ½″ H

7–58   RACETRACK

1980
Designer: Joe D'Urso
Manufacturer: Knoll International
Top: variety of woods, laminates, or stone
Legs: steel, painted or polished chrome finish; casters or glides
96″ W; 48″ D; 27 ½″ H

7–59   MC TABLE

1981
Designer: Yrjö Kukkapuro
Manufacturer: Avarte Oy
Top: birch plywood or plastic laminate
Base: steel support beams painted black
Legs: chrome-plated tubular steel
181″ W; 55″ D; 28″ H

7–60   VIENNA T

1981
Designer: Gere Kavanaugh
Manufacturer: Images of America
Top: melamine or plastic laminate on ¾-inch-thick fiber board;
   beveled edges
Legs: 1 ½-inch round steel tubes
Base: rigid polyurethane over a molded metal frame
32″ or 48″ W; 30″ D; 28″ H

Courtesy of Knoll International

7–58

Beylerian

7–59

Images of America

7–60

Courtesy of Knoll International

7–61

Gebrüder Thonet

7–62

Driade

7–63

7–61 866

1982
Designer: Richard Meier
Manufacturer: Knoll International
Top: fiberboard; hard maple veneers
Base: solid hard maple
80" W; 40" D; 27½" H

7–62 PRISM

1982
Designer: Jan Des Bouvrie
Manufacturer: Gebrüder Thonet
Top and base: plastic laminate, mahogany, oak, ash, walnut,
   or cherry; solid elm top edge
49½" W; 49½" D; 29" H

7–63 TIPPY JACKSON

1982
Designer: Philippe Starck
Manufacturer: Driade
Top: varnished turned sheet-iron
Base: bent iron tubing
47¼" Diameter; 27½" H

7–64 PRESIDENT "M"

1982
Designer: Philippe Starck
Manufacturer: Baleri Italia
Top: clear tempered glass
Wings: die-cast aluminum
Legs: steel in a silver or black baked-epoxy finish
72" or 54" W; 48" or 54" D; 29½" H

ICF, Inc.

7–64

Cadsana, Cadwallader and Sangiorgio Associates

7-65

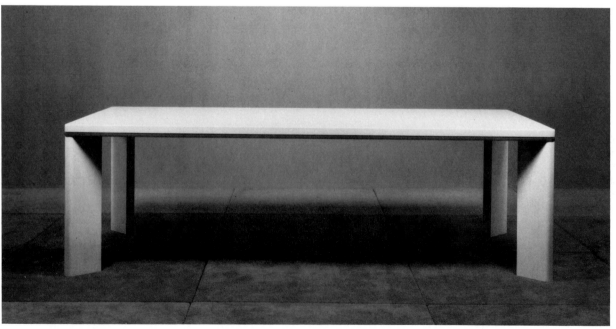

Metropolitan Furniture Corporation

7-66

Cadsana, Cadwallader and Sangiorgio Associates

7—67

Metropolitan Furniture Corporation

7—68

7—65 SORO

c. 1982
Designer: Francesco Soro
Manufacturer: Cadsana, Cadwallader and Sangiorgio Associates
Top: glass, Pentelico marble, stone with a polyester finish, or
    white polyester
Base: rectangular tubular steel, black-fused epoxy finish
98⅜" W; 26⅜" or 31½" D; 28¾" H

7—66 BELSCHNER GROUP

1983
Designer: Andrew Belschner
Manufacturer: Metropolitan Furniture
Top and legs: cast polyester resin
78" W; 39" D; 29" H

7—67 SHADOW

1983
Designer: Cini Boeri
Manufacturer: Cadsana, Cadwallader and Sangiorgio Associates
Top: polished plate glass with a sandblasted edge
Shelf: sandblasted glass
Base: steel structure, epoxy finish
Legs: steel structure with solid oak covers in natural oak or
    black stain finish
224" W; 55⅛" D; 28¼" H

7—68 KANE GROUP

1984
Designer: Brian Kane
Manufacturer: Metropolitan Furniture
Top: cast polyester resin, wood, stone, or leather
Base: cast polyester resin
72" W; 42" D; 29" H

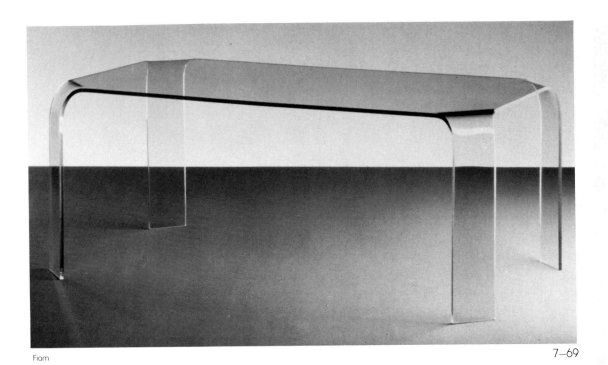

Fiam

7—69

B & B Italia

7—70

Koch + Lowy   7–71

7–69   RAGNO

1984
Designer: Vittorio Livi
Manufacturer: Fiam
Top and legs: polished plate glass
71″ W; 35½″ D; 28¼″ H

7–70   POLYGONON

1984
Designers: Afra Scarpa and Tobia Scarpa
Manufacturer: B & B Italia
Top: marble, transparent glass, or blue-cobalt glass
Base: Inox steel-plate with scratch-resistant colored film
63″ W; 51¼″ D; 28⅜″ H

7–71   MIRAGE

1985
Designer: Piotr Sierakowski
Manufacturer: Koch + Lowy
Top: ribbon-honed slate or sandblasted, pencil-edged glass
Legs: aluminum extrusion finished in Nextel
54″ or 60″ Diameter; 28½″ H

7–72   CENTRAL

1985
Designer: Angelo Mangiarotti
Manufacturer: Skipper
Top: glass
Base: marble
51¼″ diameter; 28¼″ H

Angelo Mangiarotti   7–72

Driade   7–73

Atelier International, Ltd.   7–74

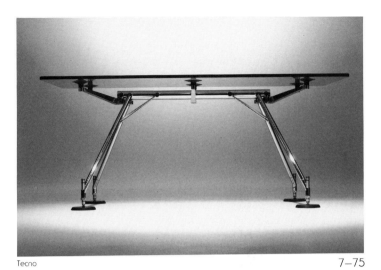

Tecno   7–75

7–73   TITOS APOSTOS

1985
Designer: Philippe Starck
Manufacturer: Driade
Top: turned sheet steel
Base: tubular steel
33" Diameter; 27½" H

7–74   SERENISSIMO

1985
Designers: Lella Vignelli, Massimo Vignelli, and David Law
Manufacturer: Acerbis International
Top: clear or semiopalescent plate glass
Support: natural finish, nonrust metal
Legs: steel covered with hand-applied colored stucco in a
    traditional encaustic technique
49.6", 57.1", 63", 88.2", or 118.1" W; 49.6", 57.1", 63", 38.6",
    or 43.3" D; 28.3" H

7–75   NOMOS

1986
Designer: Norman Foster
Manufacturer: Tecno
Top: plastic laminate, very thick melamine, wood, glass, or
    marble
Base: chrome-plated steel and die-cast aluminum
63", 86½", or 110¼" W; 39¼" or 47¼" D; 25¼"–
    28¼" H

7–76   LA BADOERA

1986
Designer: Angelo Mangiarotti
Manufacturer: Poltronova
Top: natural walnut, black lacquered ashwood, or natural
    ashwood
Base: grinstone
94½" W; 33" D; 29" H

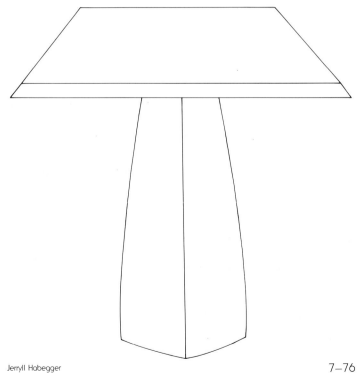

Jerryll Habegger   7–76

261

8 DESKS

Gebrüder Thonet 8—1

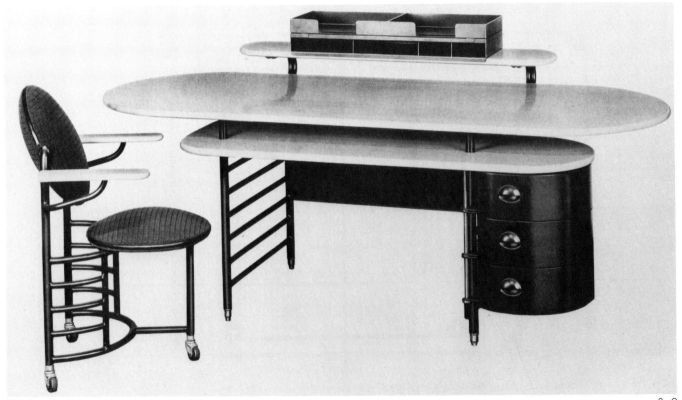

Steelcase 8—2

Courtesy of Knoll International

8–3

8–1   S 286

c. 1928
Designer: Marcel Breuer
Manufacturer: Gebrüder Thonet
Top and drawers: wood
Base: chrome-plated tubular steel
40¼" W; 19¾" D; 25½" H

8–2   JOHNSON WAX

1937
Designer: Frank Lloyd Wright
Manufacturer: Steelcase
Top: walnut
Base: aluminum and magnesite
84" W; 35" D; 33¼" H

8–3   80 D

1940
Designer: Franco Albini
Manufacturer: Knoll International
Top: clear plate glass
Drawers: wood
Base: chrome-plated squared steel tubing
48" W; 26" D; 27½" H

8–4   4658

1946
Designer: George Nelson
Manufacturer: Herman Miller
Top: wood covered in leather
Storage cabinet: tawny walnut veneer
Legal file: perforated metal
Legs: satin chrome
54" W; 28" D; 28" H

Herman Miller, Inc.

8–4

Courtesy of Knoll International

8–5

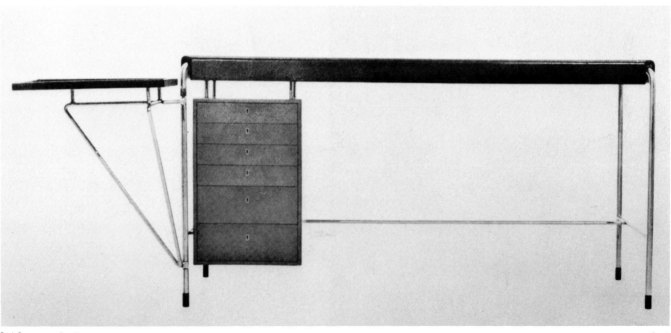

Rud. Rasmussens Snedkerier

8–6

Rud. Rasmussens Snedkerier   8–7

8–5 CANAAN

1951
Designer: Marcel Breuer
Manufacturer: Knoll International
Top and drawers: wood veneer over solid wood core
Base: solid wood
72″ W; 30″ D; 28½″ H

8–6 DESK

1952
Designer: Arne Jacobsen
Manufacturer: Rud. Rasmussens Snedkerier
Frame: chrome-plated steel tubing
Top and drawers: plywood
55″ W; 27½″ D; 27½″ H

8–7 DRAWING TABLE

1956
Designer: Poul Kjaerholm
Manufacturer: Rud. Rasmussens Snedkerier
Top and drawers: plywood
Base: flat steel
55″ or 72¾″ W; 33½″ D; 27½″ H

8–8 570

1957
Designer: Dieter Rams
Manufacturer: Vitsoe
Tops: plastic laminate
Legs: natural or anodized aluminum
47¼″ W; 19½″ D; 25¼″ H (lower top); 29″ H (upper top)

Vitsoe Kollektion   8–8

Herman Miller, Inc.   8–9

Dunbar   8–10

8–9 SWAGGED LEG (5850)

1958
Designer: George Nelson
Manufacturer: Herman Miller
Top: oiled walnut frame with plastic laminate surfaces
Base: chrome-plated steel
39" W; 28½" D; 33¾" H

8–10 ROLL-TOP DESK (2005)

c. 1959
Designer: Edward Wormley
Manufacturer: Dunbar
Top and base: solid walnut
Tambours: rosewood veneer
75" W; 28" D; 35" H

8–11 OVAL (2481)

1961
Designer: Florence Knoll
Manufacturer: Knoll International
Top: oak, walnut, mahogany, or marble
Base: steel, polished-chrome finish
96" W; 54" D; 28" H

8–12 168 AP

1961
Designers: Henning Jensen and Torben Valeur
Manufacturer: Munch Mobler
Top and base: solid oak
Fittings: chrome-plated metal with a matte finish
63" W; 31½" D; 28⅓" H

Courtesy of Knoll International

8–11

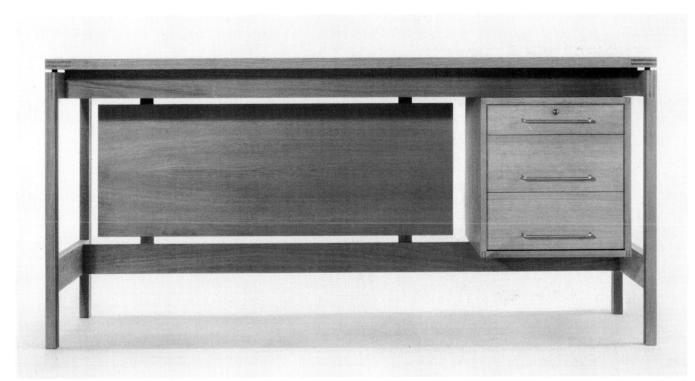

Munch Mobler

8–12

Courtesy of Knoll International

8–13

Herman Miller, Inc.

8–14

GF Furniture Systems
8–19

8–17 OFF

1968
Designer: Herbert Hirche
Manufacturer: Christian Holzapfel
Structure: chipboard with plastic laminate finish; metal rails
61½" W; 30¾" D; 30" H

8–18 2040 SERIES

c. 1968
Designer: Roger Sprunger
Manufacturer: Dunbar
Top and drawers: rosewood veneer or English oak
Base: polished stainless steel or antique bronze
84" W; 38" D; 29" H

8–19 ALLEN COLLECTION

1970
Designer: Davis Allen
Manufacturer: GF Furniture Systems
Top and base: wood or steel
60", 65", or 72" W; 32" or 38" D; 29¼" H

8–20 DJOB

1970
Designers: Arne Jacobsen and Niels J. Haugesen
Manufacturer: Scandinavian Office Organization
Top and drawers: beech or wenge wood
Frame: aluminum
60¾" W; 30½" D; 27½" H

Scandinavian Office Organization
8–20 b

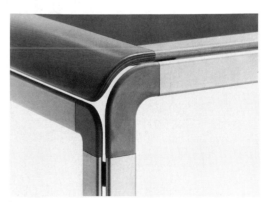

Scandinavian Office Organization
8–20 a

273

Courtesy of Knoll International

8–21

Atelier International, Ltd.

8–22

Courtesy of Knoll International

8–23

8–21   STEPHENS SYSTEM

1970
Designer: William Stephens
Manufacturer: Knoll International
Top and base: mahogany or Techgrain veneers
64" W; 20" D; 58½" H (machine station); 42" W; 30" D;
   28" H (extension)

8–22   BELLINI SYSTEM

1974
Designer: Mario Bellini
Manufacturer: Marcatre
Top and base: high-density cores covered with 0.3-mm PVC
   or wood veneer laminates
Drawers: PVC over high-density particle board core; ABS ex-
   truded handles
102.4" W; 44.5" D; 40.2" H; 28.7" Top H

8–23   GWATHMEY SIEGEL DESK

1979
Designers: Charles Gwathmey and Robert Siegel
Manufacturer: Knoll International
Top and base: hardwood with mahogany, figured Techgrain,
   or Techgrain veneer finish
Drawers: black vinyl-covered fiberboard
Pulls: stained solid mahogany
62" W; 39" D; 28" H (desk)

8–24   BURDICK GROUP

1980
Designer: Bruce Burdick
Manufacturer: Herman Miller
Top: oak, laminate, glass, or marble
Base and drawers: polished aluminum or black umber
7' and 10' W (beams); 60" W, 36" D (top); 24" W, 36" D
   (half-round); 29" H

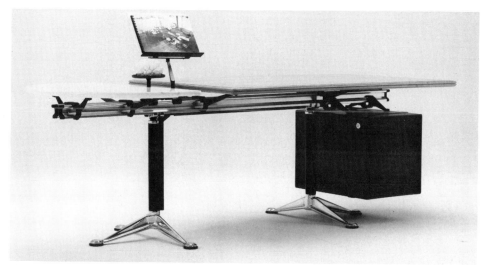

Herman Miller, Inc.

8–24

Ron Rezek

8—25

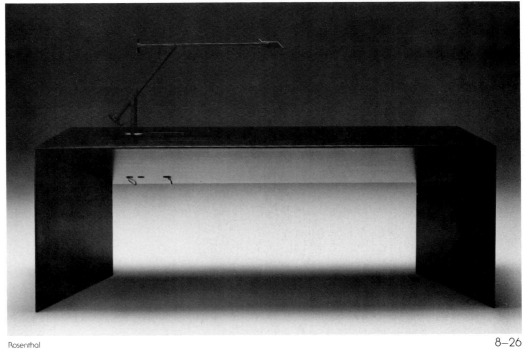

Rosenthal

8—26

8–27

8–25 TABLE GROUP

1981
Designers: Ron Rezek and Dave Potter
Manufacturer: Ron Rezek
Top: Formica Colorcore laminate
Base: heavy steel legs with plastic coating; crossed tension
    cables; tubular compression rods
72" W; 32" D; 29" H

8–26 PRISMA

1981
Designer: Cini Boeri
Manufacturer: Rosenthal
Structure: oak veneer, stained or lacquered
86 ½" W; 39 ½" D; 28 ½" H

8–27 HANNAH DESK

c. 1981
Designer: Bruce Hannah
Manufacturer: Knoll International
Top: Techgrain or plastic laminate
Pedestal frame: formed steel with black-fused finish
Drawers: black vinyl-covered fiberboard; fronts are painted,
    vacuum-formed ABS plastic
Pulls: extruded aluminum
64⅜" W; 30⅜" D; 28" H

8–28 PINSTRIPE FAMILY

1982
Designer: Walker Group
Manufacturer: ICF, Inc.
Top, pedestals, and drawers: ash, mahogany, oak, or walnut
64" W; 32" D; 29 ½" H

8–28

Modern Mode 8–29

Arflex 8–30

Rosenthal   8–31

8–29   TEK 3

1983
Designer: Modern Mode in-house
Manufacturer: Modern Mode
Top and pedestal: oak, mahogany, cherry, walnut, maple,
    or lacquered wood
Base: wood, stainless steel, or bronze
76¼" W; 60" D; 29" H

8–30   MALIBU

1983
Designer: Cini Boeri
Manufacturer: Arflex
Top: glass, wood, or plastic laminate inset with medium-
    density wood bull-nosed edge; steel column
Base: wood cabinet
67" W; 31½" D; 28¼" H

8–31   HOMMAGE À MONDRIAN

1983
Designer: Danilo Silvestrin
Manufacturer: Rosenthal
Structure: high-gloss lacquered wood
74¾" W; 46" D; 32¾" H

8–32   KANE SERIES

1984
Designer: Brian Kane
Manufacturer: Metropolitan Furniture
Top: cast polyester resin, wood, stone, or leather
Side panels: high-gloss cast polyester resin
66" W; 33" D; 29" H

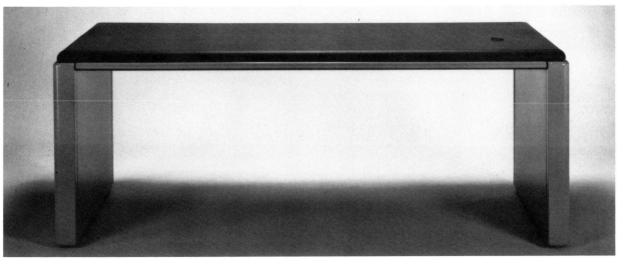

Metropolitan Furniture Corporation   8–32

9 SERVING CARTS

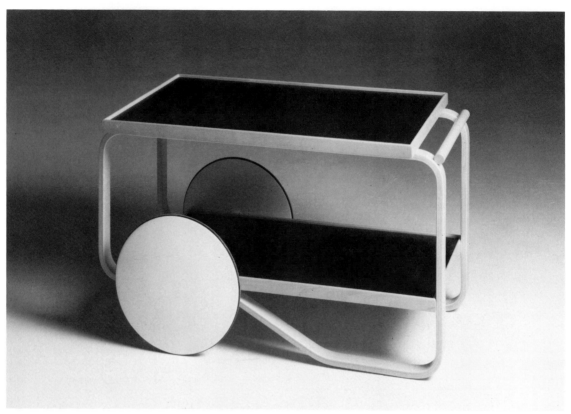

Artek   9–1

Jerryll Habegger   9–2

Rosenthal   9-3

9-1   TEA TROLLEY (98)

1936
Designer: Alvar Aalto
Manufacturer: Artek
Frame: natural birch; lacquered wheels with rubber threads
Shelf: linoleum or plastic laminate
35½" W; 19¾" D; 22¼" H

9-2   BOBY

1971
Designer: Joe Colombo
Manufacturer: Bieffeplast
Frame: injection-molded ABS; Kevi casters
17" W; 16" D; 29" H

9-3   SERVICE CART

1975
Designer: Waldemar Rothe
Manufacturer: Rosenthal
Frame: lacquered or stained beech
Trays: plastic
Handle: chrome-plated metal
22¾" Diameter; 19¾" Shelf H; 28¼" Overall H

9-4   HILTON TROLLEY

1981
Designer: Javier Mariscal
Manufacturer: Abet Laminati (Memphis)
Frame: enameled metal; rubber wheels
20½" W; 39¼" D; 31½" H

Memphis Milano   9-4

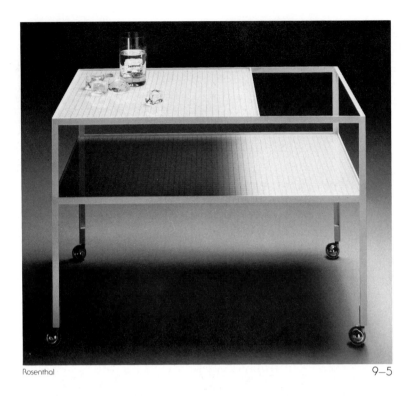

Rosenthal   9–5

Bieffeplast S.p.A./Gullans International, Inc.   9–6

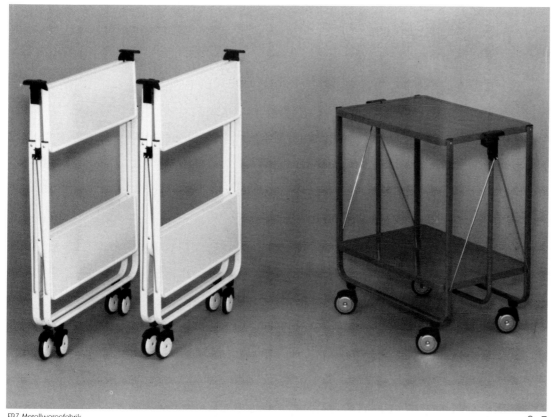

FRZ Metallwarenfabrik

9–7

9–5   SERVANT 1

1981
Designer: Herbert Hirche
Manufacturer: Rosenthal
Frame: enameled metal
Shelves: wire-reinforced glass
27½" W; 18½" D; 19¾" H

9–6   BUTLER

1982
Designer: Sottsass Associates
Manufacturer: Bieffeplast
Frame: tubular metal; Kevi casters
Shelves: plastic laminate or stainless steel
30¾" W; 19¾" D; 29½" H

9–7   FOLDING TROLLEY

1983
Designer: Louis L. Lepoix
Manufacturer: FRZ-Metallwarenfabrik
Frame and shelves: plastic-coated metal; rubber wheels
23½" W; 15¾" D; 28½" H

10 SIDE TABLES

Franz Wittmann   10—1

B.D. Ediciones   10—2

B.D. Ediciones

10—3

Cassina

10—4

10—1   NESTING

1905
Designer: Josef Hoffmann
Manufacturer: Franz Wittmann
Top and base: solid natural or limed black-stained ash
19¾″ W, 16″ D, 27½″ H; 17″ W, 14⅝″ D, 26⅛″ H;
   14¼″ W, 13¼″ D, 24¾″ H; 11½″ W, 11⅞″ D,
   23⅜″ H

10—2   1908.1

1908
Designer: Charles Rennie Mackintosh
Manufacturer: B.D. Ediciones
Top and base: black-stained and varnished sycamore; inlaid
   with mother-of-pearl
27″ W; 27″ D; 25″ H

10—3   DOMINO

1911
Designer: Charles Rennie Mackintosh
Manufacturer: B.D. Ediciones
Top and base: black-stained and varnished oak
19¾″ W; 19¾″ D; 30½″ H

10—4   DS 2

1918
Designer: Charles Rennie Mackintosh
Manufacturer: Cassina
Top and base: solid hardwood, ebony stain
29½″ W; 29½″ D; 29½″ H

Cassina 10—5

Courtesy of Knoll International 10—6

Courtesy of Knoll International

10—7

10—5 SCHROEDER 1

1923
Designer: Gerrit T. Rietveld
Manufacturer: Cassina
Top: lacquered particle board
Column and base: lacquered plywood
19.7" W; 20.3" D; 23.8" H

10—6 LACCIO

1926
Designer: Marcel Breuer
Manufacturer: Knoll International
Top: plastic laminate
Base: tubular steel, polished chrome finish
21 5/8" W; 18 7/8" D; 17 3/4" H

10—7 OCCASIONAL TABLE

1927
Designer: Ludwig Mies van der Rohe
Manufacturer: Knoll International
Top: 1/2-inch smoked float glass
Base: tubular stainless steel
27 1/2" Diameter; 19 5/8" H

10—8 E-1027

1927
Designer: Eileen Gray
Manufacturer: Images of America
Top: round-inset clear glass
Frame: steel tube, mirror-polished chrome finish
20" Diameter; 21"—35" H

Images of America

10—8

Images of America   10–9

B.D. Ediciones   10–10

Artek

10–11

10–9   OCCASIONAL TABLE

1928
Designer: Eileen Gray
Manufacturer: Images of America
Top and base: plywood
Frame: chrome-plated tubular steel
Base plate: steel
14¼" W; 16½" D; 22" H

10–10   NOVOCOMUN

1929
Designer: Giuseppe Terragni
Manufacturer: B.D. Ediciones
Structure: varnished palm root, black-lacquered oak or Corinth-
    varnished beech-veneered boards
35½" Diameter; 23¼" H

10–11   915

1932
Designer: Alvar Aalto
Manufacturer: Artek
Top: molded plywood
Frame: birch
20⅛" W; 23⅜" D; 23⅝" H

10–12   NESTING

1936
Designer: Marcel Breuer
Manufacturer: Isokon
Top and legs: plywood
24" W; 18" D; 16" H

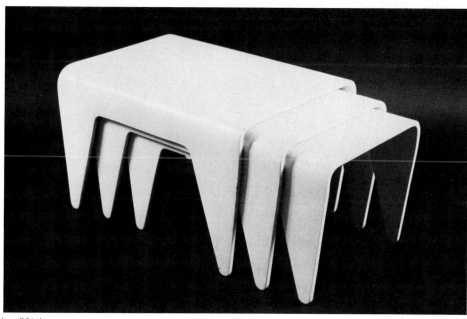

Larry Whiteley

10–12

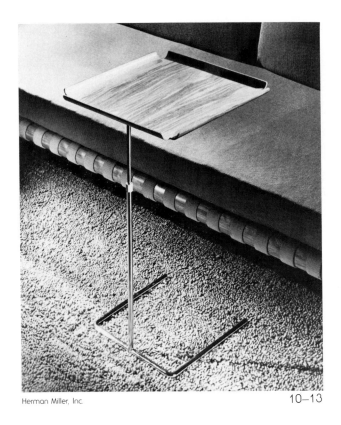

Herman Miller, Inc.   10–13

Courtesy of Knoll International   10–14

Herman Miller, Inc.   10—15

Stendig   10—16

10—13   4950

1948
Designer: George Nelson
Manufacturer: Herman Miller
Top: walnut or ash
Base: polished chrome rod
15" W; 15" D; 19" H

10—14   TABLE

1950
Designer: Isamu Noguchi
Manufacturer: Knoll International
Top: plastic laminate
Column: steel wire
Base: cast iron
24" Diameter; 20" H

10—15   LTR

1950
Designers: Charles Eames and Ray Eames
Manufacturer: Herman Miller
Top: white laminate with 20-degree angle edge
Base: bright chrome-plated steel wire
15⅝" W; 13⅜" D; 10" H

10—16   ALPHA

1956
Designer: Hans Eichenberger
Manufacturer: Swiss Design
Top: ½-inch-thick clear float glass with a polished edge
Base: flat solid stainless steel with a mirror-polished finish
18" Diameter; 21" H

Fritz Hansen   10–17

B & B Italia   10–18

Kartell

10–19

10–17   PK 71

1957
Designer: Poul Kjaerholm
Manufacturer: Fritz Hansen
Top: acrylic
Base: matte chrome-plated steel
11 ¼" W; 11 ¼" D; 11 ½" H

10–18   GATTI

1966
Designer: Mario Bellini
Manufacturer: B & B Italia
Top and legs: stamped Fiberglas
17 ⅜", 18 ⅛", 18 ⅞", and 19 ¾" W and D; 10" H

10–19   NESTING SET (4905)

1968
Designer: Giotto Stoppino
Manufacturer: Kartell
Top and legs: ABS
19" Diameter; 12 ⅝", 14 ⅝", and 16 ½" H

10–20   CIARLY BAR

c. 1970
Designer: Carlo Urbinati
Manufacturer: Tulli Zuccari
Top and frame: Baydur rigid foamed polyurethane; insulation;
  steel weight-bearing pin; four wheels
21 ⅝" W; 21 ⅝" D; 30 ¾" H

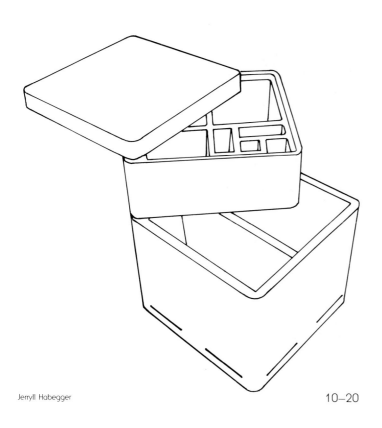

Jerryll Habegger

10–20

Rud. Rasmussens Snedkerier   10—21

Brickel Associates   10—22

Brickel Associates

10–21 STACKING

c. 1970
Designer: Jørgen Rud. Rasmussen
Manufacturer: Rud. Rasmussens Snedkerier
Top: mahogany
Frame: oak
17¾″ W; 17¾″ D; 17¾″ H

10–22 I-BEAM (3078)

c. 1970
Designer: Ward Bennett
Manufacturer: Brickel Associates
Structure: black steel pedestal
12″ or 16″ W; 12″ or 16″ D; 15″ H

10–23 ANGLE-ROUND (3020)

c. 1970
Designer: Ward Bennett
Manufacturer: Brickel Associates
Top: glass, polished edge
Frame: stainless steel
20″ W; 20″ D; 18″ H

10–23

10–24 771

c. 1971
Designers: Afra Scarpa and Tobia Scarpa
Manufacturer: Cassina
Top: reversible in wood (walnut or rosewood) or plastic
Frame: walnut or rosewood
29½″ W; 29½″ D; 15¼″ H

Cassina

10–24

Zanotta   10—25

Fiam   10—26

Zanotta   10–27

Zanotta   10–28

10–25   SERVOMUTO

1974
Designer: Achille Castiglioni
Manufacturer: Zanotta
Top: stratified plastic laminate or stiff lacquered polyurethane
Stem: fire-lacquered metal
Base: ABS
19¾" Diameter; 33¾" H

10–26   ONDA

1975
Designer: Vittorio Livi
Manufacturer: Fiam
Top and legs: plate glass
22" W; 13¾" D; 16½" H

10–27   CUMANO

1978
Designer: Achille Castiglioni
Manufacturer: Zanotta
Top: fire-lacquered metal
Frame: steel rod
21½" Diameter; 27½" H

10–28   TREVI

1981
Designer: Enzo Mari
Manufacturer: Zanotta
Top: marble, silvered stone, or plastic laminate
Base: aluminum alloy and steel
21" Diameter; 27½" H

Driade   10–29

Atelier International, Ltd.   10–30

Rosenthal   10–31

10–29 MICKVILLE

1983
Designer: Philippe Starck
Manufacturer: Driade
Frame: tubular steel
Top: turned sheet steel
15" Diameter; 31½" H

10–30 KICK

1983
Designer: Toshiyuki Kita
Manufacturer: Atelier International
Top: oval, lacquered, medium-density wood with a rubber
    bumper edge
Base: enameled steel; two casters; pneumatic height
    adjustment
19.7" W; 19.7" D; 15.7"–20.7" H

10–31 HOMMAGE À RIETVELD

1983
Designer: Danilo Silvestrin
Manufacturer: Rosenthal
Structure: lacquered wood
27" W; 18" D; 23½" H

10–32 TEA FOR TWO

1986
Designers: François Scali and Alain Domingo
Manufacturer: Nemo
Top: removable circular glass
Base: gray epoxy metal
15¾" Diameter; 21¾" H

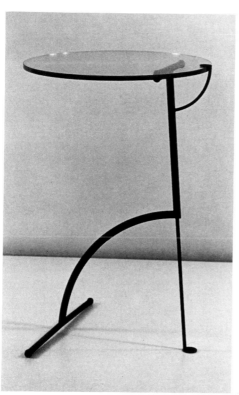

Nemo   10–32

11 STOOLS

Thonet Industries 11—1

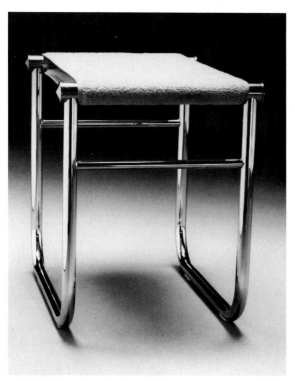

Cassina 11—2

11—1   WIENER POSTPARKASSE SERIE
1904
Designer: Otto Wagner
Manufacturer: Thonet Industries
Seat: three-ply elm-veneer molded plywood; perforated design and hand hold
Base: steam-bent ⅞-inch square American elm with aluminum cap detailing
16¼" W; 16¼" D; 18½" H

11—2   LC/9
1928
Designer: Le Corbusier
Manufacturer: Cassina
Frame: polished chrome tubular steel
Top: beige terrycloth fabric
14.2" W; 19.7" D; 17.7" H

11—3   BARCELONA
1929
Designer: Ludwig Mies van der Rohe
Manufacturer: Knoll International
Seat: foam-rubber cushions covered in leather
Base: stainless steel, polished finish; saddle leather straps
23" W; 22" D; 14½" H

11—4   AMADEUS
1929
Designer: Robert Mallet-Stevens
Manufacturer: Images of America
Seat: foam covered in leather
Base: tubular steel
15" W; 15" D; 30½" H

Courtesy of Knoll International   11–3

Images of America   11–4

Rud. Rasmussens Snedkerier   11–5

Artek   11–6

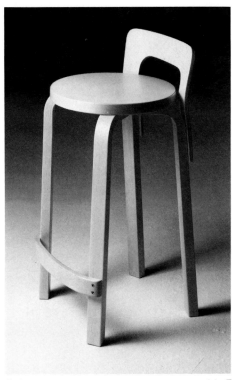

Artek   11–7

11–5   FOLDING CHAIR (8783)

1930
Designer: Kaare Klint
Manufacturer: Rud. Rasmussens Snedkerier
Seat: canvas or oxhide
Base: natural ashwood
22¾″ W; 19¼″ D; 17″ H

11–6   3-LEGGED (60)

1933
Designer: Alvar Aalto
Manufacturer: Artek
Seat: natural birch, linoleum, or plastic laminate
Legs: natural birch
13¾″ W; 13¾″ D; 17¼″ H

11–7   K 65

1935
Designer: Alvar Aalto
Manufacturer: Artek
Seat: natural birch, linoleum, or plastic laminate
Legs and back: natural birch
13¾″ W; 16½″ D; 27½″ H; 23⅝″ SH

11–8   SGABILLO

1950
Designer: Max Bill
Manufacturer: Zanotta
Top and legs: stratified birch
15¾″ W; 11¼″ D; 17¾″ H

Zanotta   11–8

Antti Nurmesniemi

11–9

Sori Yanagi

11–10

Artek   11−11

11−9   SAUNA

1952
Designer: Antti Nurmesniemi
Manufacturer: Vuokko
Seat: birch veneer
Legs: pine
17" W; 16" D; 17" H

11−10   BUTTERFLY

1954
Designer: Sori Yanagi
Manufacturer: Tendo Mokko
Frame: molded plywood; metal crossbar
16½" W; 12¼" D; 15½" H; 13¼" SH

11−11   FAN-LEGGED (X600)

1954
Designer: Alvar Aalto
Manufacturer: Artek
Seat: natural ash
Legs: natural birch
15" W; 15" D; 17½" H

11−12   MEZZADRO

1957
Designers: Achille Castiglioni and Pier Giacomo Castiglioni
Manufacturer: Zanotta
Seat: lacquer or chrome-plated steel
Stem: chrome-plated steel
Footrest: natural beech
19¼" W; 20" D; 20" H

Zanotta   11−12

Fritz Hansen

11–13

Fritz Hansen

11–14

Fritz Hansen   11—15

11—13   PK 33

1959
Designer: Poul Kjaerholm
Manufacturer: Fritz Hansen
Seat: leather cushion
Base: matte chrome-plated steel
21" W; 21" D; 13½" H

11—14   PK 91

1961
Designer: Poul Kjaerholm
Manufacturer: Fritz Hansen
Seat: canvas or leather sling
Base: matte chrome-plated steel
23½" W; 17¾" D; 14½" H

11—15   3169/70

1965
Designer: Fritz Hansen
Manufacturer: Fritz Hansen
Seat: laminated, molded wood in natural teak or lacquered
Base: chromed steel tubing
17¼" W; 17¼" D; 23½" H (Model 3169); 13½" W;
    13½" D; 17¼" H (Model 3170)

11—16   OTTOMAN (1709)

1966
Designer: Warren Platner
Manufacturer: Knoll International
Seat: foam cushion over molded Fiberglas shell, covered in
    fabric
Base: steel rod, nickel finish; molded rubber suspension unit
24½" W; 24½" D; 15" H

Courtesy of Knoll International   11—16

313

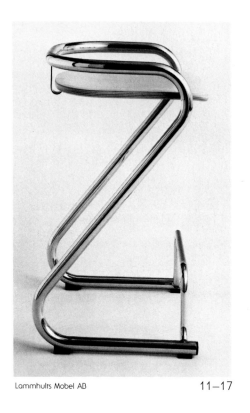

Lammhults Mobel AB   11–17

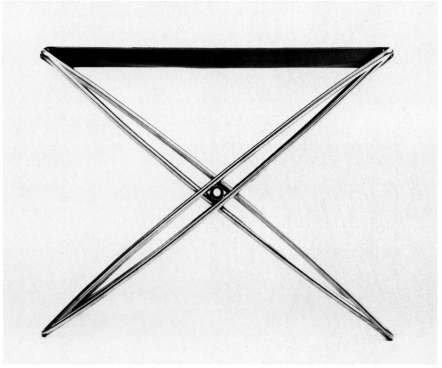

Johannes Hansens Møbelsnedkeri, Copenhagen, Denmark   11–18

Zanotta   11–19

11–17   S 70-3

1968
Designers: Borge Lindau and Bo Lindekrantz
Manufacturer: Lammhults Mobel AB
Seat: plywood, natural birch or lacquered
Frame and base: 32-mm chrome-plated or enameled tubular
    steel
19" W; 17¼" D; 28" H; 24¾" SH

11–18   STOOL

1970
Designer: Jørgen Gammelgaard
Manufacturer: Design Forum
Seat: PVC-coated Fiberglas fabric
Base: chrome steel
21¾" W; 19" D; 17" H

11–19   PRIMATE KNEELING

1970
Designer: Achille Castiglioni
Manufacturer: Zanotta
Seat and knee pad: Baydur (polyurethane foam covered in
    fabric or leather)
Base: black polystyrene
Stem: polished stainless steel
19¾" W; 31½" D; 18½" H

11–20   BIRILLO

1971
Designer: Joe Colombo
Manufacturer: Zanotta
Seat and back: foam-filled, covered in leather or vinyl
Frame: stainless steel
Base: Fiberglas, self-return swivel
18½" W; 18½" D; 42" H; 30¼" SH

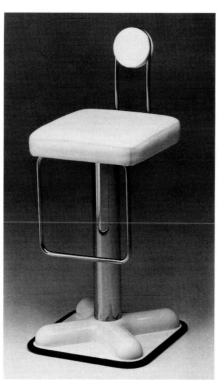

Zanotta   11–20

Krueger   11–21

Rudd International   11–22

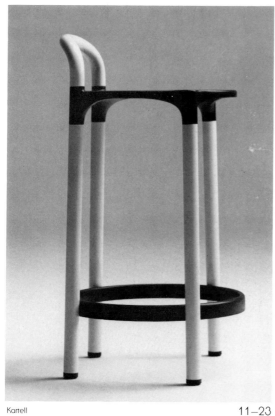

Kartell   11—23

11—21   BAND SERIES
c. 1972
Designer: Unknown
Manufacturer: Krueger
Structure: Fiberglas
18″ W; 18″ D; 16″ H

11—22   DONUT
1974
Designers: Rud Thygesen and Johnny Sorensen
Manufacturer: Magnus Olesen
Seat: laminated beech with black laboratory stain
Legs: laminated beech with white oak veneer
14″ W; 14″ D; 17½″ H

11—23   5/4825
1979
Designer: Anna Castelli Ferrieri
Manufacturer: Kartell
Seat: expanded polyurethane
Back: curved PVC tube
Legs: stone-enameled metal tube
Footrest: pressed polystyrol
Feet: black rubber
15⅝″ Diameter; 34⅝″ H; 29½″ SH

11—24   STOOL
1980
Designer: Gunnar A. Andersen
Manufacturer: E. Kold Christensen
Seat and legs: edge-placed ash slats
28″ W; 14¼″ D; 14¼″ H

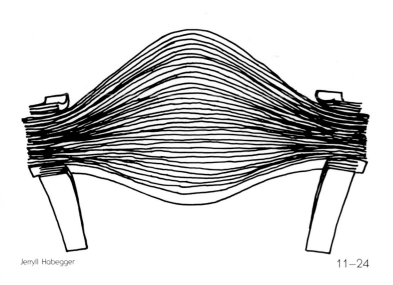

Jerryll Habegger   11—24

11—25

11—26

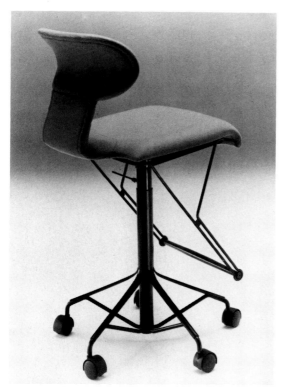

ICF, Inc.   11–27

11–25   LOW STOOL (820)

1982
Designer: Richard Meier
Manufacturer: Knoll International
Seat and base: laminated hard maple veneers and solid hard
    maple
17 5/8" W; 17 5/8" D; 15 1/4" H

11–26   HIGH STOOL (822)

1982
Designer: Richard Meier
Manufacturer: Knoll International
Seat and base: laminated hard maple veneers and solid hard
    maple
Footrest: stainless steel, polished finish
15 3/8" W; 15 3/8" D; 27 1/2" H

11–27   OSCAR DRAFTING

1983
Designer: Oscar Tusquets
Manufacturer: Casas
Seat and back: molded foam over molded Fiberglas, covered
    in fabric
Column: epoxied steel
Base: black-epoxied or chrome-plated steel
Foot bar: beech
17" W; 19" D; 35"–37 1/2" H; 24 3/4"–27 1/4" SH

11–28   SARAPIS

1985
Designer: Philippe Starck
Manufacturer: Driade
Frame: square tubular steel
Seat: steel mesh
14" W; 18" D; 33 1/2" H; 24" SH

Driade   11–28

12 COFFEE TABLES

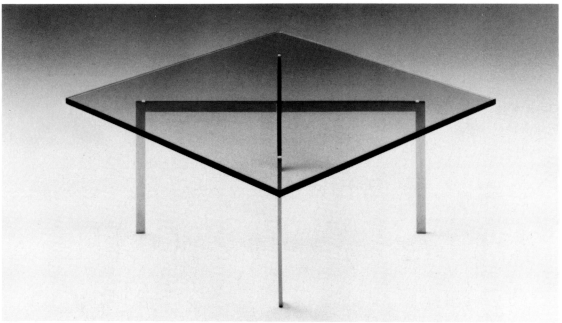

Courtesy of Knoll International   12–1

Artek   12–2

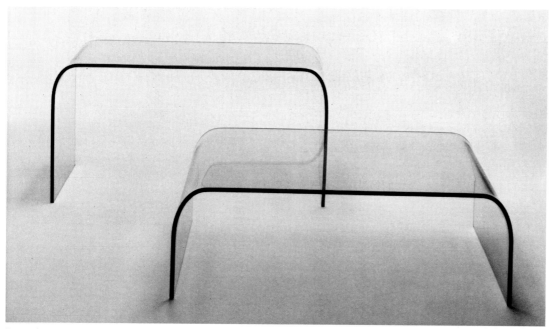

Fontana Arte

12—3

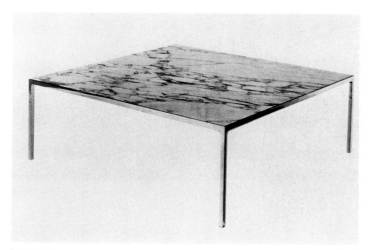

Scope Furniture

12—4

12—1   BARCELONA

1929
Designer: Ludwig Mies van der Rohe
Manufacturer: Knoll International
Top: ¾-inch polished float glass
Base: stainless steel
40" W; 40" D; 17" H

12—2   BENCH (153)

1935
Designer: Alvar Aalto
Manufacturer: Artek
Top and legs: natural birch
28½" or 44¼" W; 15¾" D; 17¼" H

12—3   2633

1937
Designer: Pietro Chiesa
Manufacturer: Fontana Arte
Top and legs: ¾-inch clear crystal glass
55" W; 27½" D; 15¾" H

12—4   CT SERIES

1937
Designer: William Armbruster
Manufacturer: Scope Furniture
Top: ¾-inch marble and granite or ½-inch Solar bronze
    glass
Base: stainless steel, Imron, polished bronze, or statuary bronze
30", 36", or 40" W; 30", 36", or 40" D; 16" H

Herman Miller, Inc.   12–5

Herman Miller, Inc.   12–6

Artek 12—7

12—5   PLATFORM BENCH
1946
Designer: George Nelson
Manufacturer: Herman Miller
Top: primavera or ebonized wood
Base: ebonized wood
48", 56¼", 68", or 72" W; 18½" D; 14" H

12—6   CTM
1946
Designers: Charles Eames and Ray Eames
Manufacturer: Herman Miller
Top: black ash
Base: chrome-plated metal rod
34" Diameter; 15" H

12—7   Y 805
1947
Designer: Alvar Aalto
Manufacturer: Artek
Top: clear glass with radius corners
Base: natural birch
31 ½" W; 31 ½" D; 17 ¼" H

12—8   NOGUCHI
1947
Designer: Isamu Noguchi
Manufacturer: Herman Miller
Top: plate glass
Base: solid walnut or poplar in an ebony finish
50" W; 36" D; 15¾" H

Herman Miller, Inc. 12—8

Herman Miller, Inc.

12–9

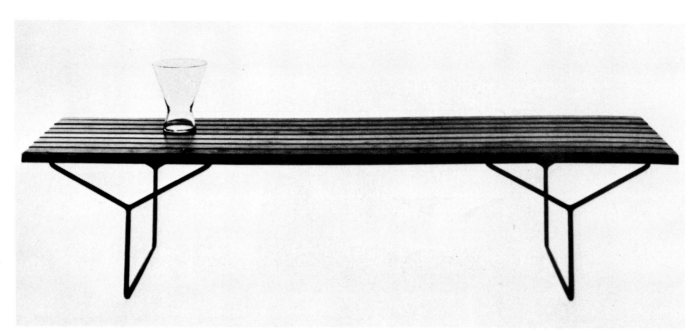

Courtesy of Knoll International

12–10

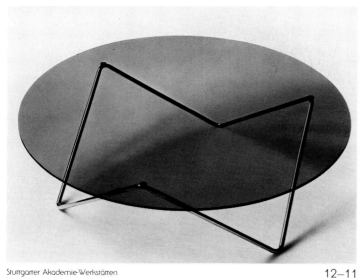

Stuttgarter Akademie-Werkstätten   12–11

12–9   ETR

1951
Designers: Charles Eames and Ray Eames
Manufacturer: Herman Miller
Top: laminate top with 20-degree angle
Base: bright chrome-plated steel wire
84″ W; 29″ D; 10″ H

12–10   SLAT BENCH

1952
Designer: Harry Bertoia
Manufacturer: Knoll International
Top: wooden slats, painted finish
Base: steel rods, polished chrome or painted finish
71½″ W; 19″ D; 15½″ H

12–11   COFFEE TABLE

1953
Designer: Herbert Hirche
Manufacturer: Stuttgarter Akademie-Werkstätten
Top: glass
Base: chrome-plated steel tube
39¼″ Diameter; 13″ H

12–12   PK 61

1955
Designer: Poul Kjaerholm
Manufacturer: Fritz Hansen
Top: glass, slate, or flint-rolled marble
Base: matte chrome-plated steel
31½″ W; 31½″ D; 12½″ H

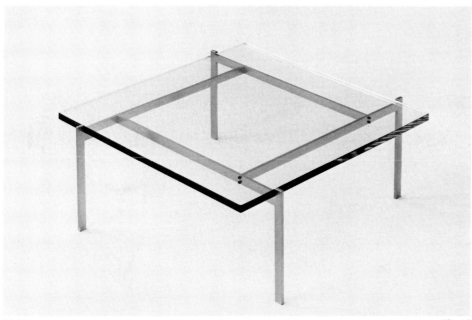

Fritz Hansen   12–12

327

Herman Miller, Inc.

12–13

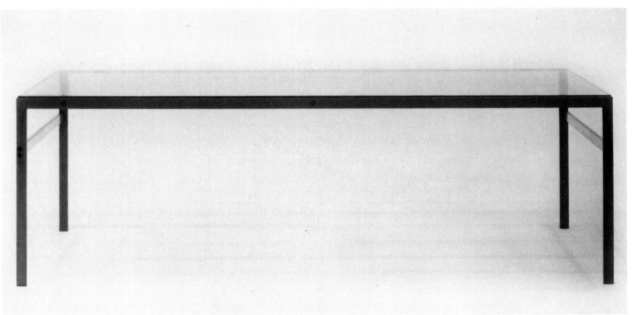

Do-Ex

12–14

Courtesy of Knoll International   12–15

12–13   CATENARY

1963
Designer: George Nelson
Manufacturer: Herman Miller
Top: clear plate glass laminated to a tinted plastic core
Base: chrome-plated epoxy-glued steel
36" W; 36" D; 15" H

12–14   BO 551

1964
Designers: Preben Fabricius and Jørgen Kastholm
Manufacturer: Bo-Ex
Frame: matte chrome-plated steel
Top: 20-mm glass, cleft slate, marble, or wood
55" W; 30⅛" D; 17" H

12–15   JUMBO

1965
Designer: Gae Aulenti
Manufacturer: Knoll International
Top and base: solid marble, polished finish
44¾" W; 44¾" D; 14½" H

12–16   3714

1966
Designer: Warren Platner
Manufacturer: Knoll International
Top: float glass, beveled edge
Base: steel wire, bright nickel finish
42" Diameter; 15" H

Courtesy of Knoll International   12–16

Courtesy of Knoll International   12–17

Habitat/Intrex   12–18

Zanotta   12–19

12–17 ANDRE

1967
Designer: Tobia Scarpa
Manufacturer: Knoll International
Top: ½-inch clear or smoked float glass
Base: tubular steel, polished chrome finish
45″ W; 45″ D; 15¼″ H

12–18 KNOCK-DOWN

c. 1968
Designer: Paul Mayen
Manufacturer: Habitat
Top: clear glass
Base: polished chrome
36″ W; 36″ D; 15¾″ H

12–19 MARCUSO

1969
Designer: Marco Zanuso
Manufacturer: Zanotta
Top: ⅝-inch clear glass
Legs: 4-inch diameter polished stainless steel
35½″ W; 35½″ D; 15¾″ H

12–20 CAORI

1969
Designer: Vico Magistretti
Manufacturer: Knoll International
Top: stainless steel, satin finish
Frame: plywood, lacquer finish
Drawer and side cabinet door: solid wood, lacquer finish
50⅝″ W; 37¾″ D; 15¾″ H

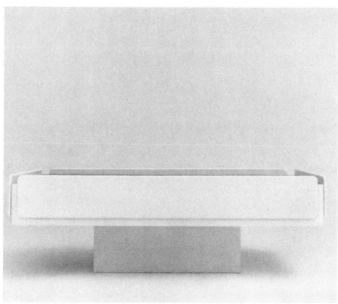

Courtesy of Knoll International   12–20 a

Courtesy of Knoll International   12–20 b

Brickel Associates   12–21

B & B Italia   12–22

Courtesy of Knoll International

12–23

12–21   TWO-TIER (3039)

c. 1971
Designer: Ward Bennett
Manufacturer: Brickel Associates
Top: ¾-inch marble
Frame: mirror-finished stainless steel
36" W; 36" D; 16½" H

12–22   SCACCHI

1972
Designer: Mario Bellini
Manufacturer: B & B Italia
Top and frame: polystyrene embedded in a cold-molded
    polyurethane batting with a polyurethane cover
Base: rigid injection-stamped polyurethane
35½" W; 11⅞" D; 21¾" H (Horse); 35½" W; 11⅞" D;
    14½" H (Tower); 35½" W; 11⅞" D; 14⅜" H (Queen)

12–23   LUNARIO

1972
Designer: Cini Boeri
Manufacturer: Knoll International
Top: ½-inch tempered glass with inset steel cap, polished
    chrome finish
Base: steel, polished chrome finish with counterbalance
    weights
59" W; 43¼" D; 11" or 15¾" H

12–24   4-LEG CLAW (3054)

c. 1972
Designer: Ward Bennett
Manufacturer: Brickel Associates
Top: ¾-inch glass, polished edge
Base: mirror-finished stainless steel
40" W; 40" D; 15½" H

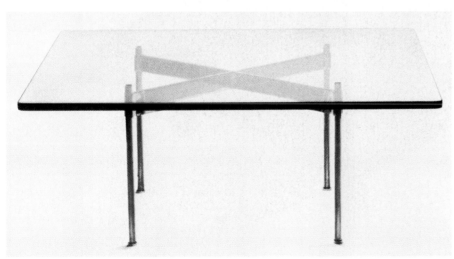

Brickel Associates

12–24

Cassina   12—25

Sunar Hauserman   12—26

Cadsana, Cadwallader and Sangiorgio Associates   12—27

12—25   WADDELL (713)

1973
Designer: Theodore Waddell
Manufacturer: Cassina
Top: ⅝-inch-thick clear, polished plate glass with bull-nosed edges
Base: chrome steel compression tubes; stainless steel tension wires; ball connector joints
38.3" Diameter; 15.7" H

12—26   KIOTO

1974
Designer: Gianfranco Frattini
Manufacturer: Ghianda
Top: fitted ⁵⁄₁₆" x 2" beech strips in a natural finish with rosewood inlays on ends
Legs: beech in a natural finish
45" W; 45" D; 14" H

12—27   PARALLEL

1975
Designer: Ross Littell
Manufacturer: Cadsana, Cadwallader and Sangiorgio Associates
Top: glass, Calacatta marble, or Pietra Serena
Base: chrome-plated or black-fused-epoxy rectangular steel
23⅝", 31½", or 39⅜" W; 23⅝", 31½", or 39⅜" D; 19¾" or 16½" H

12—28   DOMINO

1979
Designers: Alexander Blomberg and Jan Wichers
Manufacturer: Rosenthal
Top and frame: lightweight building board coated with 3-mm Plexiglas; PVC edging; plastic runners
36.8" W; 36.8" D; 18.4" H (18.4" x 18.4" x 18.4" cube)

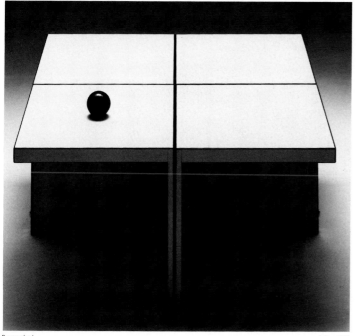

Rosenthal   12—28

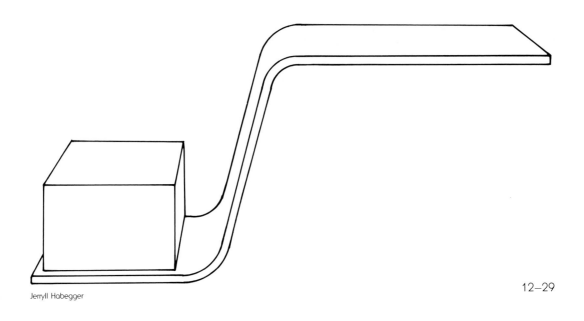

Jerryll Habegger

12–29

Cassina

12–30

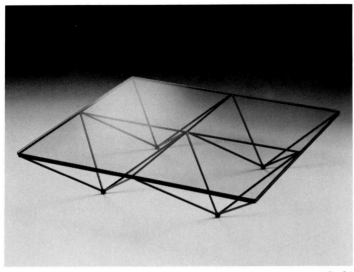

B & B Italia   12–31

12–29   K 3

c. 1980
Designer: Stefan Wewerka
Manufacturer: Tecta Möbel
Top and column: Plexiglas
Base: wood counterweight
49 ¼" W; 19 ¾" D; 20" H

12–30   NAVIGLIO

1981
Designer: Piero De Martini
Manufacturer: Cassina
Top: natural cleft slate
Frame: natural ashwood or natural Italian walnut
Legs: steel, finished in matte black lacquer
44.9" W; 44.9" D; 13.7" H

12–31   ALANDA

1982
Designer: Paolo Piva
Manufacturer: B & B Italia
Top: ½-inch clear polished glass with rounded edges
Base: solid steel rod with black enamel finish
47 ¼" W; 47 ¼" D; 9 ⅞" H

12–32   HANKY

1982
Designer: Gabriele Regondi
Manufacturer: Rimadesio
Structure: curved crystal glass; ABS feet
37 ¾" W; 37 ¾" D; 14 ½" H

Rimadesio   12–32

Courtesy of Knoll International

12–33

Courtesy of Knoll International

12–34

ICF, Inc.   12–35

12–33   ROLLING TABLE

c. 1982
Designer: Joe D'Urso
Manufacturer: Knoll International
Top: 1-inch-grid clear wire glass, inset in black vinyl gaskets
Base: stainless steel or painted steel; mounted on concealed
    casters
48″ W; 48″ D; 14½″ H

12–34   MERCER COLLECTION

1983
Designer: Lucia Mercer
Manufacturer: Knoll International
Top and base: solid granite; stainless steel rod connection
63″ W; 50″ D; 12″ H

12–35   DE MENIL

1983
Designers: Charles Gwathmey and Robert Siegel
Manufacturer: ICF, Inc.
Top: veneered cherry, mahogany, walnut, ebonized elm,
    natural or rosewood-stained ash
Base: solid cherry, mahogany, walnut, ebonized elm, natural
    or rosewood-stained ash
37½″ W; 37½″ D; 18″ H

12–36   MAYA

1984
Designer: Gino Vardi
Manufacturer: Images of America
Top: ashwood with a matte black polymeric lacquer, rounded
    edges
Frame: steel
Legs: 5-inch square tubular steel
50″ W; 50″ D; 16″ H

Images of America   12–36

Vecta   12–37

12–37   POLLOCK TABLE

1985
Designers: Charles Pollock and William Jaremko
Manufacturer: Vecta
Top: ⅜-inch-thick gray-tinted glass, polished edges
Base: solid-cast polyester resin
50⅜″ W; 27⅞″ D; 14″ H

13 HANGING LAMPS

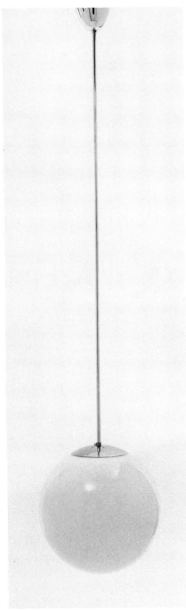

Technolumen   13–1

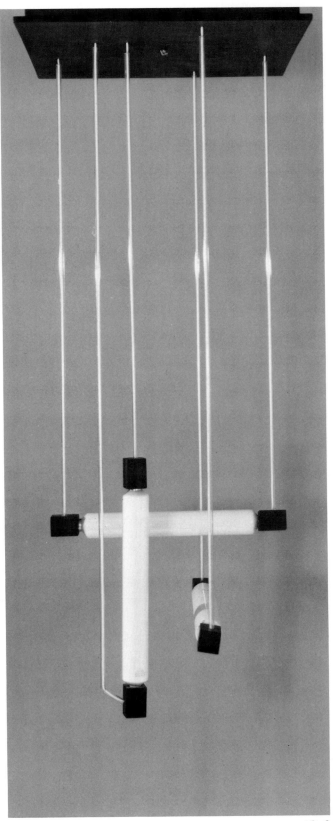

13–2

Louis Poulsen   13–3

13–1   OPAL PENDANT

c. 1900
Designer: Unknown
Manufacturer: Technolumen
Globe: opal glass
Stem and ceiling plate: chrome-plated metal
8", 10", or 12" Diameter; 47", 49", or 51" Overall H

13–2   HANGING LAMP

1920
Designer: Gerrit T. Rietveld
Manufacturer: Gerrit T. Rietveld
Structure: ebonized oak terminals; neon tube lights
13¾" W; 13¾" D; 51¼" H

13–3   PH 4½-4

1926
Designer: Poul Henningsen
Manufacturer: Louis Poulsen
Diffuser: opal glass or white aluminum
Support: chrome-plated metal
17¾" Diameter; 11¼" H

13–4   0024

1931
Designer: Gio Ponti
Manufacturer: Fontana Arte
Diffuser: glazed glass
Discs: crystal or glazed crystal
Mount: chrome-plated brass
21" Diameter; 21" H; 86½" Overall H

Fontana Arte   13–4

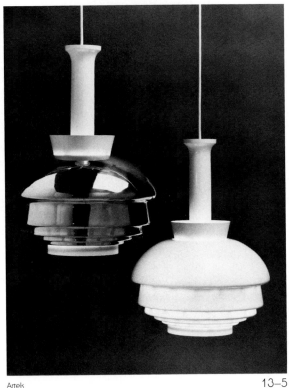

Artek   13–5

13–5   A 335B

1952
Designer: Alvar Aalto
Manufacturer: Artek
Reflector: polished brass
Support: matte white aluminum
11¾" Diameter; 16½" H

13–6   BUBBLE LAMP (CC727)

1952
Designer: George Nelson
Manufacturer: Gossamer Designs in Lighting
Structure: self-webbing white vinyl spray over a steel wire
    frame; chrome or brass fittings
36" Diameter; 14" H

13–7   RA 337

1954
Designer: Alvar Aalto
Manufacturer: Artek
Reflector: matte white aluminum
Support: interior brass louvers
23¼" Diameter; 9" H

13–8   JL 341

c. 1954
Designer: Juha Leiviska
Manufacturer: Artek
Reflector: aluminum
23¼" Diameter; 6¾" H

Jerryll Habegger   13–6

Artek
13–7

Artek
13–8

Louis Poulsen

13–9

Louis Poulsen

13–10

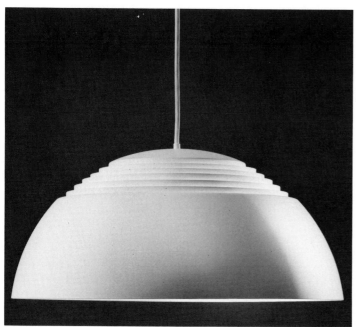

Louis Poulsen   13–11

13–9   PH 5

1958
Designer: Poul Henningsen
Manufacturer: Louis Poulsen
Diffuser: metal
19¾" Diameter; 9⅞" H

13–10   ARTICHOKE

1958
Designer: Poul Henningsen
Manufacturer: Louis Poulsen
Diffuser: matte copper or matte stainless steel
23½", 28¼", or 33" Diameter; 18½", 24¼", or 27¼" H

13–11   AJ ROYAL PENDANT

1960
Designer: Arne Jacobsen
Manufacturer: Louis Poulsen
Structure: metal
14½" or 19¾" Diameter; 6¼" or 8¾" H

13–12   PH CONTRAST

1962
Designer: Poul Henningsen
Manufacturer: Louis Poulsen
Diffuser: polished aluminum
Reflector: metal
17¾" Diameter; 15¾" H

Louis Poulsen   13–12

Louis Poulsen   13–13

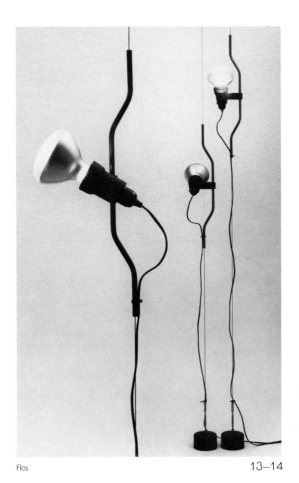

Flos   13–14

Lyfa-Fog & Morup

13—15

13—13   PH 4/3

1966
Designer: Poul Henningsen
Manufacturer: Louis Poulsen
Diffuser: metal
15¾" Diameter; 7¼" H

13—14   PARENTESI

1970
Designers: Achille Castiglioni and Pio Manzu
Manufacturer: Flos
Support and base: black rubber
Extender column: stainless steel wire
157.5" Max. H

13—15   SEMI-PENDANT

1970
Designers: Torsten Thorup and Claus Bonderup
Manufacturer: Lyfa-Fog & Morup
Reflector: aluminum
10"—27½" Diameter

13—16   AREA 50

1974
Designer: Mario Bellini
Manufacturer: Artemide
Diffuser: heat-resistant textured Fiberglas
Counterweight: white-lacquered metal
Ceiling mount: Makrolon
19¾" Diameter

Artemide

13—16

Flos   13–17

Ron Rezek   13–18

Atelje Lyktan   13–19

13–17 FRISBI

1978
Designer: Achille Castiglioni
Manufacturer: Flos
Diffuser/Reflector: Plexiglas
Reflector: polished-chrome metal
Ceiling plate: black plastic
Support: stainless steel wires
23.6" Diameter; 28.7" H

13–18 200

c. 1978
Designer: Ron Rezek
Manufacturer: Ron Rezek
Diffuser: perforated steel
24" Diameter; 8" H

13–19 VEGA

1979
Designer: Per Sundstredt
Manufacturer: Atelje Lyktan
Reflector: lacquered aluminum
40½" or 52½" W; 9¾" H

13–20 LINEARE 850/880

1981
Designer: Studio Tecnico
Manufacturer: O-Luce
Reflector: lacquered extruded aluminum
Support: stainless steel wires
39½", 78¾", or 118" W; 4" D; 2" H

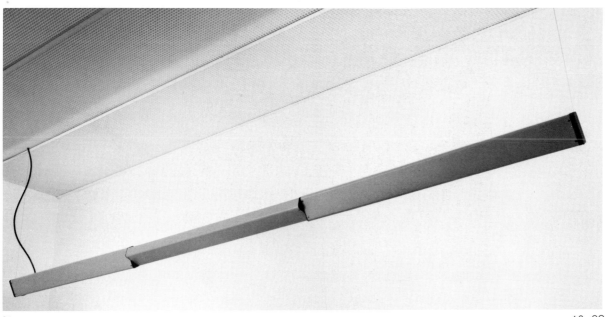

O-Luce   13–20

Artemide   13–21

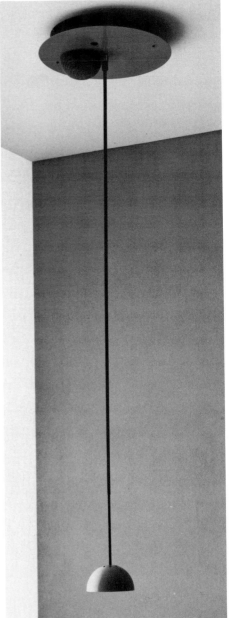

Artemide   13–22

Artemide   13–23

13–21 ATON

c. 1981
Designer: Ernesto Gismondi
Manufacturer: Artemide
Reflector: extruded or anodized aluminum
Connector/Support: black impact-resistant thermoplastic
Support: steel cable
40", 64", 82¾", or 112¼" W; 4¾" D; 2" H

13–22 ALESIA

1982
Designer: Carlo Forcolini
Manufacturer: Artemide
Structure: metal
4½" Diameter; 43"–82" H; 12½" Diameter (ceiling plate)

13–23 ABOLLA

1982
Designer: CP & PR Associati
Manufacturer: Artemide
Reflector and counterweight: metal
Support: steel wires
7" Diameter; 155" Max. H

13–24 ELLIPS

1982
Designer: Dag Holmgren
Manufacturer: Atelje Lyktan
Structure: extruded aluminum; neon tube
39¼" or 59" W; 21¾" or 31½" H

Atelje Lyktan   13–24

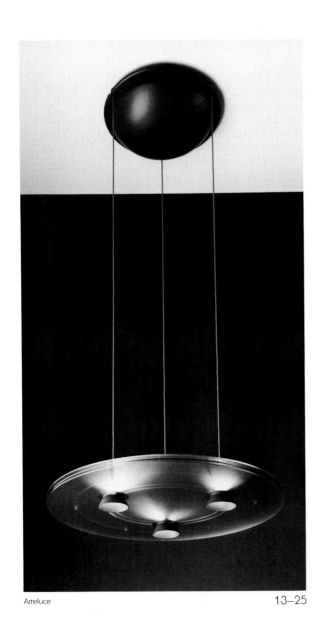

Arteluce   13–25

Sirrah   13–26

Ingo Maurer/Design M   13—27

13—25   AURORA

1983
Designers: Perry A. King and Santiago Miranda
Manufacturer: Arteluce
Reflector: enameled spun-steel cones
Pendant: textured, circular glass plate, polished edge
Support: braided copper wire enclosed in an insulating plastic
   sheathing
Ceiling plate: spun aluminum
23.6" Diameter; 12"—92" H

13—26   DISKOS

1983
Designer: Giovanni Offredi
Manufacturer: Sirrah
Reflector: translucent Vedril disc
Support and ceiling plate: ABS
26½" W; 23½" D; 3" H (Reflector)

13—27   LIGHT STRUCTURE

1983
Designers: Peter Hamburger and Ingo Maurer
Manufacturer: Ingo Maurer
Structure: plastic with six incandescent light tubes
19¾" W; 19¾" D; 19¾" H

13—28   OLAMPIA

1984
Designer: Daniela Puppa
Manufacturer: Fontana Arte
Structure: chrome-plated brass tube
Diffuser: white opal glass
Reflector: sandblasted crystal glass disc
28¾" Diameter; 50"—73½" H

Fontana Arte   13—28

Ron Rezek   13–29

13–29 SPHEDRON (300)

1985
Designer: Ron Rezek
Manufacturer: Ron Rezek
Structure: aluminum
Diffuser: crystal glass
9" Diameter; 5" H

13–30 CYCLOS

1985
Designer: Michele De Lucchi
Manufacturer: Artemide
Reflector, support, and ceiling plate: painted metal
Diffuser: cut glass, frosted center
26⅜" Diameter; 67" Max. H

Artemide   13–30

14 WALL LAMPS

Louis Poulsen 14—1

Artemide 14—2

Louis Poulsen

14–3

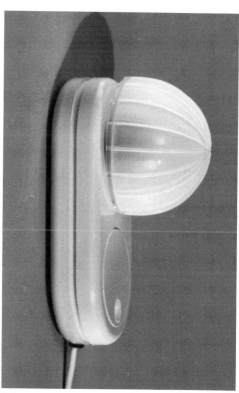

Gullans International, Inc./Bieffeplast S.p.A.

14–4

14–1   DISCOS

1956
Designer: Arne Jacobsen
Manufacturer: Louis Poulsen
Diffuser: opal glass
Wall plate: white metal
8¾", 13¾", or 17¾" Diameter; 4½", 4", or 5¼" Projection

14–2   MANIA

1964
Designer: Vico Magistretti
Manufacturer: Artemide
Structure: Makrolon
9½" or 11" W; 4" or 5½" D

14–3   P-HAT

c. 1967
Designer: Poul Henningsen
Manufacturer: Louis Poulsen
Structure: metal
9" or 11" Diameter; 5½" or 6¾" Projection

14–4   FARSTAR

1973
Designer: Adalberto Dal Lago
Manufacturer: Francesconi
Diffuser: molded and sanded glass
Structure: injection-molded ABS
4¾" W; 5¼" D; 9½" H

Stilnovo   14—5

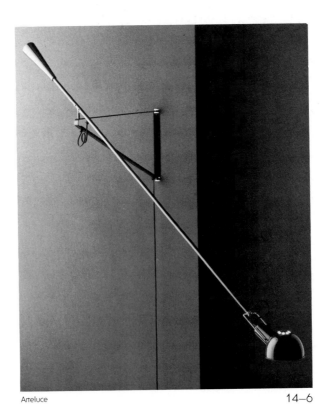

Arteluce   14—6

Flos

14–7

14–5 SPHERE
1973
Designers: Danilo Aroldi and Corrado Aroldi
Manufacturer: Stilnovo
Structure: Vedril
Support: chromed metal
11¾" W; 6" D; 6" H

14–6 265
1973
Designer: Paolo Rizzatto
Manufacturer: Arteluce
Structure: enameled metal
33½" D; 80¾" (arm length); 14¼" H (wall bracket)

14–7 QUARTO
1974
Designer: Tobia Scarpa
Manufacturer: Flos
Reflector: enameled metal or polished nickel
Diffuser: clear polycarbonate
15.7" W; 8.25" D; 7.25" H

14–8 MANIGLIA
1977
Designers: Jonathan De Pas, Donato D'Urbino, and Paolo
   Lomazzi
Manufacturer: Stilnovo
Reflector and transformer holder: Makrolon
Stem: chromed metal
30" Projection

Stilnovo

14–8

Stilnovo   14–9

Stilnovo   14–10

Arteluce

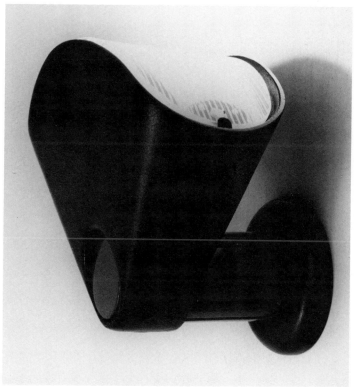

Flos

14–9 GOMITO
1977
Designer: Gae Aulenti
Manufacturer: Stilnovo
Reflector: metal
Structure: antistatic ABS resin
10" Diameter; 10" H

14–10 ZAGAR
1978
Designer: S. Carpani
Manufacturer: Stilnovo
Reflector: lacquered die-cast aluminum
Structure: lacquered extruded aluminum
8⅔" Projection; 13¾" H

14–11 WALL
1978
Designers: Perry A. King, Santiago Miranda, and Gianluigi
    Arnaldi
Manufacturer: Arteluce
Diffuser: elliptical cast colored glass
Structure: enameled metal
15" W; 10.5" D; 8.8" H

14–12 BOLLO
1979
Designer: Tobia Scarpa
Manufacturer: Flos
Diffuser: convex glass
Structure: enameled cast aluminum
8.2" W; 6.7" D; 7.5" H

14–11

14–12

Stilnovo   14—13

Artemide   14—14

IPI Lighting   14–15

14–13   OBLO

1979
Designers: Mazzucchelli and Fiorin
Manufacturer: Stilnovo
Diffuser: pressed glass; black rubber gasket
Wall plate: metal
18″ Diameter; 4¼″ D

14–14   MEGARON

1980
Designer: Gianfranco Frattini
Manufacturer: Artemide
Structure: lacquered extruded aluminum
11″ D; 14½″ H

14–15   IL W

1981
Designer: Marco Zotta
Manufacturer: Eleusi
Structure: baked enameled cast aluminum
5″ W; 8″ D; 13″ H

14–16   GIOVI

1982
Designer: Achille Castiglioni
Manufacturer: Flos
Structure: enameled metal
11″ Diameter; 6¼″ D

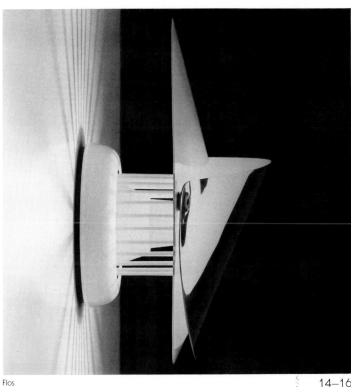

Flos   14–16

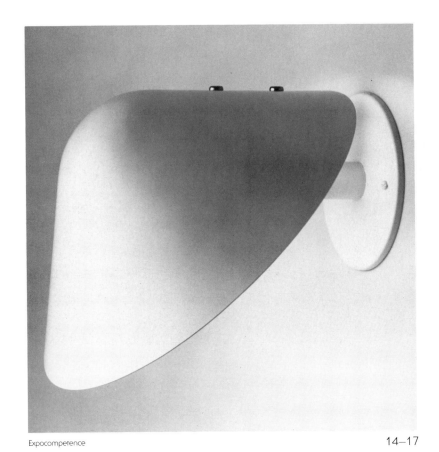

Expocompetence   14—17

Boyd Lighting   14—18

Nessen Lamps

14–19

Koch + Lowy

14–20

14–17   WALL VIP

1983
Designer: Jørgen Gammelgaard
Manufacturer: Design Forum
Reflector: aluminum
Support: stainless steel
13¾" Diameter; 16½" D; 28" H

14–18   WALL BRACKET

1983
Designer: Charles Pfister
Manufacturer: Boyd Lighting
Reflector: precast, glass-reinforced concrete disc or solid marble
Armature and plate: sand-etched or polished brass or bronze
10" Diameter; 12" Projection; 4⅝" H

14–19   ALA

1984
Designer: Gianfranco Frattini
Manufacturer: Luci
Structure: aluminum
7" W; 14" D

14–20   WAVE

1984
Designer: Charles Gevers
Manufacturer: Koch + Lowy
Structure: polished brass or chrome, white-lacquered enamel,
  or black or gray Nextel
12" W; 3" D; 7½" H

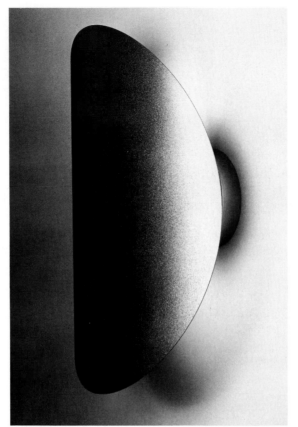

Martinelli-Luce   14—21

Martinelli-Luce   14—22

Bellagamba   14–23

14–21 SCUDO (1258)
1984
Designer: Elio Martinelli
Manufacturer: Martinelli-Luce
Reflector: silvery metal
Wall plate: chrome-plated steel
13 ½" Diameter

14–22 SISTEMA LE RONDINI (1249/3)
1984
Designer: Elio Martinelli
Manufacturer: Martinelli-Luce
Structure: lacquered metal; chrome conductor
63¾" W; 10½" D

14–23 PENTAX SYSTEM
1984
Designer: Giovanni Bellagamba
Manufacturer: Bellagamba
Structure: extruded aluminum
8" W; 27½" D; 39½" H

14–24 PAN-A-LUX
c. 1984
Designer: Rambusch
Manufacturer: Rambusch
Reflector: polished extruded aluminum
Structure: glass-reinforced polymerized gypsum
10¾" W; 13¼" D; 5½" H

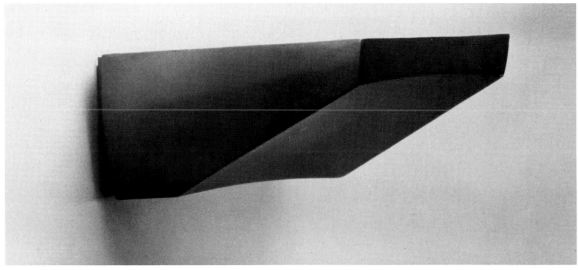

Rambusch   14–24

Artemide   14–25

Artemide   14–26

Ron Rezek

14–27

14–25   CLIPEO

1985
Designer: Eric Gottein
Manufacturer: Artemide
Structure: painted metal
12¼" W; 7" D; 7" H

14–26   STRIA

1985
Designer: Ernesto Gismondi
Manufacturer: Artemide
Wall-mounting bracket: molded, heat-resistant, black, glassfiber-
  reinforced polyester
Reflectors: white-painted metal
14⁹⁄₁₆" W; 5½" D; 15⅜" H

14–27   SCONCE (430)

1985
Designer: Gere Kavanaugh
Manufacturer: Ron Rezek
Structure: painted metal
12" W; 9" D; 5" H

14–28   DAMOCLE

1985
Designer: Mitchell Mauk
Manufacturer: Artemide
Base and reflector: black molded thermoplastic
Supports: black flexible metal rods
7⅞" W; 8²¹⁄₃₂" D; 14¼" H

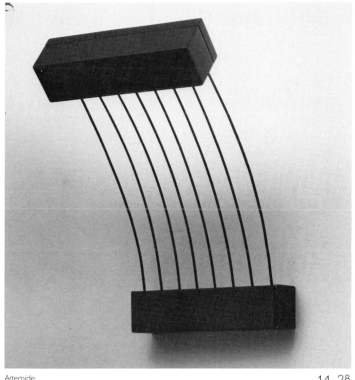

Artemide

14–28

15 TABLE LAMPS

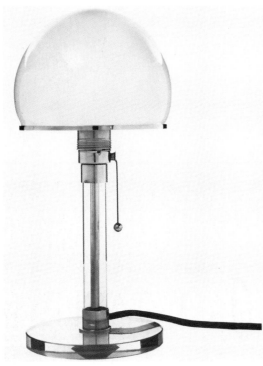

Technolumen   15–1

15–1   WAGENFELD

1924
Designer: Wilhelm Wagenfeld
Manufacturer: Technolumen
Diffuser: opaque glass shade
Stem and base: clear glass; nickel-plated metal
7″ Diameter; 14″ H

15–2   TABLE LAMP

1924
Designer: Frank Lloyd Wright
Manufacturer: Heinz & Co.
Frame: oak or mahogany
Reflector: glass
14″ W; 16″ D; 20″ H

15–3   TABLE LAMP

1925
Designer: Gerrit T. Rietveld
Manufacturer: Gerrit T. Rietveld
Reflector and base: painted metal
Diffuser: glass
Stem: chrome-plated steel
4¾″ W (base); 6″ D (base); 15″ H

15–4   L 1

1937
Designer: Jac. Jacobsen
Manufacturer: Luxo Italiana
Reflector: sheet steel
Stem and base: tubular steel; hardened steel springs
6¾″ Diameter (shade); 47″ Max. H

Heinz & Co.   15–2

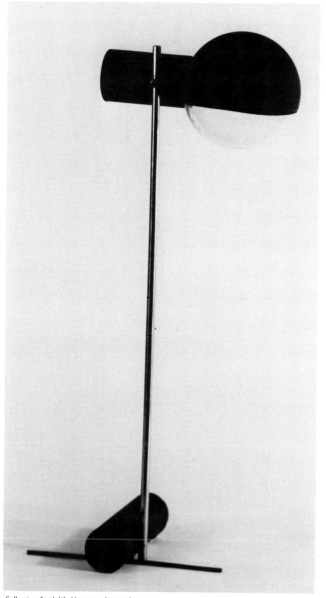

Collection Stedelijk Museum, Amsterdam

15–3

Luxo Italiana

15–4

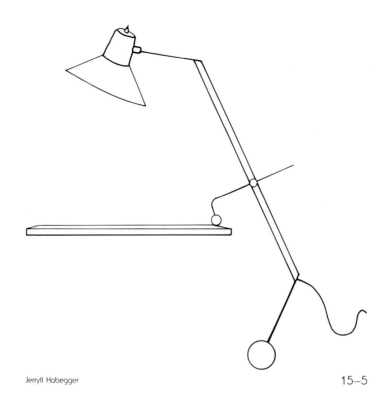

Jerryll Habegger

15–5

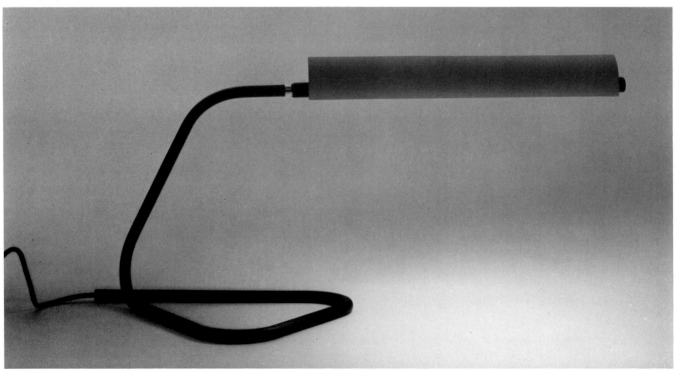

Flos

15–6

Nessen Lamps   15–7

Koch + Lowy   15–8

15–5 LIBRALUX

1948
Designer: Roberto Menghi
Manufacturer: Lamperti
Reflector: enameled aluminum
Stem and counterweights: brushed brass
29½" H

15–6 TUBINO

1950
Designers: Achille Castiglioni and Pier Giacomo Castiglioni
Manufacturer: Flos
Reflector: anodized aluminum
Stem and base: lacquered metal
10½" W; 26½" D; 11½" H

15–7 ANYWHERE

1952
Designer: Greta von Nessen
Manufacturer: Nessen Lamps
Reflector and dome: aluminum, baked enamel finish
Stem and base: bright chrome metal
14" Diameter; 14½" H

15–8 HALF NELSON

c. 1955
Designer: George Nelson
Manufacturer: Koch + Lowy
Structure: polished brass or aluminum
15½" Diameter; 19" H

Louis Poulsen   15—9

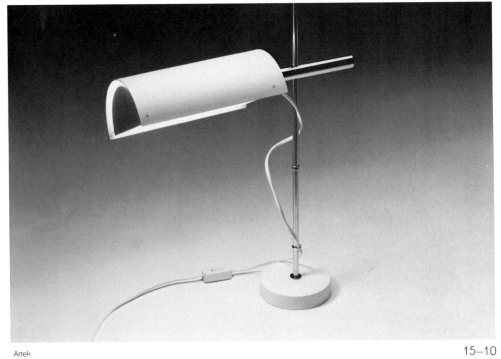

Artek   15—10

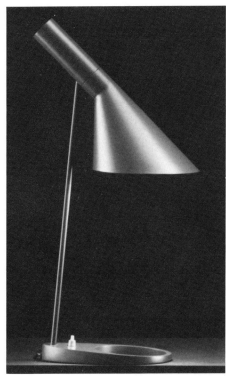

Louis Poulsen   15—11

15—9   PH 80

1958
Designer: Poul Henningsen
Manufacturer: Louis Poulsen
Diffuser: opal acrylic
Stem: chrome-plated metal
Base: black metal
21¾″ Diameter; 26½″ H

15—10   BS 712

c. 1959
Designer: Ben af Schultren
Manufacturer: Artek
Reflector and base: aluminum
Stem: chrome
16″ Diameter; 20½″ H

15—11   AJ VISOR

1960
Designer: Arne Jacobsen
Manufacturer: Louis Poulsen
Structure: metal
7″ Diameter; 21¼″ H

15—12   COLOMBO (281)

1962
Designer: Joe Colombo
Manufacturer: O-Luce
Diffuser: Perspex
Base: lacquered steel
10¼″ W; 9½″ D; 9″ H

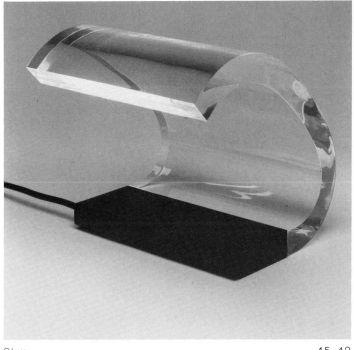

O-Luce   15—12

Flos   15–13

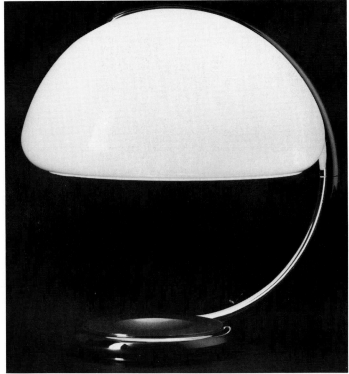

Martinelli-Luce   15–14

15–13   TACCIA

1962
Designers: Achille Castiglioni and Pier Giacomo Castiglioni
Manufacturer: Flos
Reflector: enameled spun aluminum, resting on a clear
    handblown glass bowl
Base: extruded aluminum
19.3" Diameter; 21.2" H

15–14   SERPENTE

1965
Designer: Elio Martinelli
Manufacturer: Martinelli-Luce
Reflector: white opal methacrylate
Stem and base: lacquered or chrome-plated metal
17¾" Diameter; 17¾" H

15–15   PH 5

1965
Designer: Poul Henningsen
Manufacturer: Louis Poulsen
Diffuser: metal
Stem and base: polished chrome
19¾" Diameter; 26¼" H

15–16   ECLISSE

1966
Designer: Vico Magistretti
Manufacturer: Artemide
Structure: lacquered aluminum
4¾" Diameter; 6¾" H

Louis Poulsen

15—15

Artemide

15—16

Louis Poulsen   15–17

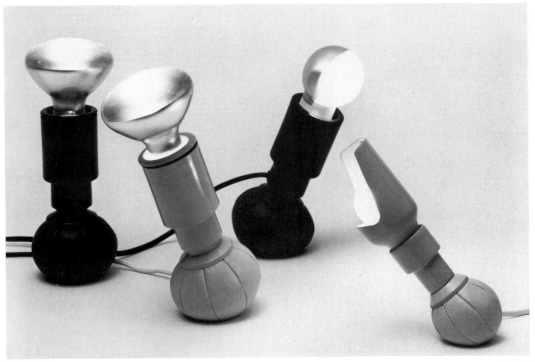

Arteluce   15–18

Martinelli·Luce   15–19

15–17 PH 4/3

1966
Designer: Poul Henningsen
Manufacturer: Louis Poulsen
Diffuser: white metal
Stem and base: chrome
17¾" Diameter; 21¾" H

15–18 600

1966
Designer: Gino Sarfatti
Manufacturer: Arteluce
Reflector and structure: enameled metal
Base: vinyl
2¾" Diameter; 8" H

15–19 PIPISTRELLO

1967
Designer: Gae Aulenti
Manufacturer: Martinelli·Luce
Reflector: white opal methacrylate
Telescope: stainless steel
Base: lacquered metal
21½" Diameter; 26"–33¾" H

15–20 LESBO

1967
Designer: Angelo Mangiarotti
Manufacturer: Artemide
Reflector and stem: blown smoked glass
Base: metal
20½" Diameter; 14½" H

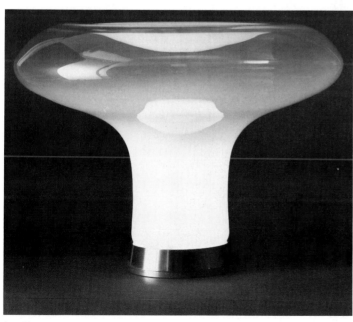

Artemide   15–20

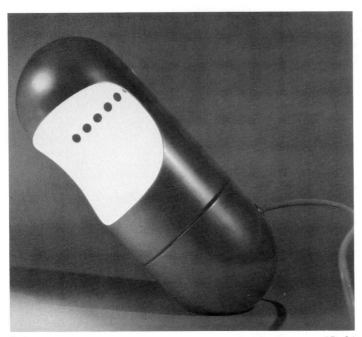

Arteluce   15—21

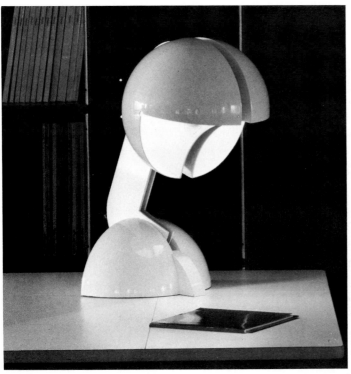

Martinelli-Luce   15—22

15—21   537

1967
Designers: Vittorio Gregotti, Lodovico Meneghetti, and Giotto
    Stoppino
Manufacturer: Arteluce
Structure: lacquered aluminum
3¾" Diameter; 8" H

15—22   RUSPA (633)

1968
Designer: Gae Aulenti
Manufacturer: Martinelli-Luce
Structure: lacquered metal
13" W; 8½" D; 22⅞" H

15—23   BOALUM

1970
Designers: Livio Castiglioni and Gianfranco Frattini
Manufacturer: Artemide
Structure: tubular plastic; metal power-conductor coil
2¼" Diameter; 78¾" Length

15—24   LAMPIATTA

1971
Designers: Jonathan De Pas, Donato D'Urbino, and Paolo
    Lomazzi
Manufacturer: Stilnovo
Reflector: white lacquered metal
Base: ABS
11" Diameter; 19¾" Max. H

Artemide   15—23

Stilnovo   15—24

Arteluce   15—25

Artemide   15—26

Sirrah

15—27

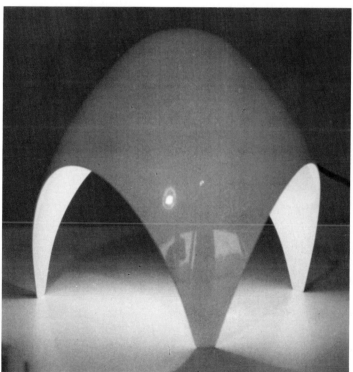

Martinelli-Luce

15—28

15—25 607

1971
Designer: Gino Sarfatti
Manufacturer: Arteluce
Structure: lacquered aluminum
10" Diameter; 12¼" H

15—26 TIZIO

1972
Designer: Richard Sapper
Manufacturer: Artemide
Reflector: Durethane
Stem: anticorrodal aluminum; counterweights in metal alloy
Base: ABS
42½" Projection; 4⅜" Diameter (base); 46½" Max. H

15—27 KAORI

1975
Designer: Kazuhide Takahama
Manufacturer: Sirrah
Structure: metal; stretched white fabric cover
14¼" W; 7" D; 9" H

15—28 COQUE (686)

1975
Designer: Elio Martinelli
Manufacturer: Martinelli-Luce
Structure: lacquered metal
9⅞" Diameter; 8⅝" H

Flos

15—29

O·Luce

15—30

Artemide

15–29 IPOTENUSA

1976
Designer: Achille Castiglioni
Manufacturer: Flos
Reflector: formed, enameled aluminum
Diffuser: injection-molded methacrylate
Stem: chrome
Base: enameled die-cast aluminum
3½" W; 6" D; 24½" H

15–30 ATOLLO

1977
Designer: Vico Magistretti
Manufacturer: O-Luce
Structure: lacquered aluminum
19¾" Diameter (reflector); 8" Diameter (base); 27½" H

15–31 SINTESI

1978
Designer: Ernesto Gismondi
Manufacturer: Artemide
Reflector: anodized aluminum; black metal grille
Stem and base: anodized aluminum
22" Max. D; 22" Max. H

15–31

15–32 RING

1979
Designer: Bruno Gecchelin
Manufacturer: Arteluce
Structure: cast aluminum, enamel finish
22.8" D; 15.2" H

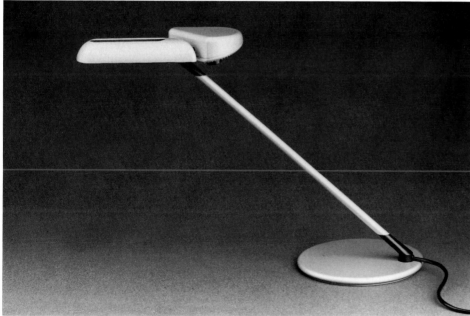

Arteluce

15–32

389

Arteluce

15–33

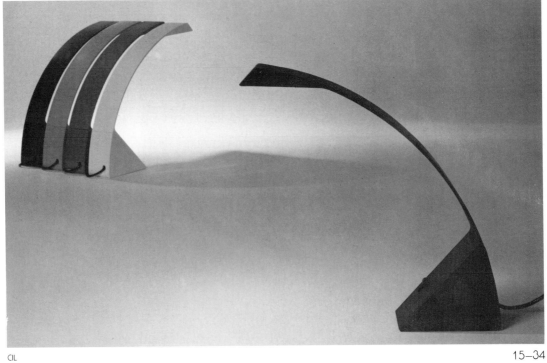

CIL

15–34

O·Luce   15—35

15—33 MANTIS

1979
Designers: Perry A. King, Santiago Miranda, and Gianluigi Arnaldi
Manufacturer: Arteluce
Reflector: methacrylate
Stem: extruded aluminum
Base: cast aluminum
16.9" W; 16" H

15—34 ARCOBALENO

1979
Designer: Marco Zotta
Manufacturer: CIL
Structure: epoxy-coated die-cast aluminum
3⅜" W; 15¾" D; 16½" H

15—35 KUTA

1980
Designer: Vico Magistretti
Manufacturer: O-Luce
Reflector: lacquered aluminum
Stem and base: lacquered metal
11¾" Diameter (plate); 6¼" D; 12¼" H

15—36 TURISELLA

c. 1980
Designer: Alberto Besana
Manufacturer: Sem Luci
Reflector and base: aluminum
Stem: black anodized aluminum
30¼" D; 24¾" H

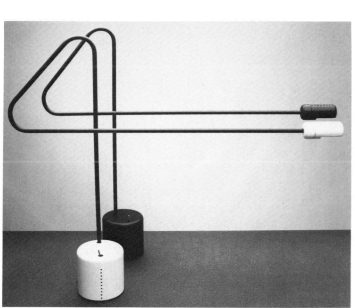

Sem Luci   15—36

Jerryll Habegger

15–37

15–37   MULTIPLICA

c. 1980
Designers: Jonathan De Pas, Donato D'Urbino, and Paolo
    Lomazzi
Manufacturer: Stilnovo
Reflector: Plexiglas or lacquered metal
Stem and base: lacquered metal with stamped rubber fittings
48″ D; 40½″ H; 15¾″ Diameter (reflector)

15–38   ALA

c. 1980
Designer: Rodolfo Bonetto
Manufacturer: Guzzini
Structure: aluminum
6¾″ W; 15¼″–36″ D; 12¼″–32¼″ H

15–39   STRING LINE

1981
Designer: Knud Holscher
Manufacturer: Solar Belysning
Reflector: aluminum
Stem and base: tubular stainless steel
10¼″ W; 15¾″ D; 19″ H

15–40   MIA

1981
Designer: Carlo Frigerio
Manufacturer: Eleusi
Structure: brass with a lacquer finish or a polished, satin, or
    chrome finish
5″ W; 26″ D; 16″ H

Guzzini

15–38

Knud Holscher

15–39

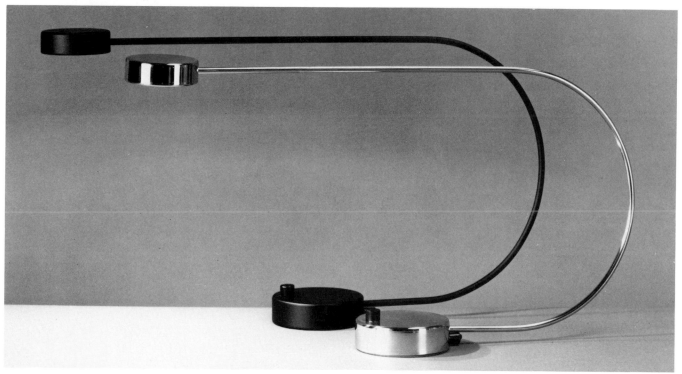

IPI Lighting

15–40

Flos   15–41

15–41   GIBIGIANA

1981
Designer: Achille Castiglioni
Manufacturer: Flos
Reflector: circular polished-steel mirror
Base: enameled steel; injection-molded plastic dimmer and
    thumbwheel
3.8" or 4.1" Diameter; 16.4" or 20.5" H

15–42   MINI-BOX

1981
Designers: Gae Aulenti and Piero Castiglioni
Manufacturer: Stilnovo
Structure: lacquered metal
6¼" H

15–43   ORBIS

1982
Designer: Ron Rezek
Manufacturer: Ron Rezek
Reflector and stem: stainless steel
Base: cast aluminum
32" D; 13" H

15–44   SLALOM

1982
Designer: Vico Magistretti
Manufacturer: O-Luce
Reflector: lacquered aluminum
Stem and base: black lacquered metal
9¾" Diameter (base); 19¾" H

Stilnovo   15–42

Ron Rezek

15–43

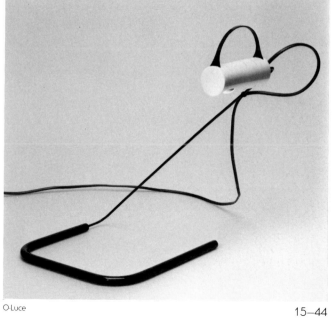

O·Luce

15–44

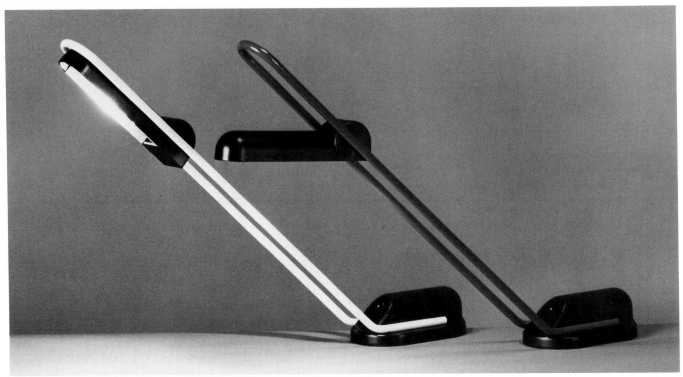

IPI Lighting

15–45

Luxo Italiana

15–46

Ledu   15–47

Stilnovo   15–48

15–45   PRIAPO
1982
Designer: Carlo Vietri
Manufacturer: Eleusi
Base and reflector: cast Macrolon
Arms: baked enamel aluminum
4" W; 24" D; 17" H

15–46   STRINGA
1982
Designer: Hans Ansems
Manufacturer: Luxo Italiana
Reflector: aluminum
Stem: aluminum enclosing a steel tension spring
Base: steel
17" W; 20" H

15–47   IPL 600
1983
Designer: Achim Willing
Manufacturer: Ledu
Reflector: injection-molded ABS
Stem and base: painted metal
12" W (reflector); 6" D (reflector); 28" Max. H

15–48   NASTRO
1983
Designer: Alberto Fraser
Manufacturer: Stilnovo
Reflector and base: Makrolon
Stem: multicolored plastic
5 ½" D; 4 ½" H (base); 8 ¼" D; 1 ½" H (reflector)

Ron Rezek

15–49

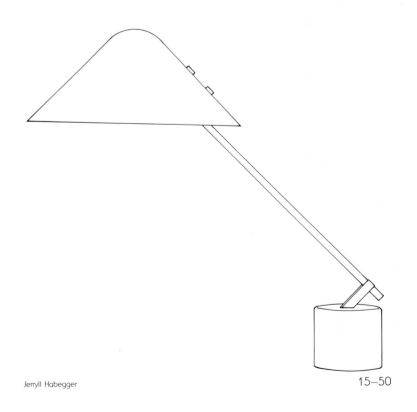

Jerryll Habegger

15–50

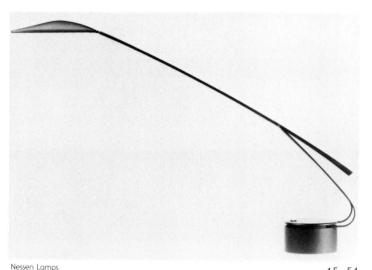

Nessen Lamps

15–51

15–49   110
1983
Designer: Ron Rezek
Manufacturer: Ron Rezek
Diffuser: perforated steel
Stem and base: sheet metal
9″ W; 14″ D; 18″ H

15–50   SWING VIP
1983
Designer: Jørgen Gammelgaard
Manufacturer: Design Forum
Reflector and base: aluminum
Stem: stainless steel
13¾″ Diameter (reflector); 4½″ Diameter (base); 23½″ D;
    22½″ H

15–51   DOVE
1984
Designers: Mario Barbaglia and Marco Colombo
Manufacturer: Paf
Reflector and stem: injection-molded plastic
Base: die-cast metal alloy
4¾″ Diameter (base); 7½″–23″ Extension; 11″–27½″ H

15–52   THOLOS
1984
Designer: Ernesto Gismondi
Manufacturer: Artemide
Structure: lacquered metal
3⅜″ W (base); 6″ D (base); 23½″ Max. H

Artemide

15–52

Luxo Italiana   15—53

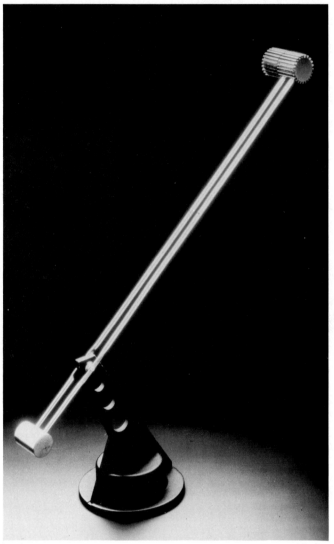

Luxo Italiana   15—54

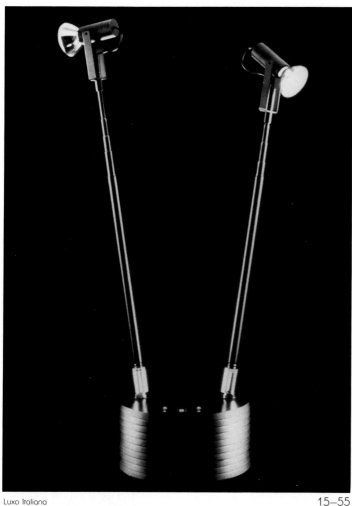

Luxo Italiana   15—55

15—53 PICCHIO

1984
Designer: Isao Hosoe
Manufacturer: Luxo Italiana
Structure: ABS
Inner reflector: polished aluminum
3½" W; 15" D (open); 16¼" H (closed); 26¼" H (open)

15—54 ALTALENA

1985
Designers: Pep Sant and Ramon Bigas
Manufacturer: Luxo Italiana
Reflector: Ryton; polished aluminum inner reflector
Arms: black-painted or chrome-plated brass
Base: ABS
6" W; 25¼" D; 15¾" H

15—55 SCIOPTICON

1985
Designer: Hans Ansems
Manufacturer: Luxo Italiana
Base: ABS
Telescopic arms: black-painted brass
5½" Diameter; 43¼" H

15—56 JACK (D 10)

1985
Designer: Alberto Meda
Manufacturer: Luce Plan
Structure: black anodized aluminum
13¾" D; 19¾" H

Luce Plan   15—56

16 FLOOR LAMPS

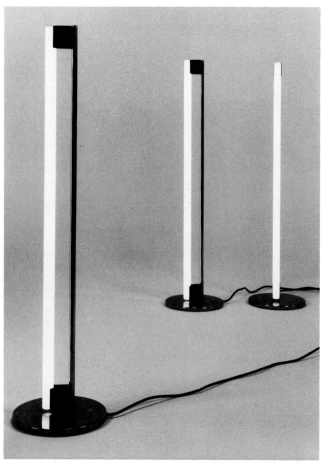

Images of America

16–1

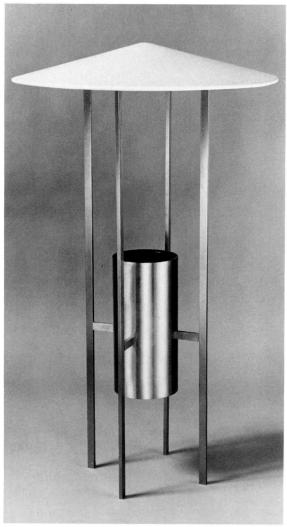

Peter L. Goodman/Edison Price

16–2

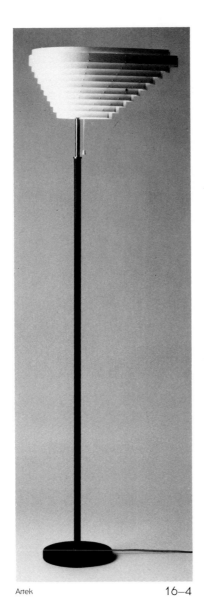

16–1   TUBE LIGHT
1927
Designer: Eileen Gray
Manufacturer: Images of America
Stem and base: polished chrome; exposed incandescent tube
10" Diameter; 40" H

16–2   FLOOR LAMP
1950
Designer: Philip Johnson
Manufacturer: Edison Price
Structure: brass
Reflector: white enameled metal
42" H

16–3   1063
1954
Designer: Gino Sarfatti
Manufacturer: Arteluce
Stem and base: lacquered metal; exposed slimline bulb
84¾" H

16–4   A 805
1954
Designer: Alvar Aalto
Manufacturer: Artek
Diffuser: iron
Stem and base: metal; brass fittings
20½" Diameter; 68½" H

Arteluce   16–3

Artek   16–4

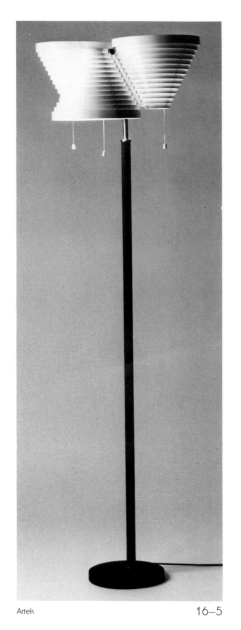

Artek   16—5

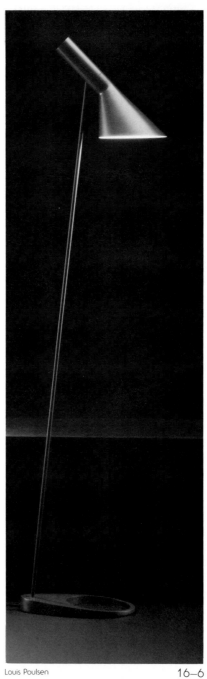

Louis Poulsen   16—6

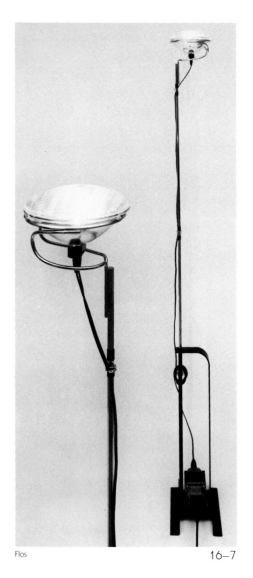

Flos   16—7

16—5   A 809

1954
Designer: Alvar Aalto
Manufacturer: Artek
Diffuser: iron
Stem and base: metal; brass fittings
22 ½" Diameter; 66" H

16—6   AJ VISOR

1960
Designer: Arne Jacobsen
Manufacturer: Louis Poulsen
Structure: metal
6 ⅛" Diameter; 51 ⅛" H

16—7   TOIO

1962
Designers: Achille Castiglioni and Pier Giacomo Castiglioni
Manufacturer: Flos
Stem: hexagonal brass, nickel-plated and polished
Base: enameled steel
8.3" Diameter; 67"–78.8" H

16—8   ARCO

1962
Designers: Achille Castiglioni and Pier Giacomo Castiglioni
Manufacturer: Flos
Reflector: spun aluminum
Stem: stainless steel
Base: white marble
78.6" Diameter; 95" H

Flos

16—8

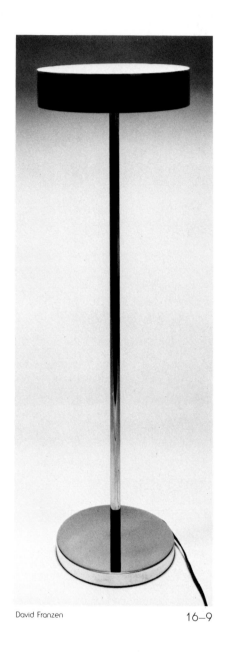

David Franzen   16–9

Cedric Hartman Inc.   16–10

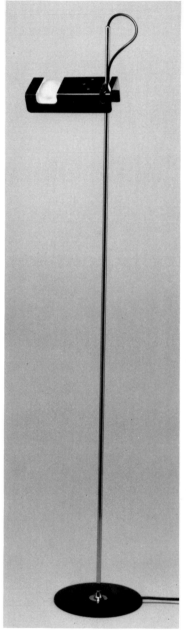

O·Luce   16–11

16–9 FRANZEN FLOOR LAMP

1965
Designer: Ulrich Franzen
Manufacturer: Egli Company
Structure: chrome-plated steel; interior of shade is spray painted
13″ W (shade); 39½″ H

16–10 1U WV

1966
Designer: Cedric Hartman
Manufacturer: Cedric Hartman Inc.
Reflector and base: polished chrome
Stem: polished stainless steel
10.8″ W (base); 13″ D; 36″–42″ H

16–11 SPIDER

1966
Designer: Joe Colombo
Manufacturer: O-Luce
Reflector: lacquered aluminum
Stem: chrome-plated steel
Base: lacquered steel
9″ Diameter (base); 55″ H

16–12 CHIMERA

1969
Designer: Vico Magistretti
Manufacturer: Artemide
Diffuser: white Plexiglas
Base: white-lacquered metal
8¾″ Diameter; 70⅞″ H

Artemide

16–12

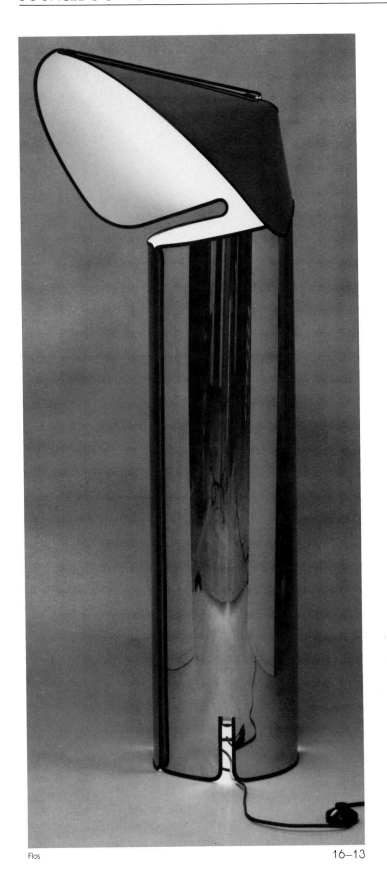

Flos   16—13

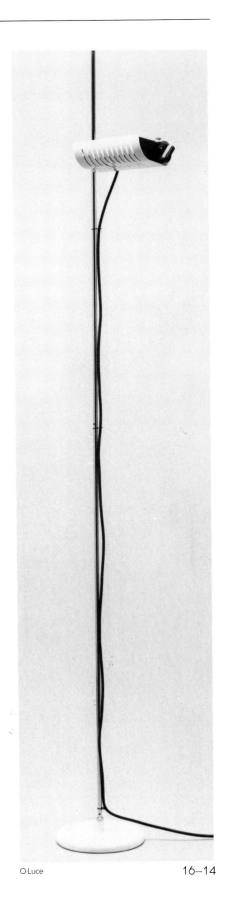

O·Luce   16—14

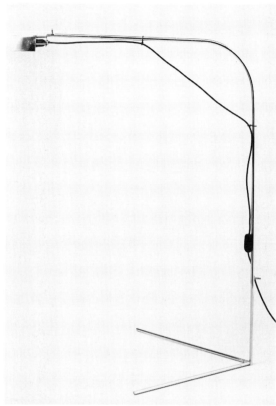

B.D. Ediciones   16–15

16–13   CHIARA

1969
Designer: Mario Bellini
Manufacturer: Flos
Structure: stainless steel
29½" W; 20" D; 56¼" H

16–14   626

1972
Designer: Joe Colombo
Manufacturer: O-Luce
Reflector and base: lacquered steel
Stem: chrome-plated metal
9½" Diameter (base); 82¾" H

16–15   FLAMINGO

1972
Designer: A. Siza Vieira
Manufacturer: B.D. Ediciones
Structure: chrome-plated steel tubes and rods
Reflector: stainless steel wings
20¼" W; 30"–36¼" D; 33½"–47¼" H

16–16   PILEO

1972
Designer: Gae Aulenti
Manufacturer: Artemide
Reflector: polycarbonate
Base: ABS
17¼" Diameter; 55" H

Artemide   16–16

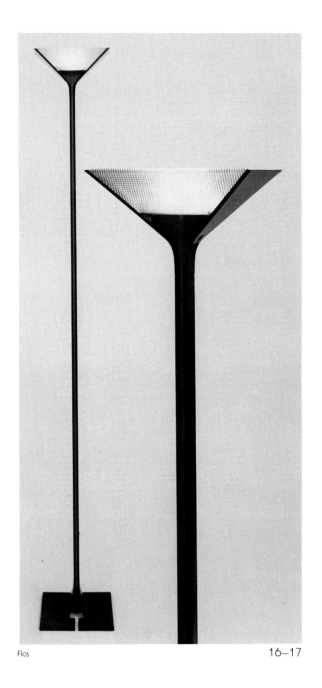

Flos   16–17

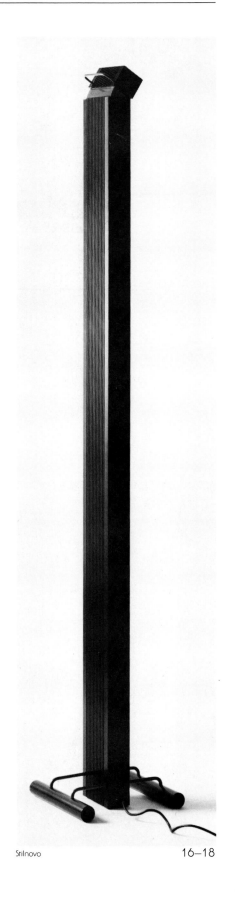

Stilnovo   16–18

Arteluce   16–19

16–17   PAPILLONA

1977
Designer: Tobia Scarpa
Manufacturer: Flos
Reflector and base: die-cast aluminum
Diffuser: metalized glass
Stem: aluminum with an extruded-plastic accent
9.7″ W; 9.7″ D; 75.5″ H

16–18   ZAGAR

1978
Designer: S. Carpani
Manufacturer: Stilnovo
Reflector: lacquered die-cast aluminum
Structure: lacquered extruded aluminum
Base: lacquered metal
5½″ W; 2½″ D; 71″ H

16–19   JILL

1978
Designers: Perry A. King, Santiago Miranda, and Gianluigi
   Arnaldi
Manufacturer: Arteluce
Diffuser and base: colored cast glass
Diffuser cradle: enameled cast aluminum
Stem: enameled steel
11″ Diameter (base); 15″ W; 5.9″ D (reflector); 76″ H

16–20   FLOOR LAMP

1979
Designers: Torsten Thorup and Claus Bonderup
Manufacturer: Focus Form
Structure: enameled metal
17″ D; 54⅜″ H

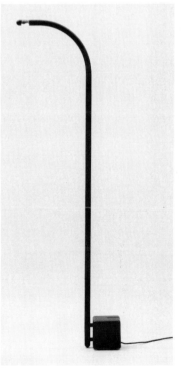

Focus Form   16–20

Luce Plan   16–21

16–21   D 5

1979
Designers: Paolo Rizzatto and Sandra Severi Sarfatti
Manufacturer: Luce Plan
Screen: lacquered aluminum
Reflector: bright-finished Renal
Stem: stove-enameled steel
Base: Serena stone
19¾" W; 74¾"–88½" H

16–22   POOL (620)

c. 1979
Designer: Ron Rezek
Manufacturer: Ron Rezek
Structure: metal
6" W; 26" D; 39" H

16–23   610

1980
Designer: Ron Rezek
Manufacturer: Ron Rezek
Reflector, stem, and base: sheet metal
Diffuser: perforated steel
15" W; 10" D; 44" or 72" H

16–24   600

c. 1981
Designer: Ron Rezek
Manufacturer: Ron Rezek
Structure: metal
24" Diameter (shade); 12" Diameter (base); 70" H

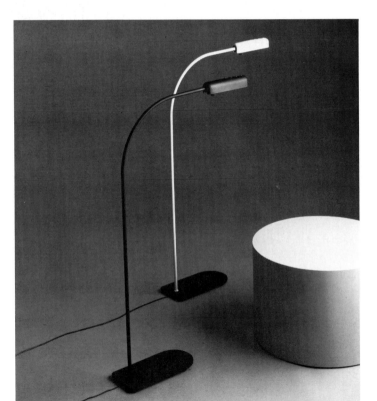

Ron Rezek   16–22

Ron Rezek   16—23

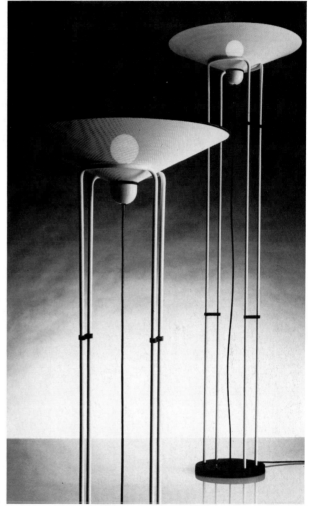

Ron Rezek   16—24

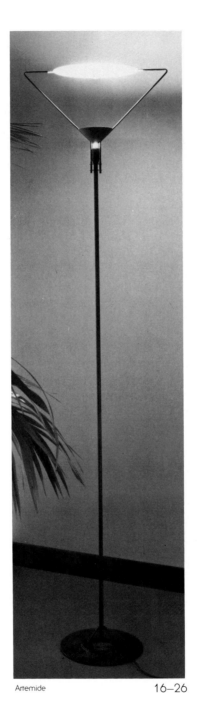

Koch + Lowy   16—27

Tecta Möbel   16—25

Artemide   16—26

16–25   L 30

1982
Designer: Stefan Wewerka
Manufacturer: Tecta Möbel
Structure: chrome-plated metal with a leather-covered support
22 ½" W; 78 ¾" H

16–26   POLIFEMO

1983
Designer: Carlo Forcolini
Manufacturer: Artemide
Reflector: glass
Stem and base: matte black metal
11 ¾" Diameter (base); 19 ¾" Diameter (reflector);
    84 ½" H

16–27   DELTA

1983
Designer: Piotr Sierakowski
Manufacturer: Koch + Lowy
Structure: Nextel suede
9" Diameter (base); 14" D; 44" H

16–28   ILIOS

1983
Designers: Ingo Maurer and Franz Ringelhan
Manufacturer: Ingo Maurer
Reflector: glass
Support and base: metal
7 ⅛" W (base); 7 ⅛" D (base); 74 ¾" H

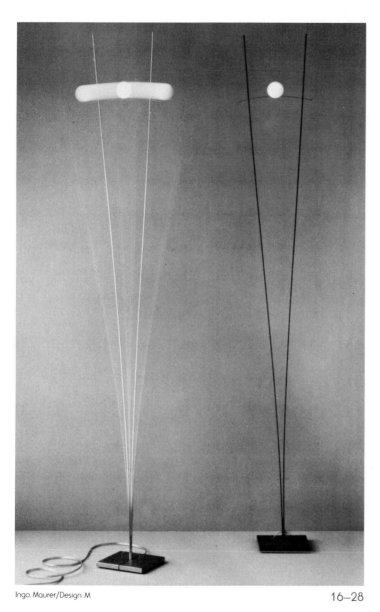

Ingo Maurer/Design M

16–28

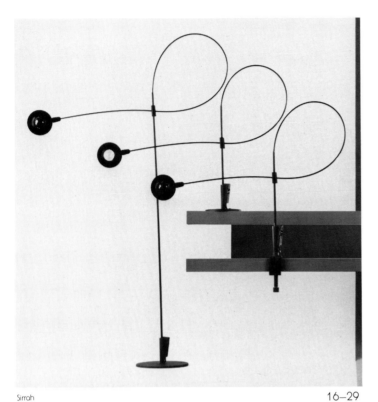

Sirrah

16–29

16–29 SIGLA

1985
Designer: René Kemna
Manufacturer: Sirrah
Structure: Fiberglas
Base: painted metal
9" Diameter; 4"–31 ½" Projection; 53"–59" H

16–30 FLAMINGO

1985
Designer: Fridolin Naef
Manufacturer: Luxo Italiana
Reflector and transformer box: plastic
Structure: steel
78¾" H

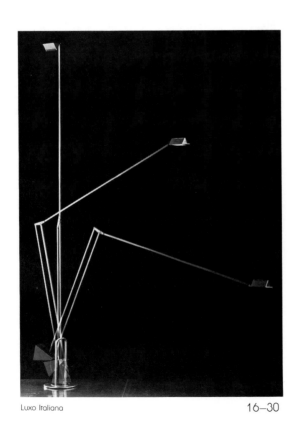

Luxo Italiana

16–30

17 STORAGE

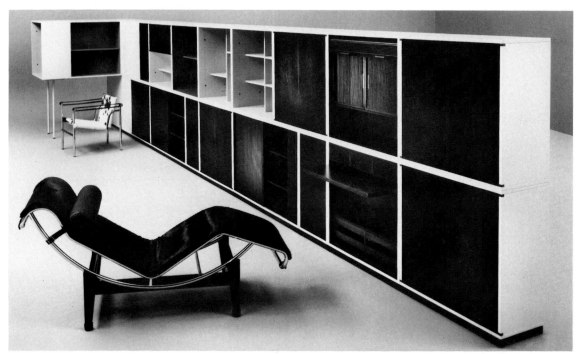

Cassina

17—1

Misura Emme

17—2

Angelo Mangiarotti

17-3

17-1   CASIERS STANDARD

1925
Designer: Le Corbusier
Manufacturer: Cassina
Structure: white-painted wood
15¾" or 31½" W; 11¾", 15¾", or 23½" D; 15¾",
    31½", or 63" H

17-2   ELEGIE

1949
Designer: Ignazio Gardella
Manufacturer: Misura Emme
Uprights: black fire-painted metal
Shelves and casings: semipolished lacquered wood
Doors and drawers: polished polyester-lacquered wood
Feet and knobs: brass
43" W; 12½" D; 86½" or 102¼" H

17-3   ADJUSTABLE BOOKSHELVES

1952
Designers: Angelo Mangiarotti and Bruno Morassutti
Manufacturer: Fratelli Frigerio
Support: black-lacquered steel tubes
Shelves: molded plywood
55" W; 17¾" D; Variable height

17-4   STEELFRAME GROUP (4012)

1954
Designer: George Nelson
Manufacturer: Herman Miller
Frame: steel; baked enamel finish
Top: plastic laminate
Drawers: lacquered wood
Pulls: polished chrome
33½" W; 17¼" D; 29⅜" H

Herman Miller, Inc.

17-4

Herman Miller, Inc.   17—5

Haller Systems   17—6

Vitsoe Kollektion   17–7

17–5   CSS

1959
Designer: George Nelson
Manufacturer: Herman Miller
Poles: aluminum
Cabinets, shelves, and drawers: wood
32" or 48" W; 14⅛" or 18½" D; 75¼" H

17–6   606

1960
Designer: Dieter Rams
Manufacturer: Vitsoe
Frame: E-profiles of anodized aluminum
Shelves and cabinets: maple, veneered beech, white wood,
   gray Formica, or heavy-duty metal
25¾" or 35½" W (cabinets); 15½" D; 62½" H

17–7   HALLER FURNITURE SYSTEM

1961
Designer: Fritz Haller
Manufacturer: Haller Systems
Frame: chrome-plated 19-mm steel tubes; chrome-plated
   25-mm steel ball joints
Shelves, panels, and doors: 1-mm sheet metal with a baked
   enamel finish
30" W; 14" or 20" D; 14" H (basic module)

17–8   40 SN

1966
Designers: Walter Muller and Peter Maly (1985)
Manufacturer: Interlubke
Structure: lacquered wood
22⅛" or 36¼" W; 15" or 24" D; 88½" or 95¾" H

Interlubke   17–8

423

Kartell   17–9

Habitat/Intrex   17–10

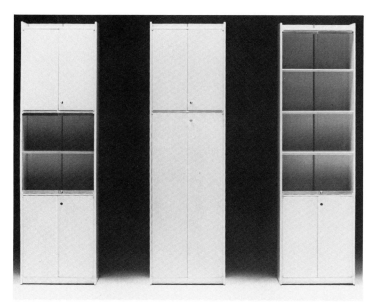

B & B Italia

17—11

17—9   MULTI-BOX SYSTEM

1967
Designer: Anna Castelli Ferrieri
Manufacturer: Kartell
Structure: ABS
15″ W; 15″ D; 9½″ H (Model 4970); 15″ W; 15″ D; 15⅛″
    H (Model 4982)

17—10   KATONAH

c. 1968
Designer: Paul Mayen
Manufacturer: Intrex
Structure: polyester epoxy or wood
37″ W; 20″ D; 80″ H

17—11   OLINTO 12

1970
Designer: Kazuhide Takahama
Manufacturer: B & B Italia
Structure: polyester-lacquered particle board; PVC edge
    bumpers
26½″ W; 13″ D; 91½″ H

17—12   LINEAR HML SYSTEM

1970
Designer: Rodolfo Bonetto
Manufacturer: Elco Bellato
Structure: polyurethane-lacquered wood or Tanganyika walnut
25″ or 37″ W; 18″ D; 31″, 56″, or 82″ H

Elco Bellato

17—12

Behr   17—13

Herman Miller, Inc.   17—14

Artemide

17–13 1600 PANEL

1971
Designer: Jürgen Lange
Manufacturer: Behr
Rails: anodized aluminum with plastic extrusion joint covers
　to hide wall fastening
Shelves: enameled wood
35½", 47¼", or 82¾" W; 12½", 19", or 25¼" H; 2" D
　(panel); 12½" D (shelf); 6¼" H (panel)

17–14 CO/STRUC (ACTION ENVIRONMENTS)

1971
Designer: Robert Propst
Manufacturer: Herman Miller
Structure: high-impact, injection-molded thermoplastic
22⁷⁄₁₆" W; ⅝" D (rail); 13⅛" or 17⁵⁄₁₆" D (shelf); 2" H
　(rail); 6" H (rail spacing)

17–15 DODONA 300

1971
Designer: Ernesto Gismondi
Manufacturer: Artemide
Structure: extruded ABS resin
27½" W; 11¾" D; 27½", 55⅛", or 82⅝" H

17–16 OIKOS

1973
Designer: Antonia Astori
Manufacturer: Driade
Structure: plastic laminate
Baskets and trays: nylon-coated metal wire
11¾", 17¾", 23¾", or 35½" W; 11¾", 17¾", or
　23¾" D; 16½", 29¼", 54¼", 79½", 92", 104¾", or
　117¼" H

Driade

17–16

427

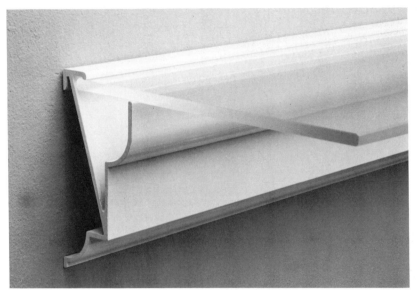

B.D. Ediciones   17—17

Interlubke   17—18

Interlubke   17—19

17—17 HIALINA

1973
Designers: Lluís Cloret and Oscar Tusquets
Manufacturer: B.D. Ediciones
Shelf: 5–6-mm-thick glass with polished edges
Support bracket: anodized aluminum
118" Max. W (support bracket); 6" or 9½" W (shelf)

17—18 GLIDING DOOR

1974
Designer: Team Form
Manufacturer: Interlubke
Structure: lacquered wood, cherrywood, or mahogany
Front: lacquered wood, wood veneer, fabric-covered, clear
    mirror or bronze mirror
61⅝" W; 28" D; 97⅞" H

17—19 MEDIUM PLUS

1974
Designer: Team Form
Manufacturer: Interlubke
Structure: lacquered wood, black-stained ash, natural ash,
    cherrywood, or mahogany
Top: granite or travertine
Hardware: chrome- or bronze-plated
18⅞" or 37¾" W; 18⅞" D; 14¼", 26¾" or 39⅜" H

17—20 ANTRO PLUS

1975
Designer: Team Form
Manufacturer: Interlubke
Structure: lacquered wood or cherrywood
Finger grips: satin chrome or cherrywood
12⅝", 25¼", or 33" W; 7½", 15¾", or 19" D; 19¾" or
    35½" H

Interlubke   17—20

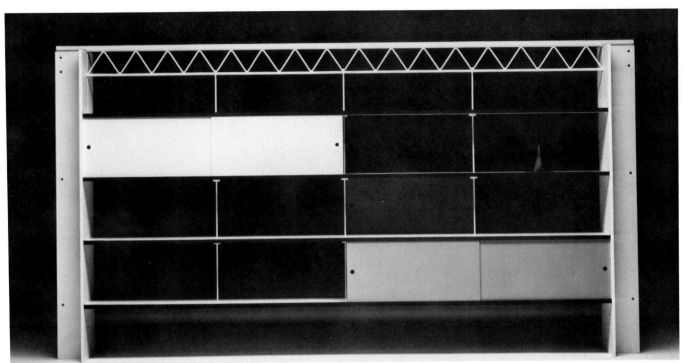

Acerbis International

17—21

Interlubke

17—22

Driade   17–23

17–21 BROOKLYN

1976
Designers: Lodovico Acerbis and Giotto Stoppino
Manufacturer: Acerbis International
Post structure: bilaminate or natural ashwood
Girders: lacquered steel
Doors: laminated or natural ashwood
85", 119¼", or 153½" W; 15" D; 82" H

17–22 STUDIMO PLUS

1977
Designer: Team Form
Manufacturer: Interlubke
Structure: lacquered wood, black-stained ash, natural ash,
    oak, cherrywood, or mahogany
Hardware: satin chrome or bronze
14½", 23⅛", or 36¾" W; 9½", 14⅛", or 19¼" D;
    72⅛" H

17–23 BRIC

1978
Designers: Enzo Mari and Antonia Astori
Manufacturer: Driade
Drawers and cabinets: white plastic laminate
Shelves: marble or birchwood
15¾" or 31½" W; 12", 15¾", or 24" D; 16", 31¼", or
    63½" H

17–24 HILTON

1978
Designers: Lodovico Acerbis and Giotto Stoppino
Manufacturer: Acerbis International
Cabinets: high-density particle board with a polyurethane lac-
    quer finish or walnut veneer
Doors, tops, and bases: injection-molded plastic frames with
    a polyurethane lacquer finish
Top and door/drawer faces: clear glass, lacquered opaque
    glass, or walnut veneer
Shelves: clear glass or fabric-covered particle board
35.5" W; 16.8" D; 18.4" H

Acerbis International   17–24

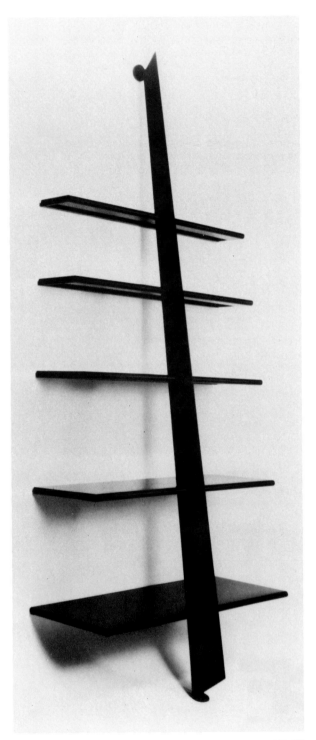

ICF, Inc.

17–25

Pastoe

17–26

B.D. Ediciones

17–27

17–25 MAC GEE (LEANING)

1978
Designer: Philippe Starck
Manufacturer: Baleri Italia
Structure: steel in a silver or black baked epoxy finish
39 ½" W; 17" D; 92 ⅛" H

17–26 AMSTERDAMMER

1979
Designer: Aldo van den Nieuwelaar
Manufacturer: Pastoe
Structure and shelves: medium-density fiberboard
Tambour doors: vacuum-formed polystyrene
14" or 29" W; 14" or 20" D; 53", 67", 87", or 94" H

17–27 HYPÓSTILA

1979
Designers: Lluís Clotet and Oscar Tusquets
Manufacturer: B.D. Ediciones
Support and shelves: anodized aluminum
40 ⅛"–177 ½" W; 6 ⅛"–9 ¾" D (shelf); 78 ¾"–157 ½" H

17–28 20" MODULE SYSTEM

1980
Designer: Pirkko Stenros
Manufacturer: Muura Me Oy
Structure: lacquered wood or natural birch
20 ½" W; 20 ½" D; 21 ½", 43 ¼", or 65" H

Muura Me Oy

17–28

Jerryll Habegger 17–29

B & B Italia 17–30

Memphis Milano   17–31

Angelo Mangiarotti   17–32

17–29 ALVA

c. 1980
Designers: Afra Scarpa and Tobia Scarpa
Manufacturer: Goppion
Top: cleft slate or clear glass with polished edges
Back, sides, and shelves: clear glass with polished edges
Doors: clear tempered glass with polished edges
Base: cleft slate
Hardware: steel with black chrome finish
23⅝" W; 13⅜" or 19¾" D; 73⅝" H

17–30 QUADRANTE

1981
Designers: Antonio Citterio and Paolo Nava
Manufacturer: Xilitalia (B & B Italia)
Case: glossy, polyester-varnished wood
Back of cabinet, sliding doors, and shelves: transparent glass
Frame of sliding doors and legs: shiny, light-colored, anodized
    aluminum finish
106⁵⁄₁₆" W; 18½" D; 54⅛" H

17–31   CARLTON

1981
Designer: Ettore Sottsass
Manufacturer: Abet Laminati (Memphis)
Structure: wood covered with colored plastic laminate
74¾" W; 15¾" D; 77" H

17–32 ESTRUAL

1981
Designer: Angelo Mangiarotti
Manufacturer: Skipper
Structure: extruded anodized aluminum
12", 23½", or 35½" W (modules); 13¾" D; 80¾" or
    104¾" H

Fiam   17—33

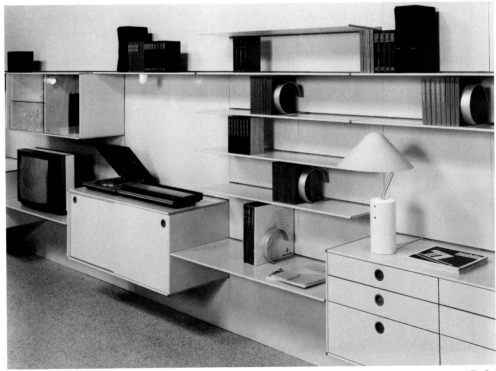

Expocompetence   17—34

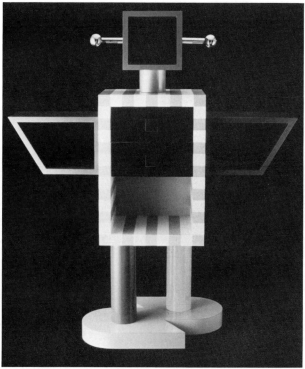

Memphis Milano   17–35

17–33   ERRE

1982
Designer: Studio L/V
Manufacturer: Fiam
Top and base: painted wood
Structure and shelves: glass
Support: steel with a black chrome finish
46½" W; 15¾" D; 59" H

17–34   ACCENTA

c. 1982
Designer: Jørgen Michaelsen
Manufacturer: Expocompetence
Support post: extruded aluminum
Mounting plates: steel
Panels: high-density particle board in a Nextel finish
Shelves and cabinets: high-density particle board covered in
    aluminum sheet
23⅝" W; 5⅛" D (panel); 11", 15", or 19" D (shelf); 30¾"–
    94½" H

17–35   GINZA

1982
Designer: Masanori Umeda
Manufacturer: Abet Laminati (Memphis)
Structure: wood covered with colored plastic laminate; chrome-
    plated metal
21¾" W; 16½" D; 69" H

17–36   WOGG I

1983
Designer: Gerd Lange
Manufacturer: Wogg
Structure: plastic laminate
Slotted fasteners: plastic
23½" W (module); 11¾" D; 26¾" H (module)

Cumberland Furniture   17–36

B.D. Ediciones

17—37

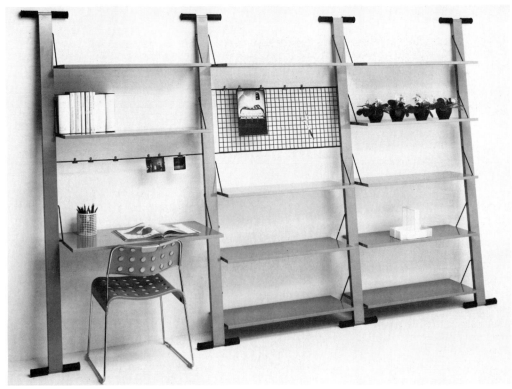

Bieffeplast S.p.A./Gullans International, Inc.

17—38

Saporiti Italia   17–39

ICF, Inc.   17–40

17–37   ROBERTO

1983
Designer: Pepe Cortés
Manufacturer: B.D. Ediciones
Top: 10-mm-thick lacquered polished plate glass
Support and drawers: lacquered wood
Handles: anodized aluminum
100⅜″ W; 40⅛″ D; 25½″ H

17–38   GRAFFITI

c. 1983
Designer: Rodney Kinsman
Manufacturer: Bieffeplast
Structure: epoxy-painted steel
36¼″ or 42½″ W; 12½″, 15¾″, or 19½″ D; 78¾″, 86½″, or 94½″ H

17–39   SILOS

1984
Designer: Giovanni Offredi
Manufacturer: Saporiti Italia
Top: marble
Cylinders: wood veneer
54¼″ W; 19″ D; 55½″ H; 50¼″ H (counter top)

17–40   A-1

1985
Designer: Luigi Massoni
Manufacturer: Boffi
Structure: plastic laminate or polyester epoxy
Base plate and finger recesses: aluminum
6″, 18″, 24″, 36″, or 48″ W; 18″ or 24″ D; 1′–5′ H

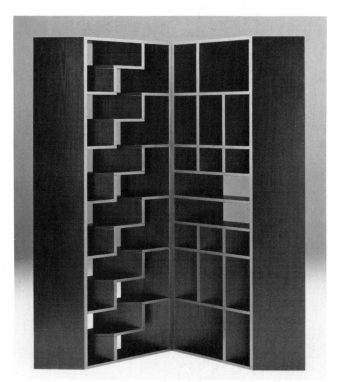

Rosenthal   17–41a

Rosenthal   17–41b

Rosenthal   17–42

17–41   CORNER

1985
Designer: Marcello Morandini
Manufacturer: Rosenthal
Structure: black-stained ash or white- or silver-lacquered finish
22″ W; 31″ or 42″ D; 85¾″ H

17–42   LIFE SERVICE

1985
Designer: Jochen Flacke
Manufacturer: Rosenthal
Structure: medium-strength board finished in a high-gloss
        lacquer
Top: synthetic-resin-bonded laminate or polished stainless steel
82″ W; 20½″ D; 39″ H

17–43   QUINTA

1985
Designer: Franco Bazzani
Manufacturer: Alberto Bazzani
Frame: black-semishine-lacquered wood
Doors and top: white-lacquered wood
Shelves: crystal glass
77⅛″ W; 22¾″ D; 58¼″ H

Alberto Bazzani   17–43

BIBLIOGRAPHY

Alison, Filippo. *Charles Rennie Mackintosh as a Designer of Chairs.* Milan: Casabella, 1973.

Ambasz, Emilio. *Italy: The New Domestic Landscape.* New York: Museum of Modern Art, 1972.

Aver, Ernst Josef. *Furniture Design.* Stuttgart: Design Center of Stuttgart, 1985.

Baroni, Daniele. *The Furniture of Gerrit Thomas Rietveld.* Woodbury: Barron's, 1978.

Blaser, Werner. *Mies van der Rohe Furniture and Interiors.* Woodbury: Barron's, 1980.

Burkhardt, François, and Inez Franksen. *Design: Dieter Rams.* West Berlin: Gerhardt Verlag, 1981.

Busch, Akiko. *Product Design.* New York: PBC International, 1984.

Clark, Robert Judson. *Design in America: The Cranbrook Vision, 1925–1950.* New York: Harry N. Abrams Inc., 1983.

De Fusco, Renato. *Le Corbusier Designer—The Furniture of 1929.* Milan: Casabella, 1976.

Dorfles, Gillo. *Furniture Design from Italy.* Rome: Julia, 1980.

Emery, Marc. *Furniture by Architects.* New York: Harry N. Abrams Inc., 1983.

Ferrari, Paolo. *Achille Castiglioni.* Milan: Electa International, 1985.

Gandy, Charles D. *Contemporary Classics.* New York: McGraw Hill Book Company, 1981.

Garner, Philippe. *Twentieth-Century Furniture.* New York: Van Nostrand Reinhold, 1980.

Glaeser, Ludwig. *Ludwig Mies van der Rohe: Furniture and Furniture Drawings.* New York: Museum of Modern Art, 1977.

Gramigna, Guiliana. *1950/1980 Repertory.* Milan: Arnoldo Mondadori Editore, 1985.

Greenberg, Cara. *Mid-Century Modern.* New York: Harmony Books, 1984.

Hiesinger, Kathryn B. *Design Since 1945.* Philadelphia: Philadelphia Museum of Art, 1983.

Hogben, Carol. *Modern Chairs.* London: Lund Humphries Publishers, 1970.

Johnson, J. Stewart. *Eileen Gray, Designer.* New York: Museum of Modern Art, 1979.

Kremerskothen, Josef. *Moderne Klassiker: Mobel die Geschichte Machen.* Hamburg: Gruner + Jahr AG, 1983.

Larrabee, Eric and Massimo Vignelli. *Knoll Design.* New York: Harry N. Abrams Inc., 1981.

McFadden, David Revere. *Scandinavian Modern Design 1880–1980.* New York: Harry N. Abrams Inc., 1982.

Mastropietro, Mario. *An Industry for Design.* Milan: Edizioni Lybra Immagine, 1986.

Meadmore, Clement. *The Modern Chair.* New York: Van Nostrand Reinhold, 1975.

Nielsen, Johan Moller. *Wegner, Sitting Pretty.* Copenhagen: Gyldendal, 1965.

Pallasmaa, Juhani. *Alvar Aalto Furniture.* Helsinki: Museum of Finnish Architecture, 1984.

Sembach, Klaus-Juergen. *Contemporary Furniture.* New York: Architectural Book Publishing Co., 1982.

Stern, Robert A.M. *The International Design Yearbook.* New York: Abbeville Press, 1986.

Wichmann, Hans. *Industrial Design Unikate Serienerzeugnisse.* Munich: Prestel-Verlag, 1985.

Wilk, Christopher. *Marcel Breuer Furniture and Interiors.* New York: Museum of Modern Art, 1981.

LIST OF SUPPLIERS

ABET LAMINATI
Viale dell Industria 21
I-12042 Bra, Cueno
Italy
(Available through Artemide)

ACERBIS INTERNATIONAL
via Brusaporto 31
I-24068 Seriate, Bergamo
Italy
(Available through Atelier
    International)

ADD INTERIOR SYSTEMS
515 Crocker Street
Los Angeles, CA 90013

ADELTA OY
Tunturikatu 9 A 1
SF-00100 Helsinki
Finland
(Available through ICF, Inc.)

AIRBORNE
140 Rue-Paul-Doumer
B.P. 7
33702 Merignac Cedex
France

AIRON
via Don Sturzo 10
20050 Triuggio
Milano
Italy

ALBERTO BAZZANI
via Pusterla 37
I-20030 Bovisio, Milano
Italy

ALFRED KILL GmbH
Schorndorferstrasse 33
D-7012 Fellbach
West Germany
(Available through Davis Furniture
    Industries)

ALIAS
via Respighi 2
I-20122 Milano
Italy
(Available through ICF, Inc.)

ALTAFORM
Gladsaxevej 311
DK-2860 Soborg
Denmark
(Available through DSI)

AMERICAN SEATING
901 Broadway N.W.
Grand Rapids, MI 49504

ARCONAS CORPORATION
580 Orwell Street
Mississauga, Ontario
Canada L5A 3V7

AREACON
7973 Beverly Boulevard
Los Angeles, CA 90048

ARFLEX S.p.A.
via Monte Rosa 27
I-20051 Limbiate, Milano
Italy
(Available through Beylerian Ltd.)

ARKITEKTURA
1240 West Long Lake Road
Bloomfield Hills, MI 48013

ARTEK OY AB
Keskuskatu 3
SF-00100 Helsinki
Finland
(Available through ICF, Inc.)

ARTELUCE
via Moretto 58
I-25121 Brescia
Italy
(Available through Atelier
    International)

ARTEMIDE
IDCNY
528 Center One
30-30 Thomson Avenue
Long Island City, NY 11101

ARTEMIDE S.p.A.
via Brughiera
I-20010 Pregnana Milanese, Milano
Italy
(Available through Artemide)

ARTIFORT
St. Annalaan 23
6214 AA Maastricht
Holland
(Available through Castelli Furniture)

ASKO OY
PL/Box 45
SF-15101 Lahti 10
Finland
(Available through Stendig
    International)

ATELIER INTERNATIONAL
IDCNY
30-20 Thomson Avenue
Long Island City, NY 11101

ATELJE LYKTAN AB
S-296-00 Aahus
Sweden

AUGUST
Box 43
Centerville, OH 45459

AVARTE OY
Kalevankatu 16
SF-00100 Helsinki
Finland
(Available through Beylerian Ltd.)

AXIOM DESIGNS
110 Greene Street
New York, NY 10012

B & B AMERICA
745 Fifth Avenue
4th floor
New York, NY 10022

B & B ITALIA S.p.A.
Strada Provinciale
I-22060 Novedrate, Como
Italy
(Available through B & B America)

B.B.B. OVER
Viale Brianza, 42
I-20036 Meda, Milano
Italy
(Available through Beylerian Ltd.)

B.D. EDICIONES DE DISENO
Carrer Mallorca, 291
08037 Barcelona
Spain

BALERI ITALIA
via Trento 10
24100 Curno, Bergamo
Italy
(Available through ICF, Inc.)

BEHR PRODUKTION
Postfach 1254
D-7317 Wendlingen/Neckar
West Germany

BELLAGAMBA
via Visconti di Modrone 27
20122 Milano
Italy
(Available through Berichi
    International)

BERICHI INTERNATIONAL
485 Madison Avenue
New York, NY 10022

BEYLERIAN LTD.
305 East 63rd Street
New York, NY 10021

BIEFFEPLAST
via Marconi
I-35030 Caselle di Selvazzano
Italy
(Available through Gullans
    International)

BO-EX
Frederikssundsvej 157
2700 Bronshoj
Denmark

BOFFI
via Oberdan, 70
20030 Lentate sul Seveso, Milano
Italy
(Available through ICF, Inc.)

BONACINA
via Madonnina, 15
I-22040 Lurago D'Erba, Como
Italy
(Available through Beylerian Ltd.)

BOTIUM ApS
Bonderup
DK-4700 Naestved
Denmark
(Available through Rudd
   International)

BOYD LIGHTING
56 12th Street
San Francisco, CA 94103-1293

BRAYTON INTERNATIONAL
P.O. Box 7288
High Point, NC 27264

BRICKEL ASSOCIATES
515 Madison Avenue
New York, NY 10022

BROWN JORDAN
9860 Gidley Street
P.O. Box 5688
El Monte, CA 91734

BRUNATI
Strada Statale 342
I-22040 Alzate Brianza
Italy
(Available through Axiom Designs)

CADSANA, CADWALLADER AND
   SANGIORGIO ASSOCIATES
East Middle Patent Road
Greenwich, CT 06831

CAMPANIELLO IMPORTS
225 East 57th Street
New York, NY 10022

CARL HANSEN
Kochsgade 97/Boks 225
DK-5100 Odense C
Denmark

CARLO POGGI
via Campania 5
27100 Pavia
Italy

CASAS
Milagro 40
08028 Barcelona
Spain
(Available through ICF, Inc.)

CASSINA S.p.A.
Casella Postale 102
via Busnelli 1
I-20036 Meda, Milano
Italy
(Available through Atelier
   International)

CASTELIJN COLLECTION
Vrouwenweg 1C
3864 DX Nijkerkerveen
Netherlands

CASTELLI FURNITURE
116 Wilbur Place
Bohemia, NY 11716

CASTELLI S.A.S.
via Torreggiani 1
I-40128 Bologna
Italy
(Available through Castelli Furniture)

CEDRIC HARTMAN INC.
1116-18 Jackson
Box 3842
Omaha, NE 68102

CHRISTIAN HOLZAPFEL
Postfach 1280
7240 Horb
West Germany

CI DESIGNS
574 Boston Avenue
P.O. Box 191
Medford, MA 02155

CIL
via Prospero Santacroce, 128
I-00167 Roma
Italy

COLLEZIONE SIMON LTD.
22 Madison Avenue
Paramus, NJ 07652

COMFORT
via Seveso 19
20036 Meda, Milano
Italy
(Available through Stendig
   International)

COMFORTO
P.O. Box 917
Lincolnton, NC 28092

CUMBERLAND FURNITURE
36-35 Thirty-Sixth Street
Long Island City, NY 11106

DAVIS FURNITURE INDUSTRIES
602 West Linden Avenue
P.O. Box 2065
High Point, NC 27261

DE SEDE
CH-5313 Klingnau
Switzerland
(Available through Stendig
   International)

DESIGN FORUM
Praestemarksvej 8
Box 264
DK-4000 Roskilde
Denmark
(Available through Expocompetence)

DOMUS ITALIA
149 Wooster Street
New York, NY 10012

DREVOUNIA
(Available through Stendig
   International)

DRIADE S.p.A.
via Padana Inferiore 12/A
I-29012 Fossadello di Caorso,
   Piacenza
Italy
(Available through Interna Designs)

DSI
150 East 58th Street
New York, NY 10155

DUNBAR FURNITURE CORPORATION
601 South Fulton Street
Berne, IN 46711

DUX INTERNATIONAL
S-23100 Trelleborg
Sweden
(Available through Dux International
   in America)

DUX INTERNATIONAL
305 East 63rd Street
New York, NY 10021

E. KOLD CHRISTENSEN APS
Rygards Alle 131
DK-2900 Hellerup
Denmark
(Available through Fritz Hansen)

ECART INTERNATIONAL
111 Rue Saint-Antoine
F-75004 Paris
France

ECONOMIC-KALUSTE OY
Kiviaidankatu 11
00210 Helsinki
Finland

EDISON PRICE, INC.
409 East 60 Street
New York, NY 10022

ELAM
via Molino 27
I-20036 Meda, Milano
Italy

ELCO BELLATO
via Treviso, 87
I-30037 Scorze, Venezia
Italy
(Available through Beylerian Ltd.)

ELEUSI
via Giuseppe Verdi 7
I-22050 Lomagna, Como
Italy
(Available through IPI Lighting)

EMIL GUHL
Marktplatz 11
St. Gallen
Switzerland
(Available through Stendig
. International)

ERIK JØRGENSEN MØBELFABRIK AS
Industrivaenger 1
DK-5700 Svendborg
Denmark
(Available through Rudd
International)

EXPOCOMPETENCE
1150 Feehanville Drive
Mt. Pleasant, IL 60056

FIAM
via Ancona 1
I-61010 Tavullia, Pesaro
Italy
(Available through Pace Collection)

FIXTURES FURNITURE
1642 Crystal P.O. Box 6346
Kansas City, MO 64126

FLOS
Via Moretto 58
I-25121 Brescia
Italy
(Available through Atelier
International)

FOCUS FORM
Kongevejen 53
DK-2840 Holte
Denmark

FONTANA ARTE
via Alzaia Trieste 49
I-20094 Corsico, Milano
Italy
(Available through Interna Designs)

FRANZ WITTMANN KG
A-3492 Etsdorf am Kamp
Austria
(Available through ICF, Inc.)

FRATELLI FRIGERIO
via Degli Arconi
Cantu, Milano
Italy

FREDERICIA STOLEFABRIK
Treldevej 183
DK-7000 Fredericia
Denmark
(Available through CI Designs)

FRITZ HANSEN EFT. A/S
DK-3450 Allerod
Denmark
(Available through Rudd
International)

FRZ METALLWARENFABRIK
Gartenstrasse 22
D-6921 Zuzenhausen
West Germany
(Available through Polder Inc.)

FURNITURE OF THE TWENTIETH
CENTURY
227 West 17th Street
New York, NY 10011

GEBRÜDER THONET AG
Postfach 1520
D-3558 Frankenberg
West Germany
(Available through ICF, Inc.; Beylerian
Ltd.)

GEMLA MÖBLER
Box 1000
S-340-21 Dio
Sweden

GETAMA
DK-9631 Gedsted
Denmark

GF FURNITURE SYSTEMS
418 East Dennick
Youngstown, OH 44501

GHIANDA
(Available through Sunar Hauserman,
Inc.)

GIOVANNETTI
Casella Postale 1
I-51032 Bottegone, Pistoia
Italy

GLOBAL FURNITURE
525 Broadway
New York, NY 10012

GOPPION
via Tortona, 2
20144 Milano
Italy
(Available through Stendig
International)

GORDON INTERNATIONAL
200 Lexington Avenue
New York, NY 10016

GOSSAMER DESIGNS IN LIGHTING
593 Ottowa Avenue
Holland, MI 49423

GRUPPO INDUSTRIALE BUSNELLI
via Kennedy 34
I-20020 Misinto, Milano
Italy

GUFRAM
via I Maggio 20
I-10070 Grosso, Torino
Italy
(Available through Stendig
International)

GULLANS INTERNATIONAL
IDCNY
407 Center One
30-30 Thomson Avenue
Long Island City, NY 11101

GUZZINI
SS 77 Km 102
P.O. Box 39-59
62019 Recanati
Italy

HABITAT
341 East 62nd Street
New York, NY 10021

HÅG
P.O. Box 5055 Majorstua
N-0301 Oslo 3
Norway

HALLER SYSTEMS
17741 Cowan Avenue
Irvine, CA 92714

HASTINGS TILE & IL BAGNO
COLLECTION
201 East 57th Street
New York, NY 10022

HEINZ & CO.
Box 663
Oak Park, IL 60303

HEINZ WITTHOEFT
Traubenstrasse 51
D-7000 Stuttgart 1
West Germany

HERMAN MILLER
8500 Byron Road
Zeeland, MI 49464

HERON PARIGI
via Della Tintoria 51
P.O. Box 13
50032 Borgo San Lorenzo, Firenze
Italy
(Available through Beylerian Ltd.)

HG-MOBLER
Ostre Faelledvej
DK-9400 Norresunbdy
Denmark
(Available through Rudd
International)

ICF, INC.
305 East 63rd Street
New York, NY 10021

IMAGES OF AMERICA
829 Blair Street
Thomasville, NC 27361-1127

INGO MAURER
Postfach 400449
Kaiserstrasse 47
8 Munich 40
West Germany

INTERLUBKE
Postfach 1660
D-4840 Rheda-Wiedenbrueck
West Germany
(Available through ICF, Inc.)

INTERNA DESIGNS
Merchandise Mart 6-168
Chicago, IL 60654

INTREX
341 East 62nd Street
New York, NY 10021

IPI LIGHTING
IDCNY Center Two
30-20 Thomson Avenue
Long Island City, New York 11101

IVAN SCHLECHTER
Sogardsvej 30, Firhoj
DK-3250 Gilleleje
Denmark

JACK LENOR LARSEN
41 East 11th Street
New York, NY 10003-4685

JG FURNITURE SYSTEMS
Quakertown, PA 18951

JOHANNES HANSENS MØBELSNEDKERI
A/S
Gladsaxevej 311
DK-2860 Soeborg
Denmark

JOHN STUART INTERNATIONAL
D + D Building
979 Third Avenue
New York, NY 10022

KAFRA
via Cavour 78
I-22053 Lecco
Italy

KARTELL
via Delle Industrie 1
I-20082 Noviglio, Milano
Italy
(Available through Kartell USA)

KARTELL USA
P.O. Box 1000
Liberty Highway
Easley, SC 29641

KEBO HEALTH CARE SYSTEMS
1809 Elmdale Avenue
Glenview, IL 60025

KIMBALL/ARTEC
1549 Royal Street
Jasper, IN 47546

KINETICS
110 Carrier Drive
Rexdale, Ontario M9W5R1
Canada

KNOLL INTERNATIONAL, INC.
The Knoll Building
655 Madison Avenue
New York, NY 10021

KOCH + LOWY
21-24 39th Avenue
Long Island City, NY 11101-3687

KRUEGER
1330 Bellevue Street
P.O. Box 8100
Green Bay, WI 54308-8100

KUSCH + CO SITZMÖBELWERKE KG
Postfach 1026
D-5789 Hallenberg/Sauerland
West Germany
(Available through Kusch USA, Inc.)

KUSCH USA, INC.
24 Fort Salonga Road
Centerport, NY 11721

LAMMHULTS MÖBEL AB
Vaxjovagen Box 26
S-360 30 Lammhult
Sweden
(Available through Stendig
International)

LEDU
25 Lindeman Drive P.O. Box 358
Trumbull, CT 06611

LEHIGH LEOPOLD
2825 Mt. Pleasant Street
Burlington, IA 52601

LIGHTING ASSOCIATES
305 East 63rd Street
New York, NY 10021

LOEWENSTEIN
1801 N. Andrews Ave. Extension
P.O. Box 10369
Pompano Beach, FL 33061-6369

LOUIS POULSEN
Nylavn 11
DK-1004 Copenhagen
Denmark
(Available through Expocompetence;
Lighting Associates)

LUCE PLAN
via Bellinzona 48
I-20155 Milano
Italy
(Available through Artemide)

LUCI
via Pellizza de Volpedo 50
I-20092 Cinisello, Milano
Italy
(Available through IPI Lighting)

LUXO ITALIANA S.p.A.
via Rocca 3
24030 Presezzo, Bergamo
Italy
(Available through Luxo Lamp
Corporation)

LUXO LAMP CORPORATION
Monument Park
P.O. Box 951
Port Chester, NY 10573

LYFA-FOG & MORUP AS
Malov Byvej 229-233
DK-2760 Malov
Denmark

MAGNUS OLESEN
Toenderingvej 10 (Durup)
DK-7870 Roslev
Denmark
(Available through Rudd
International)

MARCATRE
via Sant Andrea 3
I-20020 Misinto, Milano
Italy
(Available through Atelier
International)

MARTINELLI-LUCE
via T. Bandettini 145
I-55100 Lucca
Italy

MEIDLINGER POLLACK
Hauptstrasse 56-58
A-Wien
Austria

451

METROPOLITAN FURNITURE
950 Linden Avenue
South San Francisco, CA 94080

MISURA EMME
via 4 Novembre 72
22066 Mariano Comense
Italy

MODERN MODE
P.O. Box 6667
Oakland, CA 94603

MONEL CONTRACT FURNITURE
P.O. Box 291
Oakland Gardens, NY 11364

MONTINA
Fraz. Dolegnano
33048 San Giovanni al Natisone,
    Udine
Italy
(Available through Strendig
    International)

MUNCH MOBLER
DK-4200 Slagelse
Denmark

MUURA ME OY
Keskikankaantie 5
SF-15870 Salpakangas
Finland

NEMO
17 Rue Froment
75011 Paris
France

NESSEN LAMPS
D & D Building, Space 666
979 Third Avenue
New York, NY 10022

NIENKÄMPER
300 King Street East
Toronto, Ontario
Canada M5A 1K4

NORDISK ANDELS
Jernbanegade 4
DK-1608 Copenhagen V
Denmark

NORDISKA KOMPANIET AB
Hamngatan 5
S-Stockholm
Sweden

O-LUCE
via Conservatorio 22
I-20122 Milano
Italy
(Available through AreaCon)

OLIVETTI S.p.A.
via Clerici 4-6
I-20121 Milano
Italy

P.P. MØBLER
Tofrevej 30
DK-3450 Allerod
Denmark

PACE COLLECTION
11-11 34th Avenue
Long Island City, NY 11106

PAF
via Edison 118
20019 Settimo Milanese (MI)
Italy
(Available through Koch + Lowy)

PALLUCCO SRL
via Salaria 1265
I-00138 Rome
Italy

PASTOE
Rotsoord 3, Postbus 2152
3500 GD Utrecht
Holland
(Available through Global Furniture)

PATIO SHOP
P.O. Box 31118
San Francisco, CA 94131

PIERANTONIO BONACINA
via S. Andrea, 34
22040 Lurago d'Erba, Como
Italy

POLDER INC.
One Bridge Street
Irvington, NY 10533

POLTRONA FRAU
SS 77 KM 74.5
I-62029 Tolentino, Macerata
Italy
(Available through Interna Designs)

POLTRONOVA
via Provinciale Pratese 23
I-51037 Montale, Pistoia
Italy
(Available through Poltronova
    International)

POLTRONOVA INTERNATIONAL
IDCNY Center Two
30-20 Thomson Avenue, Suite 102
Long Island City, New York 11101

RACE FURNITURE LTD.
New Road
Sheerness
Kent ME12 1AX
England

RAMBUSCH
40 West 13th Street
New York, NY 10011

RIMADESIO
via Tagliabue 91
20033 Desio, Milano
Italy

RON REZEK
5522 Venice Boulevard
Los Angeles, CA 90019
(Available through Artemide)

ROSENTHAL AG
Postfach 104
D-8672 Selb
West Germany
(Available through Rosenthal USA
    Ltd.)

ROSENTHAL USA LTD.
66-26 Metropolitan Avenue
Middle Village, NY 11379

RUD. RASMUSSENS SNEDKERIER APS
Noerrebrogade 45
DK-2200 Copenhagen N
Denmark

RUDD INTERNATIONAL
1025 Thomas Jefferson St., NW
Washington, D.C. 20007

S. HILLE AND CO. LTD.
41 Albemarle Street
London W1
England
(Available through John Stuart
    International)

SAPORITI ITALIA
via Gallarate, 23
I-21010 Besnate, Varese
Italy
(Available through Campaniello
    Imports)

SCANDINAVIAN OFFICE
    ORGANIZATION
Noeglegardsvej 12
DK-3540 Lynge
Denmark

SCOPE FURNITURE
407 West 13th Street
New York, NY 10014

SEM LUCI
via d. Scarlatti, 13
20090 Trezzano S/N (MI)
Italy

SIMON INTERNATIONAL
Superstrada KM 271-500
I-61030 Calcinelli di Saltara, Pesaro
Italy
(Available through Collezione Simon
    Ltd.)

SIRRAH
via Molino Rosso, 8
40026 Imola, Bologna
Italy
(Available through IPI Lighting)

SKANDI-FORM
Box 50
S-28013 Vinsloev
Sweden
(Available through Kebo Health Care
    Systems)

SKIPPER
via S. Spirito 14
I-20121 Milano
Italy

SOLAR BELYSNING
Industrivej Vest
DK-6600 Vejen
Denmark

STEELCASE
901 44th SE
Grand Rapids, MI 49508

STENDIG INTERNATIONAL
410 East 62nd Street
New York, NY 10021

STILNOVO
via F. Ferruccio 8
I-20145 Milano
Italy
(Available through Stilnovo America)

STILNOVO AMERICA
104 Greene Street
New York, NY 10012

STRÄSSLE COLLECTION
CH-9533 Kirchberg SG
Switzerland
(Available through Stendig
    International)

STUTTGARTER AKADEMIE-WERKSTÄTTEN
am Weissenhof 1
D-7000 Stuttgart 1
West Germany

SUNAR HAUSERMAN, INC.
8801 E. Pleasant Valley Road
Independence, OH 44131

SWISS DESIGN
(Available through Stendig
    International)

TECHNOLUMEN
Neuenstrasse 1-5
Postfach 104847
D-2800 Bremen 1
West Germany
(Available through Lighting
    Associates)

TECNO S.p.A.
via Bigli 22
I-20121 Milano
Italy

TECTA MÖBEL
D-3471 Lauenfoerde
West Germany
(Available through Global Furniture)

TENDO MOKKO
Hamamatsu-Cho 1-2-19, Minato-Ku
Tokyo 105
Japan

TEO JAKOB
Gerechtigkeitsgasse 23
3011 Bern
Switzerland
(Available through Stendig
    International)

THONET INDUSTRIES
491 East Princess Street
P.O. Box 1587
York, PA 17405

TISETTANTA
via Garibaldi 129
I-20034 Giussano, Milano
Italy

TORBEN ORSKOV & CO
Snaregade 4
DK-Copenhagen
Denmark

TULLI ZUCCARI
(Available through Hastings Tile)

UNIFOR
via Isonzo
I-22078 Turate, Como
Italy
(Available through Unifor Inc.)

UNIFOR INC.
2256 Northlake Parkway
Suite 305
Atlanta, GA 30084

VECTA
1800 South Great Southwest Parkway
Grand Prairie, TX 75051

VITSOE
Kaiserhofstrasse 10
D-6000 Frankfurt am Main
West Germany

VUOKKO
Elimaankatu 14-16
SF-00510 Helsinki
Finland

WALTER KNOLL
Postfach 1229
Bahnhofstrasse 25
7033 Herrenberg
West Germany

WILHELM SCHAUMAN
P.O. Box 240
00121 Helsinki
Finland

WINDMILL FURNITURE
Turnham Green Terrace Mews
Chiswick W4 1QU London
England
(Available through Furniture of the
    Twentieth Century)

WOGG AG MOBELIDEEN
Im Hos 10
CH-5405 Baden-Dattwil
Switzerland

ZANOTTA S.p.A.
via Vittorio Veneto 57
I-20054 Nova Milanese, Milano
Italy
(Available through ICF, Inc.; Interna
    Designs; AreaCon)

ZOGRAPHOS DESIGNS LTD.
150 East 58th Street
New York, NY 10155

INDEX OF DESIGNERS

INDEX OF MODEL NAMES

Note: Model numbers without an initial alphabetical reference are listed at the end of this index.

INDEX OF MANUFACTURERS

INDEX OF MANUFACTURERS

Notes

Notes